Advanced Praise
The Seven Strategies of M.

I have read hundreds books on Leadership. The model th.......g...... *Master Leaders* offers provides hands on insights that will help you uncover leadership strategies from some of our greatest leaders. **These real life examples will serve as tools to help you become a stronger, more effective leader in your own right.**

— Kevin Hamm
President and COO
DownEast Communications

Brad McRae's latest book, *The Seven Strategies of Master Leaders,* is filled with **inspired writing and fascinating stories that send a message to every leader and aspiring leaders about what it takes to truly be a success.**

— Jamie Baillie
President and CEO
Credit Union Atlantic

Dr. Brad McRae has researched and interviewed many of the best role-models of leadership in Canada to determine what differentiates master leaders from their less masterful counterparts. His latest book, *The Seven Strategies of Master Leaders,* **contains the essentials for leaders in troubled, ambiguous and complex times.**

— Shelle Rose Charvet,
author of the international bestseller Words That Change Minds,
2009 President of the Canadian Association of Professional Speakers

As Vice President for a team of health care professionals, my primary objective is to develop a team of professionals who focus on 'value' – not effort. Your book, *The Seven Strategies of Master Leaders,* **was made to order to help us reach our goal.**

— Tim P. Coolen
Vice President Shared Services
Medavie EMS

The importance of leadership cannot be overstated; **it is the leaders of today that provide us with hope for a better tomorrow.** As someone working hard to promote youth leadership for over 10 years, I found *The Seven Strategies of Master Leaders* to be full of valuable insights for emerging leaders of any age.

— Marc Kielburger
Co-CEO Free the Children
The Largest Organization of Children Helping Children in the World

The 32 Master Canadian Leaders who you will meet in this book were the motivational engines of their businesses, organizations and communities and truly made Canada a better place.

— Jim Reid, President & CEO
Green Solutions North America

Other books in the series by Dr. Brad McRae

The Seven Strategies of Master Negotiators
The Seven Strategies of Master Presenters

This Master Series is Also Available as E-Books along with:
- *Are You Managing Your Career or Is Your Career Managing You?*

Visit our online store at *www.BradMcRae.com* for more information.

The SEVEN STRATEGIES
of MASTER LEADERS

Leonard

Best Wishes Always

Brad McRae

Northbridge Publishing
Your bridge to publishing success
Toronto, Canada

Library and Archives Canada Cataloguing in Publication

McRae, Bradley C. (Bradley Collins), 1945-
The seven strategies of master leaders : featuring key insights from 30 of Canada's top leaders / Brad McRae.

Includes bibliographical references and index.
ISBN 978-0-9737605-6-9

1. Leadership--Canada. 2. Leadership. I. Title.

HD57.7.M445 2009   658.4'0920971   C2009-903858-7

Northbridge Publisher
488 Broadway Avenue
Toronto, ON
M4G 2R6
www.northbridgepublishng.com

Editor: Katherine Coy of Wordworks
Electronic Page Design and Composition: Herb Tucker of Covenant Technical Services
Cover Design: Webgrity
Printed and bound in Canada

Northbridge Publishing
Your bridge to publishing success

Dedication

*This book is dedicated to all of Canada's
past, present and future leaders.*

*Part of the proceeds from this book are being donated to help children
through Green Solutions' "Schools in a Box" program
and SwimJamaica.*

Acknowledgements

The 32 leaders profiled in this book provided me with their hard earned wisdom and I hope that the book will do the same for you. I also want to acknowledge all of the participants in all of my seminars who taught me at least as much as I taught them. My children, Andrew and Katie McRae are true leaders in wanting to make the world a better place and have supported me throughout the writing of all of my books. To Terrye Perlman for 30 years of Encouragement. Ideas were shared freely and debated with my wonderful colleagues Carla Angleheart, Dawn Brown, Maggie Chicoine, Mia Doucet, Claudia Hawkins, Ed Leach, Ricky Nowak, John Rocca and Rita Wuebbeler.

A special note of thanks to my book shepherd – Joan Homewood, and my editors, friends and colleagues Katherine Coy, Marilyn Christie, Carol Hill, donalee Moulton and to my trusted vice-president of everything – Lawrence McEachern.

I am deeply indebted to the students in my leadership classes and our clients at the Atlantic Leadership Development Institute who have had the courage, the will, the determination, and the commitment to face their own leadership challenges in making Canada and the world a better place.

Brad McRae
Halifax, Nova Scotia
September 2009

Contents

Foreword

Canadians tend to look to other parts of the world, especially the U.S., for leadership examples and would be hard pressed to name the top ten home-grown leaders in a variety of fields in this country. It's not for lack of great Canadian ideas or accomplished leaders, nor is it because we can't recognize true talent – it's simply because very few authors have taken the time to research and write about Canadian leaders.

As Chief Executive Officer of the largest retail industry association in the country, I have been privileged to see numerous examples of exquisite Canadian leadership. An effective and masterful leader has become the most important currency in an ever-changing and increasingly competitive retail environment. That's why this book is a gem, because it portrays real world Canadian examples of leadership that will help the reader succeed and compete on the global stage!

A case in point – a U.S. colleague asked me to suggest potential Canadian keynote speakers for an international conference. I knew full well that most of the sessions would be led by American retail executives and some high profile global players from Europe. As luck would have it, one of the Canadian leaders I chose to present as a keynote was Annette Verschuren, who is profiled in this book. She may have been selected because she oversees both Canada and Asia for Home Depot, but Annette spoke simply and passionately about "we"; about the team; about lessons learned throughout her professional journey in Canada.

Canadian leaders stand out for their ability to think in a collaborative and inclusive way, and for their willingness to take responsibility for both successes and set-backs. In my twenty-eight years heading national organizations, I have seen many executives come and go. Those who stand the test of time and rise to the level of "exceptional leader" exemplify the qualities of the Master Leadership Model developed in this book.

But the book doesn't just rely on a model to teach masterful leadership. Over and above the exceptional real life experiences showcased and the knowledge they provide, Brad McRae brings readers into the book with specifically designed, relevant exercises that will help them unlock their own leadership potential.

Great leaders are not all cut from the same cloth. As a female CEO myself, it is refreshing to note that fully one-third of the leaders profiled in this book are women. In my career, I have learned from great men and from great women who have tailored their leadership style around building trust, delivering on their promise and serving with integrity. Above all else, the most important lesson they taught me – never stop learning.

Diane J. Brisebois, President & CEO
Retail Council of Canada

Preface

As a leader you have a profound opportunity — that as a result
of your vision, perseverance and character, you can touch lives
and make the world a better place. — Brad McRae

During a visit to Rome, my friends and I lined up to go through the Sistine
Chapel. Even though we were there first thing in the morning and it was during the off season, the line to get in was still a mile long. Since it was a gorgeous
spring day, we decided not to do a scheduled tour or listen to the tour on audio-
tape. However, in the middle of the Tapestry Room, which is a beautifully long
narrow hallway, lined with tapestries, I was drawn to a tour that was standing
off to one side of the hallway. It was as if something about the tour guide's voice
and absolute passion grabbed my attention, so I decided to discreetly listen for a
minute. That is how I met the tour guide, Luigi Mazzone, who turned out to be
one of the best teachers I have ever met.

Luigi was describing the beautifully carved ceiling of the Tapestry Room,
which is one of the most intricately carved works of art that I had ever seen. The
repeating geometric shapes, the perspective and how anyone could have carved
the ceiling, lying flat on their backs was simply unbelievable. Then Luigi asked
us if we wanted to know a secret. Of course, everyone said yes. Luigi then told
us that the entire ceiling was an illusion. There was no carving – it had all been
painted on.

You could have knocked me over with a feather. I would have bet thousands
of dollars that the ceiling was carved. Luigi than asked us if we wanted to know
another secret. Of course, we all said yes. He then waited, to build the suspense,
and said that half of what we think is true is an illusion. He then asked if he
could ask one more question. Of course, we all said yes. Luigi asked why we had
come to Rome. Various members of the tour gave very thoughtful, if predictable answers. Various members of the tour had come to Rome to see the Roman
ruins, to partake of the amazing art, to look at the very foundations of our own
civilization. Luigi then said, that although all of the answers were very good, he
suggested that we had come to Rome to open up our minds.

I wrote this book to open our minds about leadership and more specifically about leadership development from a Canadian perspective. In Canada, we under-recognize, under-acknowledge and under-appreciate our own leaders. By acknowledging, recognizing and appreciating the depth of leadership talent we have, we will provide ourselves and future generations of leaders with the role models that are necessary for Canada's future.

Brad McRae
Halifax, Nova Scotia, Canada
September, 2009

Introduction

As a leader you have a profound opportunity. As a result of your vision, perseverance and character, you can touch a life and make the world a better place.

– Brad McRae

I invite you to try the following test. Test yourself first and then try it with your friends and colleagues. List 10 well-known Canadian recording artists, 10 well-known Canadian athletes, and 10 well-known Canadian leaders you admire. Time yourself or ask someone to time you. You have one minute for each list.

Whenever I try this test in my leadership classes, almost all of the people who take this test do a significantly better job of identifying Canadian recording artists and athletes than identifying Canadian leaders they admire. This reinforces my premise that Canadians under-recognize, under-acknowledge, and under-appreciate their home-grown leaders.

In this book we will learn the secrets of a cross-section of contemporary Canadian leaders. The people I profiled in the book had to meet six criteria. They had to make Canada and the world a better place and they had to have used their leadership skills to have done so. In addition, they had to have a proven track record and have come from diverse backgrounds in the private, public and volunteer sectors. By examining a diverse group of leaders, the universal principles underlying their ability to lead became clearer. Lastly, they had to have developed higher-order leadership skills and be able to use multiple skills simultaneously.

Every year there are thousands of articles and hundreds of books written on leadership. One of the most frequent questions I was asked by people who knew I was writing this book and from the publishers that I submitted the manuscript to was – "Why another book on leadership?"

This book differs from other leadership books in three significant ways. Most business books deal with leadership in the American context. Even though Canada and the United States look similar on the surface, there are major underlying differences in how we view ourselves and what we believe makes an ideal leader. The American leadership model is based on an individual's accomplishments, while the Canadian model is both more collaborative and more inclusive. Secondly, Canada needs strong Canadian role models. The in-depth interviews with the contemporary Master Canadian Leaders highlight Canadian role models we can all learn from. Thirdly, the reader will learn how to become a more masterful leader by completing the assignments and exercises that are integrated into the book. The exercises and assignments are critically important because research has demonstrated that leadership is learned more than it is taught. Research from the Center of Creative Leadership states that 50% of what we learn about leadership is based on experience, 20% is based on mentoring, 20% on failure and hardship, and 10% from formal education.[1]

Doing the research for this book has convinced me that true leadership is about wisdom, character and seasoned judgment and that it cannot be taught. It can only be learned in a manner that is similar to good parenting. For example, I was a "perfect" parent – before I had children. However, my children have taught me more about life than I could ever have taught them. In the same way, the examples of the Master Leaders in this book will profoundly change how you look at leadership in general and your own leadership competencies in particular.

I also began to realize that there were special or defining moments where the true strength of the leaders I profiled shone. As Winston Churchill said:

> There comes a special moment in everyone's life, a moment for which that person was born. That special opportunity, when he seizes it, will fulfill his mission – a mission for which he is uniquely qualified. In that moment, he finds greatness. It is his finest hour.

In their book, *Leaders: The Strategies of Taking Charge*, Warren Bennis and Burt Nanus state, "Leadership is like the abominable snowman, whose footprints are everywhere but who is nowhere to be seen."[2] I disagree. Leadership is somewhere to be seen and one of the best places to see it is in Canada. The most effective lessons in leadership often come from great leaders themselves. This book provides you with the opportunity to study and learn about leadership from in-depth interviews including:

> ➤ Rick Hansen, who became Canada's abilities awareness leader for his work in promoting accessibility, employability and a sense of community for people with spinal cord injuries, in addition to becoming a master fundraiser by raising over $178 million to help find a cure for spinal cord injuries. Rick is also the driving force in establishing the $48 million International Collaboration on Repair Discoveries (iCORD), a new spinal cord facility in Vancouver;

> ➤ Annette Verschuren grew The Home Depot Canada from 19 Canadian stores to over 179. In 2006, Annette was chosen to head Home Depot operations in Asia, and is currently transforming Home Depot's operations in China;

> ➤ David Johnston, who as president of the University of Waterloo, continues to help transform the UW, its students and faculty, surrounding communities and the ancillary cutting-edge high-tech industries into one of the more formidable brain trusts in the world; and

> ➤ Cora Tsouflidou, who transformed Cora's Restaurants from a single diner in Montreal into a national, coast-to-coast chain of 92 restaurants. In addition, Cora's philanthropic goal is to make sure every Canadian child starts the day with a healthy and nutritious breakfast.

The Master Leaders I interviewed freely shared the wisdom they have painstakingly gathered. Their insights provide the basis for the leadership skills and strategies that are examined in this book. Through in-depth interviews, you will learn about the experiences and challenges these leaders faced, and how they have been able to transform their own lives and the lives of their organizations and communities.

Along with the focus on the development and practical application of leadership strategies and skills, this book contains specifically designed exercises; each one carefully constructed to help you develop and enhance your leadership skills and strategies. By actively involving yourself in these exercises, you will be able to see yourself improve.

However, for this to truly be a book about Master Leaders, we should start with a definition of mastery. For our purposes, "Mastery" is defined as the possession of consummate strategies and skills at the highest level of proficiency. As the following example illustrates.

Pamela Walsh became the President of the College of the North Atlantic (CNA) in Newfoundland and Labrador in 1999. Like all public college systems, CNA was dependent on funding, but at that time, Newfoundland and Labrador's population was decreasing. A decreasing population meant fewer students and fewer students meant less revenue. Pamela's creative solution was, that if more students could not come to the college, the college would go to them.

Enter Qatar, a small, oil-rich nation in the Middle East that was looking for training in the fields of oil and gas, business and medical technology. The Qataris looked at programs in community colleges in the United States and Canada. In the end, they chose the college system in Canada because it was more closely aligned with their applied technological and business needs.

Once the Qataris had decided on the Canadian college model, the short list of competitors was narrowed down to four: the British Columbia Institute of Technology, the Southern Alberta Institute of Technology, the Northern Alberta Institute of Technology, and the College of the North Atlantic. How could Pamela Walsh and the College of the North Atlantic compete against three of the best community colleges in the country?

> There comes a special moment in everyone's life, a moment for which that person was born. That special opportunity, when he seizes it, will fulfill his mission – a mission for which he is uniquely qualified. In that moment, he finds greatness. It is his finest hour.
> **Winston Churchill**

Pamela rallied everyone, from clerical support staff to the vice-presidents, to become involved in trying to win the contract. She said, *"Even if we don't win the contract, working together to try to win will be good for the college."* One of the ideas that came out of a brainstorming session was to contact a seamstress in Portugal Cove, a small coastal community near St. John's, and ask her to make a copy of the Qatari flag. The Qataris arrived in late May shortly after a major snow storm. The desert-living Qataris thought they had just landed at the North Pole – but a North Pole with the Qatari flag flying over it! When the Qataris were invited for tea, they remarked that Newfoundland was not that different from their home, except that at home the flag flew over sand and in Newfoundland it flew over snow. This was the start of Pamela Walsh's and the college staff's efforts to build a strong relationship with their Qatari counterparts, and the world famous hospitality of the Newfoundlanders did not go unnoticed.

The Qataris were also impressed that CNA had developed strategic relationships with industry and government, and had put into place an accountability framework, which included surveying recent graduates about their level of satisfaction with their education, the employment they had secured, and the remuneration they were receiving. The Qataris also wanted all of the programs that would be delivered in Qatar to be certified to North American standards. The problem with this request was that the agencies that certified the programs in North America had never certified international programs before. Pamela rightly said that she could not promise this, but that she would do everything in her power to make sure that the programs were certified.

In the end, the College of the North Atlantic won the contract to set up and deliver world class college-level training in Qatar. I asked Pamela Walsh about her reaction when she heard that the college had won the contract. She said that she was at the airport in Stephenville and everyone at the airport was excited because 10 of the staff in the college's head office had just won $10 million in Lotto 6/49™. Pamela then received a telephone call telling her that CNA had won the contract to set up a campus in Doha, the capital of Qatar. Pamela let out a scream of delight. Everyone at the airport assumed that Pamela was one of the million dollar winners. Pamela was not one of the lottery winners, but she told me that she was happier than if she had won the lottery because winning the contract with Qatar afforded CNA an opportunity to grow by developing an international campus and CNA's staff now had an amazing opportunity to work abroad. Winning the contract also provided funding to put into place a state-of-the-art management information system both in Newfoundland and in Qatar. Lastly, winning this contract infused CNA with a sense of pride and a "can do" attitude.

Did CNA win the contract because of the flag? No. Did the flag help? Absolutely. Did the College of the North Atlantic win the contract because of Pamela Walsh's leadership, negotiating and presentation skills or her decision-making, opportunity-seeking, risk-taking and team-building skills? I would argue that Pamela Walsh and the College of the North Atlantic won this 10-year, $500 million dollar contract because of a seamless convergence of all these skills.

In this example, Pamela Walsh, like all of the other Master Leaders I profile in this book, demonstrated proficiency and mastery, which are also known as higher-order skills. Incidentally, at the time of this writing, the contract is valued at over $1.7 billion, and growing.

Higher-Order Skills

The concept of "higher-order skills" was developed by Francis Robinson. To explain this concept, Robinson used the analogy of learning to swim for pleasure versus preparing to swim in the Olympics. In the former, the person is learning "regular-order" swimming skills such as learning to swim and breathe at the same time. In the latter case, the person is developing "higher-order" swimming skills — that is, skills which are "based on scientific research", in this case, on how to reduce the resistance of the body in the water and on how to obtain the most powerful forward push with the least effort."[3]

Let's assume that our swimmer will be competing in the 400-metre freestyle and that she has just been assigned a new Olympic-level coach. One of the first things her coach would do is perform a differential diagnosis. The coach would ask our athlete to swim the full length of the pool, using only her arms. The coach would then ask her to swim the same distance using only her legs to propel herself through the water. The coach would then ask our athlete to swim the length of the pool using both her arms and legs.

What is the coach doing? He is looking at the relative contribution of the upper body and the lower body to the total effort. In most cases, the average swimmer uses his or her kick to remain horizontal in the water. Olympic swimmers, on the other hand, need to get six to ten percent of their forward motion from their kick. By careful measurement, the coach in this case was able to determine that our athlete was only achieving a four-percent forward thrust from her kick.

The differential diagnosis made it clear that this was a major part of the swimmer's stroke that needed improvement in order to become a world-class competitor. In other words, we all need to know which skills are working well and which skills are most in need of improvement, because we are only as good as the weakest skill. The same principle applies to improving leadership skills. An accurate differential diagnosis will help you improve your skills.

It is important to note that the idea of higher-order skills includes making improvements not only in areas where one is weak, but also continuing to improve in areas where one's skills are strong. For example, let's suppose that you are an excellent listener, but need improvement in self-control while dealing with people who appear to be rigid. Most people would assume that one would make the most gains by learning one of several self-control techniques, such as perspective management. However, you might make an equally profound impact on your leadership skills by improving your already excellent listening skills. Two things are very valuable to remember about developing higher-order skills. First, it is a proven method of development. Secondly, it reminds us that too many people put artificial ceilings on what they do well instead of developing those competencies to the fullest extent possible.

However, there can be no improvement without salient feedback. At this point, let's return to the swimming analogy to illustrate the concept of salient feedback. Salient feedback is feedback that is so compelling and personally meaningful that the person who receives the feedback will do everything that is humanly possible to change his or her behaviour. For example, let's assume that our athlete has worked exceedingly hard, both in the pool and on dry land, to develop strength in her lower body. This has resulted in an additional six-percent increase in her forward motion in the 400-metre freestyle. Along with upper-body strength-building and improvements in her technique, this has placed our swimmer among the top 10 400-metre freestyle swimmers in the world. However, she has never ranked better than a fifth-place finish, which is well outside contention for a medal. Her coach has completed another differential diagnosis, which shows that the front-arm extension of her stroke into the water needs to be a fraction of a millimeter longer and the same is true for the follow-through extension at the end of her stroke.

Although our swimmer understands this concept and has seen it demonstrated by her coach and other world-class swimmers, she just can't see that she needs to improve because she thinks she is already doing it as perfectly as possible. The coach then videotapes the swimmer. In freeze-frame, slow-motion, the coach is able to show her exactly where her arms enter and leave the water as opposed to the place where her arms *ought* to enter and leave the water. Seeing her stroke on the television monitor has acted as salient feedback for the athlete. The feedback had so much impact on our swimmer that she changed her stroke and is now in contention for an Olympic medal.

The three important elements that provide for the development of higher-order skills are:

1. An accurate assessment (differential diagnosis) of the relative strengths of the skills that make up the whole.
2. Salient feedback that is so accurate and personally meaningful that it helps us change our behaviour in the desired direction.
3. Eliminating artificial ceilings on our best skills so we can continue to develop them to the fullest extent possible.

In the above example, we looked at the development of higher-order skills in swimming the 400-metre freestyle. The rest of this book will both expand the theory of higher-order skills and illustrate it with examples of Canadian Master Leaders. However, higher-order skills by themselves are not enough. Master Leaders also have to make higher-order decisions about where and when to apply their higher-order skills.

Higher-Order Decisions

The leaders I interviewed became Master Leaders because they made seminal decisions that forever changed themselves and their organizations such as:

➢ Louise Arbour indicting the world's first sitting president of a nation for crimes against humanity;

➢ Canada Post's decision to benchmark itself against the best postal systems in the world, then setting aggressive targets for improvement, and for the first time in its history paying its unionized members a bonus for achieving set performance targets, and

➢ Bombardier's decision to build the C-Series jetliner during one of the worst downturns in aviation history. Not only will Bombardier be competing against its traditional rivals, the new 100- to 130-seat plane will compete directly with Boeing and Airbus — the world's two largest manufacturers of jet airliners.

But higher-order intentions and decisions without higher-order commitment remain unfulfilled dreams and aspirations.

Higher-Order Commitment

Perhaps no other Master Leader in Canada demonstrates higher-order commitment better than Stephen Lewis. Working 18 hours a day and giving hundreds of speeches each year, Stephen Lewis has become the world's conscience for the HIV/AIDS pandemic in Africa. In these efforts, "Lewis never stops. At an age when most people are coasting into retirement, the 67-year-old Lewis is working longer and harder than ever before, doing a job that not even Sisyphus would apply for. His mission: to get the rest of the world to pay attention to the more than 25 million people in sub-Saharan Africa who have HIV/AIDS. With 2.3 million dying a year, *Africa experiences the equivalent of a tsunami a month*. [Emphasis added]"[4]

> *The quality of a person's life is in direct proportion to their commitment to excellence, regardless of their chosen field of endeavor.*
> **Vince Lombardi**

Twenty million African children will become orphans by 2010 unless the world intervenes. Recognizing this, Stephen started the Stephen Lewis Foundation in response to the world's governments' lack of support and funding for initiatives to combat the pandemic. At the time of this writing, Lewis' foundation has distributed and committed more than $28 million to over 300 community-level initiatives in 15 sub-Saharan African countries.[5]

The foundation pays for the most basic necessities of life and death such as bars of soap, towels, blankets and funerals. It also supports local initiatives, such as buildings for orphan care, home-based palliative care, schools for orphaned girls, and a support group for grandmothers who are raising their grandchildren. In short, the foundation pays for everything from awareness and prevention programs to coffins. The foundation strategically focuses on the areas of greatest need. As Stephen Lewis states:

> *The work of the Stephen Lewis Foundation means that for people living with AIDS, or orphans or grandmothers, life has been made bearable for many who would otherwise have languished in*

isolation and despair. We've worked at the grassroots in over three hundred projects in fifteen countries, and we have a good sense of how to make an impact.

But two things happened along the way that are changing our approach. First, it became clear that the big funders involved with AIDS — from the Global Fund to the Gates Foundation to the World Bank — are making a magnificent contribution to the purchase of drugs, the creation of laboratories, the repair of health systems, the replenishment of healthcare workers, the search for a vaccine. But not a lot of the money gets to the ground ... to the grassroots communities that need it most.

Second, it became equally clear that investment at community level has had a huge impact. Over the last five years, in project after project, we saw lives and hope restored.

We began to think to ourselves that if only we had greater resources to invest, we could help to subdue the pandemic at community level; we could take the lessons we've learned and apply them across the board. This is not meant to be grandiose: it's simply meant to recognize that with enough money, we're on the precipice of creating major change right across the continent.

So we 're taking the next dramatic step in the evolution of the Foundation. We're launching a campaign called Turning the Tide. We 're going to try to raise enough funds to support all the worthy proposals that come to us — putting into operation, at country level, scores of additional projects. Our goal is to raise $100 million the next five years to fund hundreds more grassroots organizations in sub-Saharan Africa.

We believe to the depths of our being that it 's possible to Turn the Tide in this way. What we need are the numbers, and the broadening range of experience, to show everyone that it can be done; that at the grassroots, where people live and die, such energy and prevention and care can be unleashed and employed that the pandemic is reversed.[6]

For his continuing leadership in this area, Stephen Lewis was selected as *MacLean's* first annual Canadian of the Year[7] and he has not slowed down one iota since that time. In terms of his ability as presenter, Stephen Lewis is not only one of the best in Canada; he is one of the best in the world, because he is a master of eloquence in addition to being a Master Leader and a master negotiator. Stephen Lewis is truly one of our Canadian Leaders who is making a difference that makes a difference.

As this example points out, higher-order leadership is built upon the base of higher-order intentions, higher-order commitment, higher-order decisions and higher-order skills. Each leadership challenge will require a different set of higher-order skills. For example, in one situation the leader may need higher-order communication skills, while in another, higher-order creativity, while in a third, higher-order marketing, or a deft combination of all three.

Higher-order intentions, commitment, decisions and skills are necessary but not sufficient conditions to achieve significant and lasting results. There are always obstacles or resistance to overcome. Therefore Master Leaders must have higher-order follow-through. Master Leaders use the judicious combination of each of these factors to achieve success beyond what might be thought possible. Their real-life examples are used throughout this book to bring the seven strategies of Master Leaders to life.

Research by the Conference Board of Canada concluded that leadership development is more important than ever as we will need to accelerate the development of leaders in the private, public, not-for-profit and volunteer sectors as baby boomers retire in increasingly large numbers. Therefore, the purpose of this book is to help you:

➢ identify the skills and strategies Master Leaders develop and utilize,

➢ develop your own leadership skills and strategies to the highest degree possible, and

> ➤ assist others to develop their leadership skills and strategies to the fullest extent possible.

The Master Leadership Model

All of the interviews I conducted and all of the studies I have read can be summarized in the seven strategies listed in Figure I-1. Mastery is being able to use the right leadership strategies combined with the right higher-order skills such as higher-order intentions, decision-making, risk-assessment, execution, commitment and follow-through for each specific leadership challenge.

Figure I-1
The Master Leadership Model

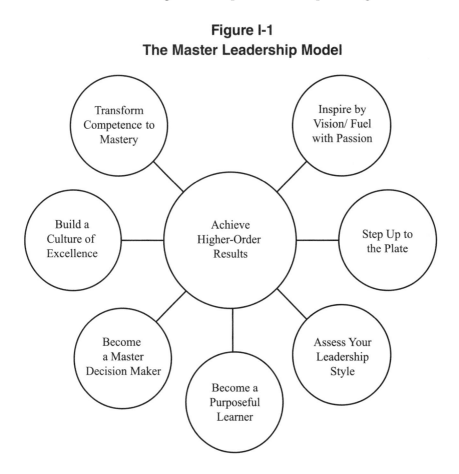

You can use this leadership model to help you develop your own higher-order leadership skills, competencies and strategies, and in turn, to help others in your organization do the same by completing the specifically designed exercises included in each chapter. Following is a brief description of the seven higher-order leadership strategies that will be explored in detail in the rest of this book. In subsequent chapters you will meet the Master Leaders I profiled and they will illustrate how these strategies and skills are applied in real life Canadian examples[1].

STRATEGY 1: Inspire by Vision/Fuel with Passion

No amount of leadership skill can save a leader if he is taking his organization in the wrong direction. Master Leaders have a clear, meaningful and compelling vision for the future that engages their organizations to take positive and decisive action. This chapter examines:

> ➢ How Master Leaders develop their vision,

> ➢ How Master Leaders articulate their vision,

> ➢ The critical difference between a motivating vision and one that isn't, and

> ➢ How Master Leaders turn their vision into reality.

STRATEGY 2: Step Up to the Plate

Over and over again, the Master Leaders interviewed for this book demonstrated their willingness to step up to the plate, take the risks and take on responsibility to get the job done. In this chapter, you will learn how Master Leaders use determination, persistence, courageous patience and focus to achieve higher-order results. We will also see how Master Leaders use Jim Collins' concept of

---

[1] In the interests of flow throughout this book, I have made every effort to alternate "he" and "she", where necessity demands a singular pronoun be used. However, please note that this is meant to refer to both women and men in these cases, and in no way is meant to suggest that sex is determinate of whether one can become a Master Leader or not.

the Flywheel – starting with small wins, and then increasing the momentum with each additional win until the organization develops the momentum necessary to carry it – not to – but past its goals.

STRATEGY 3: Assess Your Leadership Style

This chapter will help you identify some of your most important competencies and skills as a leader and formulate specific ways to improve them. We will examine two ground-breaking studies which analyzed the four factors and eight critical differences between effective leaders and their average counterparts and then give you an opportunity to rate your ability on each of these characteristics. We will then look at a process that will help you assess how others see your current abilities and highlight areas where improvement is desired.

STRATEGY 4: Become a Purposeful Learner

Groundbreaking research at the Center of Creative Leadership investigated how Master Leaders became purposeful learners. What makes this study fascinating is that the researchers were able to quantify the sources of learning. The research demonstrates that 50% of what leaders learn is learned from experience. Twenty percent is from good, bad, and flawed bosses/mentors; 20% is from failure and hardship, and the last 10% of what is learned stems from formal education. While formal education only accounts for 10%, it can be an incredibly important percentage if the education relates to the overall learning goals and objectives of the individual in question. Each of these four lessons is important, however, compound learning – which works just like compound interest – takes place when the lessons are learned in combination with other lessons.

STRATEGY 5: Become a Master Decision Maker

Master Leaders are master decision makers and in this chapter we examine how Master Leaders make crucial decisions. Reading this chapter will sharpen your understanding of how accurate and viable decision-making paid off for the Master Leaders interviewed in this book. Working through the exercises provided will help you become a more masterful decision maker.

STRATEGY 6: Build a Culture of Excellence

Three critically important questions that Master Leaders continually ask themselves are:

> ➢ How am I growing the organization?

> ➢ How am I growing the people?

> ➢ How am I growing the culture?

The one factor that most leaders do not pay enough attention to is developing a culture that will help their organizations grow and succeed long after that particular leader has moved on. In this chapter we look at how the Master Leaders profiled in this book developed seven different types of cultures and/or combinations thereof. This chapter also challenges you to look at the type of culture you are building as a leader in your own organization.

STRATEGY 7: Transform Competence to Mastery

The final chapter examines three critical differences between being competent and being a master: 1) Master Leaders set "tipping point" goals; 2) Master Leaders use compound learning to transform their skills from competency to mastery. Compound learning gives a Master Leader the advantage of integrating new experiences and lessons with their existing knowledge, which leads to exponential growth. To help you capitalize on the power of compounded growth, this chapter covers seven critical methods that will help you become a life-long learner, including the concept of salient feedback — feedback that is so personally meaningful that we actually change our behaviour, and 3) Master Leaders have the ability to apply multiple skills sets and strategies simultaneously.

STRATEGY 1

Inspire by Vision/ Fuel with Passion

All achievement is born of dreams.

– Sir Walter Raleigh

There are many people and organizations in Canada that say they are inspired by vision and fueled with passion but few really are, and there is a palpable difference between those that are and those that are not. The difference between those that are and those that are not manifests itself in ways that are big and equally important, in ways that are small. We will begin by looking closely at the big and small ways that being inspired by vision and fueled with passion manifests itself at Mountain Equipment Co-op (MEC).

Let me give a personal example of how MEC lives its values and how MEC has turned living its values into good business. Several years ago, my teenage son, Andrew, had outgrown his winter jacket. Unlike his fashion conscious younger sister, Andrew could care less. In fact, he buys 90% of his clothing second-hand. However, there was nothing at either the new or used clothing stores that appealed to him. Finally, he found "the perfect" coat at MEC and came home from MEC, very excited, but as we talked, I realized it wasn't about his new coat. When I asked him what happened, he told me that MEC had a box where customers could leave their old winter coats and MEC would donate the coats to people who could really use them. Because Andrew has a strong social conscience and MEC has a strong social conscience – and MEC *acts* on its values – MEC gained a customer for life .

Mountain Equipment Co-op is Canada's largest outdoor retail consumer cooperative. As a cooperative, it is owned by its members. In addition to goods and services, MEC "help[s] preserve the quality of the natural environment and educate[s] people on environmentally responsible outdoor adventure."[1] MEC currently has stores in Victoria, Vancouver, North Vancouver, Calgary, Edmonton, Winnipeg, Burlington, Toronto, Ottawa, Halifax, Montreal and Quebec City. Customers in other areas are served by catalog and in the spirit of conservation, MEC has a website that lets customers swap old equipment.

MEC started in 1971 with six University of British Columbia students who were into mountain climbing and were tired of having to go to the expense of driving to Seattle for purchases. They decided to form a co-op and buy the equipment that they needed directly from the suppliers. The first six members, paid $5 to join and it is still $5 to join today only now they have almost 3 million members and are, in fact, the largest co-op in the world. Incidentally, one of the original six, Sarah Golling,[2] is still on the Board (2008 to 2011) and today her ownership in the company is still valued at $5, just like it was in 1971.

MEC's original mission was to:[3]

> [Sell] good gear at fair prices for "self-propelled" recreational activities. But then as now, other agendas were at play. An unwritten part of this was to become enough of a force in the market place in Canada to make other suppliers more competitive. In this they have exceeded beyond their expectations.

Today the vision for MEC is:[4]

> ... to be the most viable, vibrant outdoor retailer in Canada. To
> help more Canadians play outdoors in self-propelled ways. To
> ensure a comprehensive, carefully nurtured network of parks,
> wilderness, and outdoor recreation areas. To inspire others
> towards environmental, social, and economic sustainability. To
> leave the world better than we found it.

In many ways these two vision statements are similar, and in fact MEC's mission to sell equipment at reasonable prices so its customers can enjoy "self-propelled" recreational activities has stayed the same. Today, and rightly so, there is a greater emphasis placed on caring for the environment. Just how MEC is bringing that vision to fruition is the next topic that will be discussed.

Caring for the Environment[5]

MEC is part of the "1% for the Planet" program whereby 1% of annual gross sales are donated to Canadian causes. However, in 2009 MEC contributed 1.5% of previous year's sales for a total of 3.6 million dollars. "Since 1987, MEC has contributed over $12.5 million to Canadian-based environmental conservation and wilderness projects, research and education." More specifically, this funding is divided into a national fund and a store fund. "The national fund supports wilderness-protection projects, research, and education such as: land acquisitions for conservation, advocacy and education, backcountry access, environmental research and studentships." In addition, each store has its own fund that "supports local environmental and conservation projects such as: educating people about environmental issues, promoting ways to reduce our ecological impact, researching local or regional environmental issues, and enhancing and conserving urban environments." In addition, "most MEC staff take earth-friendly forms of transportation to work. Many cycle and MEC provides shower facilities at most of its locations."

"In 2007, we measured our staff commuting patterns, and discovered we are not your average commuters. Almost 82% of [our] employees nationwide used alternative transportation (bike, public transit, or foot) to get to work... To encourage bike commuting we have showers and secure bike storage for staff at most locations. There is no car parking for employees at our stores, and most locations have a selection of bike tools that employees can borrow to make repairs and perform routine maintenance."

Caring for the Community.

In addition to caring for the environment, MEC cares about the community. For example, downtown Halifax has two main streets: Barrington and Spring Garden Road. Spring Garden Road is thriving with boutique stores, popular restaurants and a movie complex. It is a popular place to be for Halifax's residents and tourists alike. Barrington Street, on the other hand, was in the process of dying. Stores moved to malls and big box complexes while beautiful Victorian office buildings were boarded up. So where did Mountain Equipment Co-op locate their Halifax store? Just adjacent to Barrington Street thereby helping to redevelop a part of the city that desperately needed to be redeveloped.

Helping to rebuild Halifax's downtown community is not an isolated act for   MEC as existing and new stores are also brought in line with its environmental principles. For example, the Winnipeg location involved refitting a derelict building at a cost of $850,000 and $2.5 million to the city's CentreVenture Development Corporation, which will lease the building to MEC. Plans call for a heating and cooling system expected to boost the building's energy efficiency by as much as 64%. The store was built with as much recycled material as possible and composting toilets are used where the customers' urine is "recycled as fertilizer for a rooftop garden."

Caring for Third World Suppliers.

MEC's values also apply to ethical sourcing in the third world countries like China and Vietnam where many of its products are made. MEC's third world suppliers have to meet stringent guidelines regarding wages, employment standards, environmental and safety practices – including the number of fire exits at their facilities.

MEC's value proposition is that it is more than a store; MEC is a movement that cares about the environment, cares about its customers, cares about its community, cares about its suppliers and cares about its employees. MEC truly is an organization that is inspired by vision and fueled with passion. Now let's look at three additional examples.

Creating a Vision of a Learning Organization

Master Leaders know, at the most fundamental level, the importance of developing their people and their organization by creating a learning organization. True learning organizations use assessment, training, coaching, mentoring, on-the-job learning, e-learning, blended learning and rigorous measurement to ensure continuous performance improvement of all employees, not only for the sake of learning, but also in achieving strategic business goals. This critically important function cannot be left to chance. There has to be someone in the organization who functions as a champion of learning such as a Chief Learning Officer (CLO). Having a learning champion or CLO is not, by itself enough either. Becoming a learning organization has to be part of that organization's culture. It has to be part of an organization's DNA that is passed on from one generation of employees to the next. Speed of learning and ability to adapt rapidly to a very dynamic and constantly changing business environment demands a shift away from highly structured formal learning interventions to a more fluid and empowered learning environment. People learn as a result of a business challenge or when a customer opportunity presents itself – in other words learning on the job in real-time.

One organization that is a true learning organization based on the above criteria is Pfizer Inc. Training Magazine has chosen Pfizer as one of the top six organizations in the world for excellence in Learning and Development. The reason Pfizer earned this award is due in no small measure to its strong commitment to learning and development. In Canada, Pfizer's Director of Learning and Development is Rania Cassar-Awe. In speaking with Rania, I could hear the energy and passion in her voice and her commitment to Learning and Development as a real contributor to both the top line and the bottom line.

B.M.   *What challenges are you facing at Pfizer Canada?*

R.CA.   *Change has never been more urgent and it is clear that we need to evolve the learning environment quickly in order to adapt to what has become a new business reality. Global financial pressure, rapid technological change and a pending business merger will have a tremendous impact on how learning takes place within Pfizer.*

At the same time, our industry is becoming increasingly complex and massive amounts of knowledge have to be learned and mastered. We are also facing changing demographics and increased global competitiveness. Therefore we have to be a true learning organization in every sense of those words. For example, Pfizer is investing resources in strategic workforce planning and program development to support - for the first time – four generations of workers. A multi-generational workforce demands radically different learning and career development approaches. By modularizing and diversifying we can deliver learning in a variety of ways to improve our reach, our relevance and be a true learning organization.[6]

B.M.   *What do you mean by a true learning organization?*

R.CA.   *Pfizer's vision is to be a culture of innovation and continuous improvement. This means we have to look for novel, measurable, and sustainable methods to enhance Learning and Development. In the emerging learning world, three strategies are guiding us in meeting the increased demand for learning in Canada.*

The first is Learning Effectiveness which focuses on achieving real-time job   performance improvement in skill areas of competitive advantage, beyond the simple completion of prescribed training activities. The second is Learning On-Demand which legitimizes and capitalizes on the informal learning that happens naturally in the workplace, and the third is Learning Services which moves beyond courses in a corporate university catalogue to learning services that are scalable, accessible, affordable and easily consumed.

B.M.   *Can you tell me more about what you mean by scalable, accessible, affordable and easily consumed?*

R.CA.   *In order to get to that learning culture we have to look at the learning function in a very different way. The new model uses a variety of learning methods including e-learning and an on-demand platform allows employees from all parts of the organization to reach out, find and engage in the learning they need when they need it. It brings the learning to the job setting instead of removing the learner from the performance environment.*

Our new learning model leverages individual motivation, energy and technology to learn and grow. We have traditionally focused on identifying gaps and then push people through a set of formal interventions to fill those gaps. This approach, which is often uncomfortable and unproductive is also labour and time intensive.

Until 2 years ago, virtually all of our activities were formal classroom learning. Today we have shifted approximately 30% percent to an on-demand platform. This is important because it increases the probability that learning will be converted into performance and also stretches resources across the organization. For example, we have expanded our learning reach by 40%, and we're serving many more people. This approach recognizes that we have experts throughout the organization who can offer mentoring and coaching and facilitate peer learning – formally and informally – without making it all about the number of training sessions completed. What it all adds up to is leveraging expertise within the organization in a way that is powerful, dynamic and lets us move faster than we ever have before.

Creating a New Vision for Comprehensive Health Care

I very much wanted to interview one of Canada's most respected politicians and social activists for this book, the Honourable Roy Romanow, former Saskatchewan Premier and the former chairperson on the Future of Health Care in Canada. I hoped to find out how his vision for health care had changed since he was the chairman of the Commission on the Future of Health Care in Canada – and I can tell you that I was not disappointed. Roy Romanow is now the chairperson and chief spokesperson for the Canadian Index of Wellbeing.

I began the interview by asking how the Canadian Index of Wellbeing (CIW) related to Roy Romanow's vision for more efficient and more effective health care in Canada.

R.R.   *The CIW will promote a shared vision of what really constitutes sustainable wellbeing which is more holistic and more inclusive than healthcare per se. The CIW measures real Canadian progress toward or movement away from wellbeing, which will stimulate discussion about the types of policies and programs that would move us closer and faster toward achieving wellbeing, give Canadians a tool to promote wellbeing with policy shapers and decision makers while at the same time add momentum to the global movement for measuring societal progress.*

B.M.   **How does this work relate to the ground-breaking study of the Future of Health Care in Canada that you chaired in 2002?**

R.R.   *The overarching vision of the CIW is to make Canadians the healthiest people in the world – not only in acute care – we need a much greater emphasis than we have had to date on preventative health. Even if you implement all of the 47 recommendations from the Future of Health Care Report we would only be part way there. Now what we have to do is connect all of the dots on the upstream that would help prevent and/ or lessen the impact of many of the chronic illnesses.*

With the CIW, we will be able to measure and hopefully change the preventative socioeconomic factors from the outset that could improve our quality-of-life and make our health care system less costly and more efficient.

B.M.   **Why did you decide to spend so much of your time and energy on the CIW?**

R.R.   *The CIW is a monumental project that is much larger than it looks. If you look at the history of our country, there were times when Canada had visionary concerns that were national in scope. But given the vast size of this country, they were few and far between. Nevertheless, they are part of the glue that holds our country together. I am thinking* *about projects and events like the building of the Canadian National Railroad that linked this country from east to west. We also created a national consensus that every Canadian — regardless of his or her personal wealth or region of the country they came from — is entitled to Medicare. In many ways the CBC holds our country together and helps us learn about each other and our concerns. And certainly, Expo 67 was a celebration of Canada – I can still remember standing in the Bell Pavilion, which showcased a 360-degree screen that took us on a virtual flight across this vast and beautiful country of ours. The CIW will be another of those projects of which all Canadians will be proud.*

Creating a New Vision for Higher Education

David Johnson is the visionary president of the University of Waterloo. During our interview, it soon became obvious that David's vision goes way past the University of Waterloo. David has a very strong and very articulate vision for higher education, research and innovation for the entire country.

B.M.   *Roy Romanow did and is doing our country a significant service by being an articulate spokesperson for health care reform and health care accountability in Canada. It sounds like you would agree that we need to do an equally good job in studying the state of higher education in Canada so we can make sure that Canada as a whole remains both well educated and competitive.*

D.J.   *That's a lofty parallel given Roy Romanow's stature. Also there is one significant difference in that we already have the Canada Health Act and what he was doing was a substantial review of the Canada Health Act. What I am saying is that we need a Canada Learning and Innovation Act that is equivalent in scope to the Canada Health Act. We need a harmonized federal and provincial presence in the field of education because education is as important as health care if we want to be competitive in the global economy. To be competitive we have to work smarter and to work smarter we have to get smarter, and the best single way to get smarter is to ensure that we develop the talent that we have in Canada to its fullest potential in addition to attracting talent from around the world.*

The BNA Act was written in 1867 and by virtue of that Act it virtually says that education and research is a provincial responsibility and not a federal responsibility, and there are a couple of things wrong with that. One is that education and research since 1867 have become much more important priorities. Virtually every federated nation on earth including Australia, the United States, Germany and many other countries have a substantial education and research presence in their national governments, we in this country have chosen not to.

B.M.   *Would the Canada Learning and Innovation Act change that?*

D.J.   *Just as we invest in physical health care, we must invest in the intellectual health of our nation. Just as we have the Canada Health Act to protect and enhance the physical well-being of Canadians across the country, so we also need a national framework to ensure the well-being of the nation's talent. This is why I have proposed the Canada Learning and Innovation Act.*

Recognizing that different people learn best in different ways, the act will emphasize innovative techniques for helping individuals learn to the best of their capacities. A primary goal of this initiative will be to harmonize the learning and innovation opportunities across Canada and to co-ordinate the efforts of all levels of government.

> **We need to be more of an investing society than a consuming society. If we invest enough in education, we will have enough wealth to have a healthy health system. If we don't invest in our educational system, we won't have a good health care system.**
> **David Johnson**

There are some important research findings that substantiate the need for the Canada Learning and Innovation Act. The Canadian Council on Learning reports that Canada ranks 15th out of 30 in the OECD (Organization for Economic Co-operation and Development) in research and development. The Institute for Competitiveness and Prosperity noted that Canada produces 25% fewer PhDs than the US and the US produces 19 times more MA students, despite only having 9 times our population.

Canada's capacity for research and development, whether it is done by academia or by the private sector, is being threatened by shortages in our skill-based work force. For example, there is a lot of talk about the productivity gap between Canada and the US. At the present time, the chances of a student graduating with a Master's degree in Canada, on a per capita basis, is one half of a student graduating with a Masters degree in the US. This is an IQ deficit and in order to be competitive, we have to have the sophisticated and high level of skill that comes from that type of degree.

Too many people compare investing in health care and investing in education, but they miss the most fundamental point. We need to be more of an investing society than a consuming society. If we invest enough in education, we will have enough wealth to have a healthy health system. If we don't invest in our educational system, we won't have a good health care system.

In Ontario, 47% of the budget goes to health care; 25% of the budget goes to education with a larger amount going to primary and secondary education.

Twenty-five years ago, the amount of money spent on health care and education was equal and what has really gone down is the money spent on higher education. The average student faculty ratio today is 25 to 1 for all universities in Canada. Twenty years ago, it was 16 to 1. Going from 25 to 1 to 16 to 1 is a 50% decrease.

B.M.   *You stated that by 2020, Canada should seek to take the lead in the world in higher education, innovation and research. What has to happen for this to occur?*

D.J.   *I believe you need to look to Canada's innovation engines, its universities, find ways to partner with them, and reap the rewards of innovation, knowledge transfer, and the chance to shape and be shaped by the newest ideas in education. What we have achieved at UW through collaboration amongst the university, our community and our business partners must be duplicated and at the same time be responsive to differences in universities and to differences in the regions in which they serve.*

Creating a Vision for Canada's First Nations Peoples

Jawaharlal Nehru was one of the driving forces in the Indian independence movement and was India's first prime minister. Nehru said, "My most important wisdom came from Gandhi who taught me that a great teacher is one who can change the apprehensions that people have about the future into anticipations." The above quotation applies equally well to Phil Fontaine, who is the National Chief of the Assembly of First Nations.

As a leader and healer, Phil Fontaine has dedicated his life to the advancement of First Nations people. One of his greatest honours occurred when he won the National Aboriginal Achievement Award for public service. He also helped to bring to light the abuse that occurred in residential schools by revealing that he had been sexually abused by the priests who ran those schools. Phil continues to work for the betterment of all First Nations Peoples in Canada. His focus for the future is on the elimination of poverty; improvements in education, health care and housing; the strengthening of cultural identity; and the preservation of First Nations languages.

B.M.   *When did you first start being an advocate for First Nations People?*

P.F.   *My involvement started when I was quite young. My first experience was with the Canadian Indian Youth Council. I was quite inexperienced but I was very impressed with the leadership of this organization. That led to work with the Company of Young Canadians, which was made up of social activists and modeled on the US Peace Corp. It was designed to harness the incredible energy and activism of young people. I served as a project developer, which included projects in my home community of Sakeeng – and that was really the foundation of all of my future work.*

B.M.   *In a 1991 interview with CBC journalist, Bill Cameron, you said, "Let's make Canada the country it deserves to be." How much progress has been made since 1991 and what's left to do?*

P.F.   *We've made some significant progress and the most significant of those moments – if I can describe it that way – is the June 11th [2008] apology. It was historic, unprecedented; we were on the floor of the House of Commons, speaking in our own voice about our own rights to the world. It was an electric moment and the apology actually sets the stage for the transformation that Canada must undergo. A positive transformation that values culture, language and the right to govern oneself as a self-determining people. We have this incredible opportunity to take some important steps together as a country. Without the apology, this transformation was going to be very, very difficult. It is a moment in time for all of us. It sets the stage because we are now in a far better position to tackle the most important social issue of our time, which is First Nations' poverty.*

B.M.   **Do you think that the current economic problems are going to interfere with that?**

P.F.   *The current economic meltdown is a real opportunity for us because everyone is talking about and preoccupied with the stimulus package. With all of the talk of a recession or a depression, we must remember that even in the best of times we haven't shared well. Now everyone can understand the unique position we occupy as the most impoverished segment in Canadian society. We are going to have to get out of this together. When they are talking about job creation, easing credit and infrastructure initiatives, well all of that fits in with what we need in our communities: decent housing, safe drinking water, good schools, access to quality health care, shelters for battered women, job training, and rehabilitation centres.*

B.M.   **Those are all very necessary, but don't we also need more leadership and effort from the First Nations communities themselves, like the efforts that Bernd Christmas and Chief Lawrence Paul and others have made to make their communities more self-sustaining?**

P.F.   *That's very positive because when I talk about setting the stage and the stimulus package, I am talking about the next wave of wealth creation that is going to take place on our lands and our territories because that's where most of the minerals are. Hydro development is going to take place* *on our lands, as is power generation and transmission, pipelines, oil and gas, and forestry. When government talks about a 2 or 3 hundred million dollar investment in the next decade, well much of that is going to take place on our lands. In order to do this right we are going to have to look at examples like the Mi'kmaq, Membertwo, Osoyoos, Fort McKay, Westbank, the Tribal Investment Group, the Crees of Quebec, and even the casinos in Manitoba, Saskatchewan, Ontario, Quebec, etc., that's all about wealth and job creation and job training and that's all about capacity building. There is a better appreciation in the corporate sector that there has to be a new approach to partnerships so that Membertou and other experiences are very important to us because we are talking about success and we are going to have to build on success.*

B.M.   **Doesn't there need to be more people like you who take the initiative to make these things happen?**

P.F.   *I believe that the kind of understanding, knowledge, and appreciation that is needed to bring about this positive transformation is situated in so many parts of the country. It is in Millbrook, Membertou, Northern Quebec, Southern Ontario, and the golden triangle of Northern Ontario in mining. It's in Saskatchewan in agriculture and mining, Alberta in Northern development and in British Columbia with wonderful opportunities in 2010 and the treaty-making process and in the Northwest Territories where we have the diamond mines. The point I believe that's being made here is that that type of development has to be part of our experience and it has to become part of our culture but it shouldn't ever be done at the expense of the land and the environment. We are going to have to learn how to establish balance better than what we have witnessed to date. I believe we have a lot to offer in terms of traditional knowledge. For example, in the area of global warming, Sheila Watt-Cloutier is a hero to all indigenous people. She has done incredible work in trying to save the planet.*

B.M.   **Speaking of heroes, do you see the election of the first Afro-American president as having an impact on the First Nations People or as being a role-model for First Nations People?**

P.F.   *Barack Obama is an inspiration for the world. With the election of Obama as the President of the United States, the message that that sends to the world is that anything is possible. We can now talk about having an aboriginal Prime Minister. If the US can elect a black President, then we can elect an aboriginal Prime Minister or Premier, and I am certain that we will see that come to pass.*

We have looked at five different visions: MEC's vision of being a world-class leader in balancing economic and environmental sustainability, Pfizer's vision of being the best learning organization in the pharmaceutical industry, Roy Romanow's vision that Canada will have the most comprehensive health care in the world, David Johnson's vision that by 2020, Canada will lead the world in higher education, innovation and research, and Phil Fontaine's vision of developing a more self-reliant, healthier and prosperous future for Canada's First Nations peoples. I would like to add that becoming the best in the world requires tremendous forethought and vision, however, once you and your organization have developed your vision, that vision should not remain static as the following example points out.

Changing the Vision at Canadian National Railway

Canadian National Railway was the worst major national railway in North America when Paul Tellier took over in 1992. Under Paul's leadership, CN became the best major national railroad in North America and there are a number of objective criteria that attest to the fact that CN is now the best major national railroad in North America.[7] For example, "The stock market value of CN has grown from $2 billion when the Canadian government sold it to roughly $27 billion today."[8] As well, "If you had invested $75,000 when CN went public in 1995 and left this and the dividends in place, you would have $1 million today."[9]

When Paul Tellier left CN in January, 2003, to become the President of Bombardier, Hunter Harrison became the President and CEO of CN. Paul and Hunter have very different styles of leadership, however, both had one thing in common — they both had strong visions of where CN should go and they both had plans on how to get there. Under Paul Tellier, the vision for CN was to be the best railroad in North America. Under Hunter Harrison, the vision for CN is to be the best transportation company in the world. Many companies lose their way and their vision when a new President and CEO takes over. CN hasn't lost its vision – it has expanded it.

A seventh example of an organization with a strong vision is Canada Post. Many Canadians may be surprised to know that Canada Post is rated as the third most efficient postal system in the world, after the US and Australia. Given Canada's large geography, sparse population outside of the major cities, and our long cold winters, this is quite an accomplishment. Canada Post's vision is:

> Canada Post will be a world leader in providing innovative physical and electronic delivery solutions, creating value for our customers, employees and all Canadians.

If the vision provides the foundation for an organization, living its values provides a great deal of the passion. Canada Post lists it values as follows:

- We work to earn our customers' business
- We succeed by working together
- We take responsibility for our actions
- We treat each other with fairness and respect
- We strive to continuously improve
- We act with integrity in all we do

We will examine Canada Post and the large number of changes that are taking place there more closely in "Strategy 3: Assess Your Leadership Style". Now I would like to look at why vision has a mixed reputation.

Vision's Bad Rap

As we have seen in the above examples, vision can be a powerful force for organizational growth, however, the concept of visioning and writing a vision statement developed a bad reputation when it became a management fad, and like all fads, it had its day. Developing a vision was often a top down endeavour that was produced by a committee. Vision statements also tended to be long, hard to remember, and worse yet, often rang hollow. In the end, organizations ended up with one of two kinds of vision statements – living or dead. I would like to illustrate the difference between a living mission and a dead one with the tale of two hospitals.

My father had lung cancer for the second time and it was spreading throughout his body. My parents lived in California and I lived in Nova Scotia so I went to California as often and for as long as I could. My mother was the primary care giver and we kept my father home for as long as we could. However, even with hiring professional nursing assistance, his care became too much; my mother was simply worn out. Subsequently, one sad day, my father was admitted to a hospital near my parents' home.

The hospital was a new low-rise beautifully landscaped building with a view of the rolling hills. The colour scheme both inside and out was relaxing and in many ways the building resembled more a four star hotel than a hospital. I also noticed that when we went to visit, opposite the elevators on each floor, was a beautifully gold-framed mission statement for the hospital that stated how important the patient is and the exceptional level of care the patients would receive.

For our family, it was difficult to accept that their mission statement was true. As a patient with lung cancer, my father was hooked up to a constant supply of oxygen. After a while, the steady flow of oxygen causes the patient's mouth to become very dry and the hospital is supposed to have a steady supply of ice water on hand to relieve the dry mouth. Even after repeated requests, both by my father and his family, the ice water was rarely replenished. The lack of ice water was only one of the most glaring examples of the hospital's lack of attention to detail. The only area where their attention to detail excelled was that every item that could be expensed – many of which seemed totally unnecessary – were expensed to the Nth degree.

The frustration was unbearable. In the end, my tired mother, with our wonderful volunteer nurse from Home Hospice who also volunteered her two sons looked after my father at home, where he died in peace surrounded by family and familiar surroundings.

Contrast the hospital in California with the old Grace Maternity Hospital in Halifax. My son, Andrew, was born at the old — decrepit would have been a better description — Grace Maternity Hospital eight months after my father died. There was no written mission statement, or if there were one, you would not have been able to see it because the hallways were strewn with equipment and sometimes even hospital beds.

As a first-time father, who couldn't stand the sight of blood, and wasn't much good where pain is concerned either; my biggest fear was that I would faint in the delivery room. We had an amazing nurse and I still remember her name 21 years later — Mary Ann Tynes. Mary Ann told us that we were smart to choose the Grace Maternity Hospital because her hospital had the best live delivery rate of all of the hospitals in North America. She said those words with pride and then proceeded to coach us through the process. Her skill and her pride gave us the confidence to fully experience the birth of our son. This hospital did not have a "dead" gold-framed mission statement that had no meaning. This hospital had a "living" mission statement "We have the best live delivery rate of any hospital in North America." The staff didn't have to memorize it because they lived it.

There are five criteria for an outstanding vision statement. It has to be:

- Short

- Crystal Clear

- Deeply Meaningful

- Absolutely Congruent with the Organizations' Goals, Values and Objectives

- Truly Memorable

The Carter Center,[10] founded by former U.S. President Jimmy Carter and his wife Roslyn, to advance human rights and alleviate human suffering, has one of the best vision statements I have ever heard. The vision for the Carter Center is, "Waging Peace, Fighting Disease, Building Hope." What makes this statement exceptional? First, it is easy to remember; only six words. Secondly, the words are strong and powerful. Thirdly, they fully represent what the Carter Center is about, and these words absolutely ring true. In fact, it has to be crystal clear. It is like the difference in the ring when you tap an ordinary drinking glass with a fork versus when you tap a fine piece of crystal.

When an organization develops a clear and compelling vision, it becomes a living testament as to what that organization stands for while helping that organization bring its vision to fruition. Before Master Leaders can help develop their organizations' visions, they have to develop their own.

> *We know what we are, but know not what we may be.*
> **Shakespeare**

Five Methods to Help You See Your Vision More Clearly

There are five methods that can help you develop a clearer vision for yourself as a leader. It doesn't matter whether it is a personal vision or a professional vision or both.

1. Write a Vision Statement. Write a vision statement for yourself or your organization. Examples of four visions appeared at the beginning of this chapter with MEC, Pfizer, CN and Canada Post. You can gain additional insights by interviewing the most visionary leaders you know and by asking one to three people who know you well and whom you trust to give you input into and feedback on how they see your personal or professional vision.

2. List your Heroes. What do your heroes have in common? How are they different? What have they accomplished? For example, three of my heroes are Janet Conners, Fred MacGillivray and Rick Hansen. In completing this exercise, I found that they all have a strong vision on how to make the world a better place. They have developed strong self-discipline, they are persistent and committed to overcoming any and all obstacles, they are results oriented, and are magnets who have the ability to attract others in helping to bring their vision to fruition.

Which skills have you identified that you have developed and/or want to enhance? For example I would like to be as gracious as Janet Conners, as proactive as Fred MacGillivray and as self-disciplined as Rick Hansen.

A slightly different take on this exercise is to write the introduction for an event where your hero will receive a lifetime achievement award for his or her contributions as a leader. Often this person is an alter ego and what you write will apply equally well to your own life as it does to his or hers. An example of two of my heroes, Cath and Pete Moore, follows. After you read it, take some time to think about and then write your own example.

Cath and Pete Moore
Receive Lifetime Achievement Award
for Their Humanitarian Work in Jamaica

Cath and Pete spent their life savings to help establish Jamaica's first National Learn-to-Swim Program – SwimJamaica. The first goal of SwimJamaica is to teach Jamaicans to swim and help reduce the number of needless deaths from drowning. There is a special emphasis on teaching poor inner-city children from Kingston to swim. Kingston is home to some of the poorest children in the world and only half of the children graduating from elementary school are literate. Unemployment is high and poverty and crime are rampant. SwimJamaica is working to change the conditions that led to poverty and crime by helping Jamaicans change their personal metaphors from an external focus: "The world controls me and I have no power to change it", to an internal focus: "I am empowered to shape my destiny."

SwimJamaica is providing a metaphor for success. The message is, if I can learn the discipline I need in order to learn to swim, I can eventually apply that discipline to anything I undertake. Cath, who is a professional swimming instructor, wrote 140 lesson plans, assessment tests, and training and career development pathways for SwimJamaica instructors. There are SwimJamaica Programs for toddlers, children, adults and people with physical challenges. Children, even in their very early lessons, are exposed to synchronized swimming and water polo so they can see that their swimming careers can continue after they complete their lessons.

There are two avenues for future success once these children have learned to swim. They can teach others to swim, which will provide them with gainful employment and secondly, it helps them learn to take on leadership responsibilities and learn that they have the capacity to lead.

Integral to the success of SwimJamaica is the SwimJamaica infrastructure program. You cannot teach people to swim, have people teaching swimming and develop a national competitive swim program if you do not have pools in which these activities can take place. Although Jamaica is surrounded by the warm tropical Caribbean Ocean, and there are many first rate pools for Jamaica's tourists, there are very few pools for Jamaicans, and most of the few pools that do exist are in such a state of disrepair that they are not usable. Therefore, in order to bring SwimJamaica to fruition, Pete developed a five-year sponsorship program. Sponsorship was obtained not only to enable the inner-city children to join the program, but also to refurbish and re-open some of the swimming facilities.

If leadership is about influencing others in order to bring about sustainable positive change for the future, Cath and Pete are Master Leaders in every sense of those words. If leadership is about establishing metaphors for success, Cath and Pete are providing metaphors for success not only for individual Jamaicans, but for the entire country of Jamaica. They see the investment of their life savings as an investment in Jamaica, but it is also an investment in themselves because they are learning and teaching invaluable lessons about leadership in their efforts to help establish SwimJamaica and those lessons will stand them in good stead for the rest of their lives.

3. Write a Personal or Organizational Letter from the future.[11] Pick a time in the future — 5, 10, 15 years from now, or any length longer or shorter, that is meaningful to you. Date the top of the letter with the imaginary future date. Imagine that the intervening years have passed and you are writing to a good friend or colleague and use your friend's or colleague's name in the salutation. The person you write the letter to should be a person with whom you feel comfortable sharing your personal/organizational vision for the future.

Writing "the letter from the future" will feel strange at first. Most people get a feeling of uncertainty – writing about the future in the past tense just does not make sense. However, as you progress in your writing it will feel more normal. The amazing thing is, that for most people, by the time they finish their letter, usually a part of what they need to do and how to make those changes becomes clearer. In other words, we usually have more of the answer than we think we do. Writing "the letter from the future" helps all of us tap into some of our own personal wisdom that is usually hidden within us.

The purpose of dating the letter and writing it to someone you actually know is to strengthen the psychological realism of the letter. Imagine that in this future you have successfully resolved the current changes, transitions, and uncertainty in your life. Describe what helped you resolve those problems. At the time of the letter writing, you are living a wonderful, joyous, healthy, satisfying life. Describe how you are spending your time, where you are living, your relationships, beliefs, and reflections on the past and future. An example of one of my letters from the future follows.

August 28, 2020

Dear Terrye:

I have now finally and officially retired and The Atlantic Leadership Development Institute is getting along just fine without me. The big breakthrough occurred in 2009 when I published The Seven Strategies of Master Leaders. The book took off like gang busters. The cross-Canada publicity blitz did wonders for the book. In doing the PR blitz, I started doing all of my keynotes and courses through The Atlantic Leadership Development Institute. This meant that I could work significantly fewer days, but my profits and revenue went up 50%. The other major event of that year was that the website finally started paying for itself.

By the end of 2009 we were also running The Leadership Development Institute in Kingston, Jamaica. By 2015, native Jamaicans' were doing most of the work, but I consulted and helped out as much as I could.

In 2012, Ricky Nowak and I launched The Australian Leadership Development Institute. I must say that I have enjoyed working and traveling in Australia and New Zealand. And although I have not written any new books, I have been busy revising the old ones. In 2015, I turned most of the work over to my new and capable assistant and concentrated on doing volunteer work in the third world and in helping MISA (the Metropolitan Immigrant Settlement Association) accomplish its goals of getting more deserving emigrants to come to Nova Scotia and helping to make sure that the ones who do come, stay here.

Brad

A good variation to the exercise is to write down where you see yourself and your organization in two years' time. One of the advantages of the shorter time frame is that you have more control in the short term and it is easier to quantify and measure the desired results. For example:

In two years time, I will be teaching and consulting one-third of the time, doing keynotes one-third of the time, and traveling and/or writing one-third of the time. I will have quadrupled the sales of products on my website and even though I am spending less time at work, my income will have increased by twenty-five percent.

4. Draw a Picture. A picture is worth a thousand words, even if you say you can't draw. Using a large piece of paper and coloured markers, draw a picture of how you currently see yourself. Include who and what influences you, both positively and negatively. Then draw an idealized picture of how you would like to see yourself at some point in the future, for example in five or ten years. What do the differences between the two pictures suggest? How could these suggestions be translated into actionable goals? My example appears in Figure 1-1 and the suggestion was to do less volunteer work, do a better job of the volunteer work that remained and take more time for myself.

Figure 1-1
The Top Drawing Shows My Current Use of Time
And the Bottom Drawing Shows My Ideal Use of Time

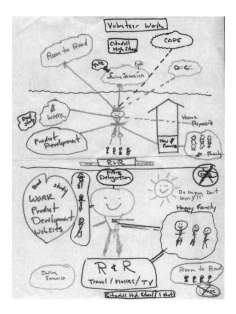

5. Make a collage. Gather some old magazines, go through them, and cut out pictures that you like. Don't spend time thinking about why you like them; just pick those that are meaningful to you. When you have finished, divide a large piece of paper in half and place both halves in front of you. The section on the left will represent your life as you currently see it, and the one on the right will be your life as you would like it. Now paste the pictures that you have cut out onto one of the two sections depending on which they represent. Often, it is best to do this with a friend because it will force you to be more articulate. This exercise also helps to make information from your abstract, conceptual, and future based part of your brain more real and more concrete, which also makes it more likely that you will be able to move forward and act on your vision.

Exercise 1-1: Now that you have completed all five of the above exercises, can you identify common themes? What are you learning about your goals, your life and your vision? Then, write down the goals and the vision for your life that seem to emerge from these five exercises.

Next, write down a plan to help you ensure you accomplish those goals that are most important to you and will help you bring your vision to fruition, including: What will you do? Who will help you? What resources do you have? What is your timeline?

What do you need to stop doing, start doing, and continue doing?

How do I Find My Passion?

All the Master Leaders I interviewed for *The Seven Strategies of Master Leaders* were fueled by passion: from Roy Romanow's vision for Canada to have the most efficient and effective comprehensive health care system in the world, to David Johnston's vision to develop the most advanced system of post-secondary education, research and innovation at the University of Waterloo, to Moya Greene's vision to transform Canada Post into the best postal system in the world.

Not surprisingly, a question I am frequently asked at the Atlantic Leadership Development Institute is, "How do I find my passion?" This is an easy question to ask, but a much more difficult question to answer – but here goes.

Your passion is related to your true purpose. When you identify your passion and articulate it, it has a crystal clear ring to it and this usually takes a great deal of time and effort. A very good place to start is to know your strengths and values in order to help you have the energy and passion to bring your vision to fruition. Three methods that can help you identify your passion are the Hedgehog Concept, the Signature Strengths test and StrengthsFinder 2.0. Each of these methods will be described below.

Transform Your Career from Good to Great

The crucial contribution of Jim Collins' seminal book, *Good to Great*, is the culmination of one of the most thorough research projects ever undertaken on business.[12] In his research, Collins identifies seven crucial factors that individually and collectively contribute to the transformation of good companies into great companies.

In his ground-breaking research, Collins looked at similar companies that were good. However, at some point, some of these companies became great and others did not. Collins then identified seven key factors that were instrumental in transforming a good company into a great company. This section of the book examines how two concepts from *Good to Great* can be applied to help leaders and potential leaders reach levels of peak performance that they would not otherwise have thought possible.

The two concepts, "The Hedgehog Concept" and the "Concept of the Flywheel," are explained in more detail in Collins' book. For our purpose, exercises and action steps to help you apply these techniques to your own specific circumstances are included.

Collins defines "The Hedgehog Concept" as follows:

> The essential strategic difference between the good-to-great and comparison companies lay in two fundamental distinctions. First, the good-to-great companies founded their strategies on deep understanding along three key dimensions — what we came to call the three circles. Second, the good-to-great companies translated that understanding into a simple, crystalline concept that guided all their efforts... [13]

Whereas Collins uses the three circles of "The Hedgehog Concept" to look at good-to-great companies, I have applied these concepts to understand the transformation from good-to-great performance on an individual level. The three circles, as applied to individual performance, are shown in Figure 1-2.

Figure 1-2

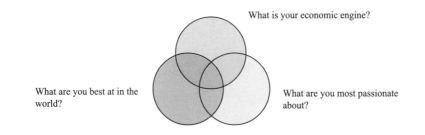

What is your economic engine?

What are you best at in the world?

What are you most passionate about?

What are you most passionate about?

It may take years to fully define the content of each circle. You can define it through reflection, by observing the activities that lead to flow and glow, and/ or by getting feedback from others. For example, I have been teaching *The Seven Strategies of Master Negotiators* for the past 20 years. In 1998 I published a book by the same name. In the book I interviewed 21 of Canada's top negotiators. However, it wasn't until after I finished the book that I realized that everyone

I had interviewed for the book was not only a Master Negotiator, but also a Master Presenter *and* a Master Leader. It was then that I realized that teaching negotiating and influencing skills was not where my true passion lay. I discovered that my passion lies where negotiation, presentation and leadership skills and strategies converge in a manner that is absolutely seamless, so seamless; in fact, that you cannot tell where one ends and the other begins. As well, my goal is that the negotiation, presentation and leadership skills have to be used to make the world a better place. I now know where my true passion lies.

You may discover what you are most passionate about in one sitting. For most of us, it takes many hours of thinking, reflection, refinement, deep discussion and salient feedback from people who know us well, until we get it just right. However, when you do get it just right, it will have a crystal clear ring to it just like the mission statement for the Carter Center – "Waging Peace, Fighting Disease, Building Hope".

Exercise 1-2: What are you most passionate about? Take a moment and think about what makes you passionate: at work, in your home life or volunteer work. Write down what comes to mind.

What are you best at?

The next circle is what you are best at. In other words, we want to obtain maximum synergy by doing what we are most passionate about and to use our best skills, talents and abilities to help us pursue that passion.

Here again, it may take years of thinking, reflecting, refining and obtaining significant feedback from others to determine what we are best at in the world. And once again, when we have articulated what we are best at in the world, it will have a crystal clear ring to it.

For example, I am best at finding ideas backed by scientific evidence and translating those ideas so they can be readily understood. I then use metaphors and mnemonics (memory techniques) so they can be easily remembered and provide an easy-to-use implementation system so these ideas can be readily applied to produce real-world results. For people who are retired or partially retired, this is an ideal time to start something new, especially if you have the economic freedom to fund it yourself. There are also many opportunities to make a difference by doing what you are best at through volunteer work and/or through mentoring others.

If you still want or need paid work, there are opportunities to apply your talents. All you need to do is to look where you can find funding and/or downsize your lifestyle and fund, or partially fund, those things that you would most enjoy doing. For example, I met two dentists, Neil and Anna, while hiking with my son in the Peruvian Andes. They had just spend two weeks volunteering in the Amazon rain forests on a medical boat that provided medical services for the indigenous people who only saw a doctor or dentist once a year. Both Neil and Anna said that this was among the most meaningful experiences they had ever had.

Exercise 1-3: What are you best at? What feedback have you received that supports that you are best at this? What other kinds of feedback do you need to obtain to help you refine what you are best at?

What is your economic engine?

Your economic engine supplies you with the financial means so you can do what you are most passionate about. If you are self-employed, your economic engine is your own business. For example, my economic engine is my course, "Become a Master Negotiator" and 50% of my income is derived from doing keynotes and teaching seminars on that subject. However, as much as I love teaching this particular course, I am now in the process of re-branding my business as the *Atlantic Leadership Development Institute*™. In this institute, we focus on developing our clients' abilities where negotiating, presenting and leadership strategies and skills merge as a unified whole. When the change in my economic engine is complete, the three circles will perfectly align.

If you work for someone else, or for a company or an organization, your economic engine is how you perceive your current job, but it is also your career path — that is, where your current job can take you. In the past, the only way for many individuals to move up the corporate ladder was to move into management and, in general, your pay was determined by how many people you supervised. Today's more enlightened organizations have non-traditional career paths, so someone who has expertise in a certain area also has a career ladder that recognizes his or her increasing value to the company or organization, based on his or her expertise, and the return on investment that that person brings to that particular organization. For example, a talented chemist could move to become a senior chemist, and then assistant director of research in his or her particular area, before becoming director of research.

In other cases, there is no career ladder, but enlightened employers acknowledge and reward an employee's depth of experience and/or use lateral transfers to help their employees gain valuable skills and knowledge. Another viable option is to use special assignments as opportunities for growth and development, and/or take advanced training or an advanced degree to help you move up in your career.

Exercise 1-4: What is your current economic engine? How is it measured? How well does it line up with and support your passion and abilities? Does it need to be altered, and if so how? If you work for a company or organization, what career path exists for you? What creative career path needs to be developed? Do you need to move to an organization that fully values your areas of expertise?

The Sweet Spot

The sweet spot is that space where the three circles intersect. It is a place of great synergy where 1 plus 1 is not 2, but 11. It is also the place that provides opportunities for maximum growth and development reside.

What are you most passionate about?

But passion by itself is not enough. We can be passionate about a great number of things. For example, I am very passionate about music; however I am tone deaf. Therefore music for me is a great thing to listen to, but my musically inclined children are not overly appreciative of my singing abilities.

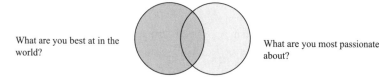

When we determine what we are best at and add this to what we are most passionate about, we narrow our focus so we can better utilize our talents. This is the place of "flow." The place where things are easy for us to learn, do and achieve higher-order results. Time just seems to stand still, until we look at the clock and realize that a great deal of time has passed.

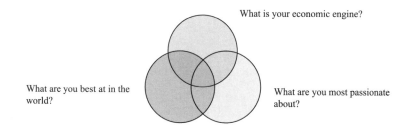

Then when we include our economic engine we have the convergence of passion, what we are best at and what supports us financially. This results in a highly focused individual who can more easily move from good to great. Another way to look at the area where the three circles intersect is the sweet spot. This is the area of maximum strength.

Finding Your Strengths

I had the distinct pleasure of attending a keynote address on Authentic Happiness by Dr. Martin Seligman.[14] Martin started his presentation with a story about being interviewed by CNN on the current state of psychology in the world. Martin was only given one word to state his answer, to which he responded by saying, *"Good."* Since this was not much of a sound bite, the reporter said he could have two words, and Martin said, *"Not Good."* The CNN reporter wasn't happy with this sound bite either, so he said he could have three words, and Martin answered, *"Not Good Enough."*

Martin then went on to state his point of view more explicitly by stating that psychology has done a good job in researching mental illness and is making strides in helping people get better. However, psychology has done a very poor job in researching happiness and helping people do a better job of attaining it. He then explained the characteristics of people who lead *"A Pleasant Life", "A Good Life"* and *"A Meaningful Life." "A Pleasant Life"* consists of having pleasant experiences such as sharing an excellent meal with a good friend; *"A Good Life"* consists of using your signature strengths (your most fundamental strengths) and *"A Meaningful Life"* consists of using your "signature strengths and virtues in the service of something much larger than you are."[15] He then told the participants, who were sitting on the edge of their seats, that we can have a *"Full Life"* which consists of a pleasant, good and meaningful life.

Martin states that, "Authentic Happiness comes from identifying and cultivating your signature strengths and using them every day in work, love, play, and parenting."[16] You can determine your Signature Strengths by reading his book *Authentic Happiness* and/or by visiting his website www.authentichappiness. org. The test, which is free, only takes about 25 minutes to complete and the results, unlike most psychological tests, are all positive. The results show your top five signature strengths and give you a percentile ranking for each one.

My own results surprised me and were most worthwhile in helping me connect with my passion. My number two strength was Industry, Diligence and Perseverance. For people who know me this comes as no surprise. Number four was Curiosity and Interest in the World and number five was Love of Learning, again no surprises. My number three was Bravery and Valor. At first I was surprised. But when I had more time to think about it, there are times when I will take a very strong stand for those things I truly believe in. What surprised me the most was that my number one was Creativity, Ingenuity and Originality. The more I thought about my number one Signature Strength, the more I knew I had to change my career. I had been extremely satisfied with one exception. I had been teaching the same course for so long that it was hard for me to think of any new or original ways to teach it better. At the same time, I had found that the books I was writing were the most original and creative thing I was doing. The answer: teach less and probably lower my dollar income, but spend more time writing and increase my passion and psychological income, which is exactly what I did.

StrengthsFinder 2.0 is another excellent way to get a clearer picture of your strengths and talents. "The philosopher Baruch Spinoza said that 'to be what we are, and to become what we are capable of becoming, is the only end of life.' You may disagree with his emphasis, but surely one of the goals of your life is to discover and apply your strengths. If your senses are numbed with delusion and denial, you will stop looking for these true strengths and wind up living a second-rate version of someone else's life rather than a world-class version of your own".[17]

The StrengthsFinder test was developed in a study of over two million people by Gallup. There are two ways to gain access to this test. One is to buy the book *StrengthsFinder 2.0.* On the inside of the back cover is a code. When you go to the website www.strengthsfinder.com and enter the code, you can take the StrengthsFinder test. You can also purchase a code on-line from the web-site, and then take the test.

The StrengthsFinder test takes approximately 30 minutes to complete. It measures 34 distinct strengths and identifies your top five strengths. For example, my top five are: 1) Learner, 2) Focus, 3) Achiever, 4) Individualization, and 5) Ideation. Numbers one and three were no surprise, but numbers two, four and five surprised me a bit, especially at first. There is no question that I am a dedicated learner. Upon reflection, I am more focused than I thought I was. My focus has helped me to achieve more than I would have ever dreamed possible. Although at times, my business associates and my family find me too focused and this is something that I have to guard against. Individualization means that I can relate well to individual people (especially when I am not too focused), discern how to best use their talents and skills and build an effective multi-disciplinary team. Ideation means that I love ideas, which helps explain why I am such an avid reader who is always in search of new ideas, concepts and information.

As an added bonus, the book tells you how to manage people who have each of the 34 strengths. This information is invaluable in managing direct reports, but it can also help peers and colleagues learn how to better appreciate and utilize their respective strengths as they work together in groups of two or more. Lastly, by reading how to manage each of the various strengths, we can look at how we can manage ourselves more effectively.

In sum, this test will help you identify your strengths and better determine how you can use them. As Buckingham and Clifton so eloquently state, "To polish even one theme so that it becomes a true strength will test your self-awareness and your resourcefulness. To hone all five is the work of a lifetime".[18]

The Signature Strengths test and StrengthsFinder 2.0 are two of the best instruments that you can use to help you find your passion.

Once you have identified — or at least have begun to identify — the elements of each of your three circles, that is what you are most passionate about, what you are best at and what your economic engine is, you then need to consider what you need to do to bring all of these efforts to fruition. In the next section, we will look at Jim Collins' "Concept of the Flywheel," which is designed to do just this.

The Flywheel

Good to great comes about by a cumulative process — step by step, action by action, decision by decision, turn by turn of the flywheel — that adds up to sustained and spectacular results.[19]

— Jim Collins

A flywheel is a large heavy metal wheel, similar to the one used to help raise the roadway within Tower Bridge in London, England. This was necessary to accommodate ships that were too tall to pass under the bridge when the roadway was down. A picture of the flywheel at Tower Bridge appears at Figure 1-3.

Figure 1-3

The analogy of the flywheel is that when we first start pushing on the flywheel to turn it, it takes a great deal of effort. If we keep pushing on the wheel, it eventually takes less effort and, inevitably, once a suitable momentum is reached, it takes very little effort to keep the flywheel going. Jim Collins states that the good-to-great companies kept taking action and making decisions until the momentum took over. This is another of the factors that helped to account for their transformation from good to great.

The same concept can also be applied to individuals who are peak performers. It is important to be aware that the concept of the flywheel is not the same as the concept of goal setting, although goal setting may be a part of it. Achieving your goals may or may not propel you to the next level of functioning. However, setting the right goals, making the right decisions and overcoming the right obstacles will help take you to the next level in your career. These activities will also help you realize the synergy that occurs, and that synergy helps create the momentum we feel when all three circles come together.

For example, to add momentum in your own career, you may need to:

1. Take on a leadership/developmental assignment at work or outside of work
2. Find a coach or mentor
3. Form or join a mastermind group
4. Work in a start up operation
5. Take over a group that isn't performing well
6. Take on an assignment in a foreign country

Exercise 1-5: What are the three to five things that you need to do, or actions that you need to take, that would bring momentum to your efforts and help you to reach your goal of taking your career to the next level?

1.

2.

3.

4.

5.

We have looked at how you can apply two of the concepts from Jim Collins' book *Good to Great* to help you as an individual move from good to great to your own career development.

These exercises and resources in this chapter will help you identify your passion. However, Master Leaders have developed something that is deeper than a passion, which is known as a calling. A calling is to do one's ultimate life's work. But how exactly do we discover our true calling? One of the most powerful analogies that author Greg Levoy uses in his book *Callings: Finding and Following an Authentic Life* is the analogy of connecting the dots. You may remember, as a child, having a book where you completed pictures by connecting the dots. At some point, enough of the dots were connected; you could clearly tell what the picture was going to be.

In the same manner, if you connect the significant events in your life, a clear picture will eventually appear and that picture will help to reveal your true calling in life. The metaphor of connecting the dots means we all have life experiences that are exceptionally meaningful for us. When we look at the connections between those events, we discover the deeper significance that can be derived from figuring out the relationship among these life experiences — which in turn will help us discover our "calling."

The following exercise helped me become more clear about my life's calling. In this exercise, I had to describe three events that were the most meaningful for me during the past year. During that year, I self-published a book, helped a man deal with panic attacks and went on the adventure of a lifetime with my son. These events require a bit of explanation to illustrate why they were so significant in helping me understand my calling.

I was in the process of finishing my first self-published book. This was the first time I had written a gift book versus my previous books which all had had a business and education focus. This meant that I had the ultimate responsibility for getting the book designed, getting it type set, printed, marketed and sold.

After a marathon brainstorming session, we agreed on just the right title — *From Our Grandmothers' Lap: Lessons for a Lifetime*. The next step was to find a warm, evocative cover that would entice potential readers to pick it up and buy it. The next step was marketing the book. One of my clients is the Credit Union Central of Nova Scotia. One of the charities they support is the Canadian Cancer Society, so they were given the book for what it cost to have the books printed. This enabled them to sell the book as a fund raiser. Copies of the book literally flew out of the credit unions and we received tremendous media publicity for the book.

Why did I list the writing and self-publishing of the gift book as one of my biggest accomplishments? Because I learned so much about publishing, sales and marketing, and this information will be of great value to me for the rest of my writing career. Also, this activity combined three of my passions – learning, creativity and humanitarian work.

The second most meaningful event of that year occurred when I was teaching in Jamaica. My friends, Cath and Pete, drove me up in the Blue Mountains to spend the night and do some hiking. The mountains were covered with tropical trees and coffee plants, the view was magnificent, and the air was fresh and clear. On that night, I was the only guest at the Starlight Hotel.

On the morning of the second day, Amy, the proprietress, asked me what I did for a living and I told her I was a psychologist. She said that she perfectly understood that I was on vacation, but wondered if I would mind talking to one of her employees. I said yes, not knowing what I might be getting myself into. As a professional speaker and consultant, I hadn't practiced as a psychologist for years. The employee Amy asked me to speak with was Dwayne (not his real name), the hotel's gardener. In a thick Jamaican accent, he told me he was having difficulty reading his Bible. He said that sometimes he could sound the words and read his Bible, but sometimes he would have spells where he couldn't read at all. He added that he was very frustrated and sometimes broke down and cried.

The first thing I thought of was a differential diagnosis, in order to develop a viable treatment plan. Did he need tutoring in how to read? Was he having panic attacks or suffering from an obsessive/compulsive disorder? I decided I would ask Dwayne some more questions to see if I could further differentiate what was preventing him from reading. So, I asked Dwayne if he understood the word diagnosis. No, he didn't. I asked him if he drove a car, hoping to use having car trouble to explain diagnosis. No, he didn't. He did, however, drive a truck at work. I was then able to explain diagnosis. If the truck wouldn't start, was it because of an electrical problem, mechanical problem, or was the truck out of gas? He then understood what I meant by diagnosis.

The next thing I asked him was if he had a doctor. No doctor. Therefore, the problem would have to be treated solely psychologically. I formulated three interventions I thought might help. First, whenever he felt anxious about reading, I suggested he do sit-ups or push-ups until he felt physically tired. The psychological principle behind this is that you can't be anxious and relaxed at the same time. Secondly, I suggested he change his thinking from "I can't read as well as I would like" to "Where can I get help to learn to read better?" He said his fiancée could help him learn to read better. Thirdly, since I knew he was deeply religious, I asked him when he met Saint Peter in heaven, if Saint Peter would be more interested in how well he read or in how good a father and husband he was. He said, "How good a father and husband." So I suggested he repeat this to himself when he started to feel anxious about reading.

Dwayne thanked me profusely, although I really didn't do very much. However, over time, I kept thinking about this encounter. One of my traditions is that at the end of every year is to ask myself what my biggest accomplishments were, and write them down. This particular year, it surprised me at first when I listed my encounter with Dwayne as one of my two biggest accomplishments. Then I asked myself why helping Dwayne made the list. It was only then that I realized that doing volunteer work, especially helping people in Third World countries had become increasingly important to me. What is the existential message behind this? Do more of it.

The following year, my son and I climbed the Inca Trail to Machu Picchu, the most famous of all of the Inca ruins in Peru. It is a 42 kilometer climb, starting in Cusco where the altitude is 3,300 metres — that means there is 40% less oxygen. On a scale of 1 to 5, with 5 being the most difficult, this hike is rated 4.5, which means that you have to be in superb condition.

Experiencing the hike and seeing Machu Picchu was truly an adventure of a lifetime, and I don't think I have ever felt more alive. Not only did I learn a great deal about the Inca civilization — I also learned a great deal about my son and myself. One of the most important lessons I learned was to spend more time honouring my spirit of adventure in both large and small ways.

When I looked at the three seminal events I had written down at the end of that year, a much clearer picture emerged of how I want to live my life — more writing, more volunteer work, more adventure, more learning, and sharing all of these activities with the people I love.

Now it is your turn to try this powerful exercise. The more often you do this exercise, the clearer you will become about your true calling.

Exercise 1-6: Connecting the Dots.

In the space below, list several events that had a lot of meaning for you in the past year or two. Then connect the dots and/or ask for feedback from others as to the pattern that they see emerging.

Sometimes we cannot see our passion or our accomplishments clearly, but others who are close to us can. Asking others how they see your passion and/or your accomplishments can also be an enlightening experience.

Exercise 1-7: How Others See My Passion/Accomplishments.

In the space below, list the names of three to five people you could ask as to how they see your passion and your accomplishments.

1.

2.

3.

4.

5.

After you have listed your passions and accomplishments, try to figure out the existential message or messages that underlie your passion and accomplishments. As you begin this process and continue to do this from one year to the next, you will begin to connect the dots. Then decide how this message or messages can be applied in your work life, volunteer work, hobbies, and/or your personal life. Lastly, develop a viable plan to implement what you have learned. If you would like to further explore finding your passion, you can order my E-book, *Are You Managing Your Career or Is Your Career Managing You?* from my website – www.BradMcRae.com.

Exercise 1-8: My Plan to Implement What I have Learned is:

Taking the Authentic Happiness Signature Strengths test, StrengthsFinder, and figuring out your Hedgehog Concept from Good to Great, and then connecting your own significant/meaningful events from year to year, and asking others what they see as your passion are excellent aids in helping you find your passion. But Master Leaders do not stop at identifying their passion. True leaders have integrated their vision and their passion into their daily life's activities. Having a vision and passion is not enough; true leaders transform them into reality. One of the best ways to change your good intentions into reality is the

100-day project, but I am getting ahead of myself. You will learn how to use the 100-day project or a series of 100-day projects in the last chapter of this book Strategy 7: Competence to Mastery. In the next chapter you will learn how the Master Leaders I profiled in this book took the next step after they articulated their vision – time and time again, they stepped up to the plate.

STRATEGY 2

Step Up to the Plate

Some believe there is nothing one man or one woman can do against the enormous array of the world's ills – against misery, against ignorance, or injustice and violence. Yet many of the world's great movements, of thought and action, have flowed from the work of a single [person]. A young monk began the Protestant reformation, a young general extended an empire from Macedonia to the borders of the earth, and a young woman reclaimed the territory of France. It was a young Italian explorer who discovered the New World, and 32-year-old Thomas Jefferson who proclaimed that all men are created equal. "Give me a place to stand," said Archimedes, "and I will move the world." These [individuals] moved the world, and so can we all.

– Robert F. Kennedy

Stepping up to the plate, taking action, and making a difference that makes a difference is one of the hallmarks of all of the Master Leaders that I have profiled in this book – and it doesn't matter one iota if we are talking about the private, public, not-for-profit or volunteer sectors. In this chapter you will meet six incredible people who stepped up to the plate and persevered, such as David Johnston who has been the president of the University of Waterloo since 1999, and has continued to help the University of Waterloo step up to the plate as Canada's most entrepreneurial university. You will meet Jim Balsillie and Michael Lazaridis who turned Research In Motion (RIM) into one of the world's premier telecommunications firm with the ubiquitous Blackberry™ in addition to funding three of Canada's most innovative institutes. You will also learn about David Cheesewright, the President of Wal-Mart Canada and David's position on sustainability at Wal-Mart, and the kudos they have received from none other than Canada's number one environmental activist, David Suzuki.

You will also be introduced to four people who stepped up to the plate to help make the world a better place through their volunteer and charitable work. They are: Warren Evans who decided to help find a cure for Huntington's disease; Craig and Marc Kielburger, who as 12- and 17-year-olds, decided to make a difference that makes a difference in the lives of disadvantaged Third-World children, and Hetty Van Gurp, who decided to turn a personal tragedy into a movement where children teach peace-making to other children both in Canada and in areas that have been affected by two of the world's most entrenched conflicts in Northern Ireland and Serbia.

Building a Different Type of University

Every year *MacLean's* magazine ranks all of the Canadian universities. The ranking includes everything from the student-teacher ratio, to the number of research grants, to the quality of teaching, and the quality of the food served on campus. Many of our universities do quite well — a few are consistently exceptional — and fewer still are seen as pioneers. One Canadian university that has time-after-time stepped up to be a pioneer in higher education in Canada is the University of Waterloo. The University of Waterloo has the largest co-op program in the world and there is a reason why Bill Gates and Microsoft come recruiting.

David Johnston has been the president of the University of Waterloo since 1999. He completed his university studies in three countries: The US (Harvard), England (Cambridge) and Canada (Queens). This may help to explain why David Johnston is such an innovative and eclectic thinker. President Johnston is also one of the strongest advocates for higher education, research and innovation at the University of Waterloo in particular and in Canada in general.

Before you read my interview with President Johnston, it is important to understand his unique perspective on post secondary education, which is illustrated in the following three examples. The first example concerns technology-mediated learning (TML).[1]

> We should strive to establish the world's leading position in technology-mediated learning. Several years ago I had the pleasure of hearing Derek Bok — the 20 year president of Harvard University — just after he had met with Harvard's presidential selection committee to advise on the choice of a successor. He said, "The committee should be seeking a president for a very different university."
>
> Bok warned that their vision of the university was too narrow — a place where 15,000 students could attend full-time and sit in lecture halls. In fact, the university is a place for 75,000 students, 60,000 of whom do not study full-time. Those 60,000 students rely far more heavily on technology-mediated learning than on traditional classroom study. And yet, universities have only barely begun to innovate in the TML area, instead leaving the field open to private enterprise in the for-profit sector.
>
> Technology-mediated learning is the future of education in Canada — to gain a world leading position by 2020, we must make inroads in this field today. [For example] the Massachusetts Institute of Technology (MIT) put all of its course offerings online at a cost of $100 million. By doing this, the university enhances the MIT brand name, and gives a glimpse of some of the world's finest courses to the rest of the world, completely free of charge.

Next is President Johnston's dedication to enhancing co-operative education.

> ➤ The co-op program eases the strain on the physical plant of universities, by using university resources year-round, and by using employers' facilities for educational purposes;

> ➤ Co-op students largely fund the cost of their education through their earnings, and make minimal demands on the student aid system;

> ➤ Co-op students contribute to provincial coffers through their taxable wages;

> ➤ Co-op graduates enjoy a $7,000 starting salary premium over their peers, and retain that premium throughout their working lifetime; and

> ➤ Co-op students and graduates enhance the productivity of their employers through the benefit of their experience.[2]

The third example is President Johnston's goal that the University of Waterloo and all Canadian universities should lead the world in the internationalization of education in order to broaden students' experience in our increasingly globalized world. More specifically:

> ➤ 50 percent of Canadian university students should spend a term abroad on an academic exchange or a co-operative work term, and

> ➤ 25 percent of our undergraduate and graduate student population should be made up of international/visa students.[3]

It became obvious to me from the interview with David Johnston and from reading many of his speeches, which are posted online, that President Johnston is the chief salesperson, cheerleader and spokesperson for the University of

Waterloo. (By the end of the interview I wanted to go to the UW to study physics!) He gives major speeches once or twice a week in which he always champions the University of Waterloo. Excerpts from my interview with David follow.

B.M.   *You said that Waterloo may not be home to a NHL hockey team, but it is becoming a world-class university. Can you please elaborate?*

D.J.   *We are a university that is 50 years old and in those 50 years, we have developed a distinctive method of education. Sixty percent of our students are co-op students and they obtain their degrees which are a combination of practical work experience plus the academic discipline. I think that's a platform for excellent educational formation for the 21st century. We see the transfer of knowledge as a two way street, for example you wouldn't start a medical school today without a teaching hospital, and I think that applies to other disciplines.*

Point two is we have the transfer of knowledge from theory to applied and back to theory because it helps us to reformulate our theory. It is not just a linear transfer from concept to the experiment to the application. Very often the refinement and the experiment help to refine and/or reformulate our theory and this is especially true at the quantum or sub-atomic level.

The third thing that is distinctive about UW and allows us to see that we are one of the leaders in the world is that we work very hard at innovation and we try to reinvent ourselves constantly. We are careful to do a relatively small number of things well and try not to cover the entire spectrum. We only have six faculties: Arts, Engineering (which is the largest in Canada), Environmental Studies, Mathematics (which is the largest faculty for mathematics and computer science in the world) and Science. We also have developed a very close interrelationship with industry, public service and the people who hire our students and who use the ideas that are generated by the university.

B.M.   *Tell me more about innovation at UW?*

D.J.   *Let me start with the Perimeter Institute for Theoretical Physics because the focus is so singular and the investment is so large. The UW is now one of the best places in North America, if not the world, to study theoretical or chalk and blackboard physics. Mike Lazaridis, the founder of RIM (Research In Motion) has personally donated $200 million. The Perimeter Institute is run by Neil Turok who worked with Stephen Hawking, who is one of the world's most renowned physicists, and Neil might have taken over from Hawking, but he decided to come to the Perimeter Institute because we had the best facilities and funding.*

> **I believe you need to look to Canada's innovation engines, its universities, find ways to partner with them, and reap the rewards of innovation, knowledge transfer, and the chance to shape and be shaped by the newest ideas in education.**
> **David Johnson**

The Quantum Computing is pure practical. Its goal is building a quantum computer – that if successful will be transformative. Moore's Law – states that the number of transistors that we can put on a micro-chip doubles every two years. However, some scientists predict that we will run into physical limits within 10 to 15 years. With Quantum Computing you calibrate the spins on the inside of atoms and those spins will be used to store pluses and minuses. What we think will happen with quantum computing in the continuing journey of the computer – is being able to analyze massive amounts of information very rapidly. Think of the multitude of projects such as monitoring climate change that could be accomplished very rapidly with quantum computing.

B.M.   *Tell me more about your approach to collaboration.*

D.J.   *Collaboration is at our core. We even have a name for it – The Waterloo Way and it comes from our Mennonite heritage. The Mennonite community has barn raisings where 100 neighbours work together – that is the spirit of collaboration and it is also the spirit of collaboration that started and nourished the University of Waterloo.*

We now have a constellation of 26 buildings, like a horseshoe surrounding the north-east corner of our campus and these industries employee 7,500 people, 1,500 of whom are co-op students or interns. In fact Mike Lazaridis was a fourth-year co-op students who didn't finish his degree because he was busy starting his company. However Mike will tell you that RIM is successful because it has learned how to use co-

op students better than any company I know of to advance its business. Mike also tells our students to finish their degrees because the reason RIM is successful is because RIM has learned how to use fundamental knowledge and principles more effectively than its competitors. So Mike says to come to RIM as a co-op student, then finish your degree and get that fundamental knowledge and then come back and work for RIM.

RIM is now the most capitalized company in the country and it only came into existence in 1992. Why in Canada? Why did this happen in southwestern Ontario? Why in an obscure little town called Waterloo? Mike says, "You build the refinery (RIM) next to the mine (UW) and in this case the mine is essentially where the talented people are." The flow of ideas goes back and forth between talented people. The best vehicle for technology transfer is a good pair of shoes – the flow of ideas back and forth and that flow is by talented people. And one of the best vehicles for technology transfer and commercialization is university convocation.

Let me go back to your question on collaboration. We have a very, very supportive community. The UW was born in 1957 because in 1956 Ira Needles, the president and CEO of BF Goodrich Tires, was also the chair of the Canadian Manufacturing Association and he said what we needed in Canada was 150,000 more engineers. There were a lot of manufactures in the community, so they started a university to meet their needs. The reason that we have the co-op program and the reason that it is so successful is that we have 36,000 employers who benefit from and support the co-op program and they value and cherish our students.

Another example of the Waterloo Way is that we have city councils donating money, land and other resources to the University of Waterloo. Most communities say that post-secondary education is a provincial responsibility – but it is different here. If you go to the site where we built a health science centre, the City of Waterloo donated $30 million plus land and $15 million from the region of Waterloo to build a health science campus, so we now have a health science centre that replaced a tire manufacturing company, a button factory and furniture textile companies – all of which were empty buildings and that is how we are developing ourselves with high value added industry in our region and this story of collaboration has been repeated six times.

The first example is a research and technology plant on the north end of the campus which is a $40 million investment by the City of Waterloo. The second is a $27 million grant by the City of Cambridge to build the School of Architecture in the old textile part of the city.

The third is the School of Pharmacy where the Cities of Waterloo and Kitchener made a $30 million investment which brings in $30 million a year into the community in terms of wages and salaries of faculty, staff, and graduate students. This will also help us attract research grants and members of the pharmaceutical industry to our community.

The fourth example is $50 million in the satellite medical school of McMaster University. Fifth, we are in discussion with the City of Stratford, the provincial and federal governments to establish $30 million investment plus land to establish a digital [imaging] medic centre.

The sixth example is that the City of Waterloo donated nine million dollars for the north campus to build housing for students and graduate students and UW provided land for a library and daycare centre for the community to enhance the quality of life which becomes a magnet for talent.

These are true partnerships and there is no dominant leader. When we began our 50th year, we organized an anniversary reception for all of the elected representatives – civic, provincial and federal. At the celebration we said "This community has built this university." At the same time, the headline in the local newspaper stated that, "This university built this community." – Both are right.

B.M.   *You stated that by 2020, Canada should seek to take the lead in the world in higher education, innovation and research. What has to happen for this to occur?*

D.J.   *I believe you need to look to Canada's innovation engines, its universities, find ways to partner with them, and reap the rewards of innovation, knowledge transfer, and the chance to shape and be shaped by the newest ideas in education. What we have achieved at UW through collaboration amongst the university, our community and our business* *partners must be duplicated and at the same time be responsive to differences in universities and to differences in the regions in which they serve.*

David Johnston is a man on a mission. He is extraordinarily personable, articulate and well informed. At the same time he is profoundly passionate about and is therefore the perfect advocate for higher education in Canada. I suspect that anyone who hears David speak, would, like me, want to follow him. The University of Waterloo and Canada are lucky that we have him. David has also forged a strong partnership with one of the University of Waterloo's most famous drop-outs.

University of Waterloo's Most Famous Drop-Out

Another story about stepping up to the plate are the stories of Jim Basillie and Michael Lazaridis who turned RIM into the fastest growing brand in the world (incidentally, the brand that is worth the most in dollar terms is fellow high-tech company Google). However, one of the world's most innovative high-tech companies, Apple, has RIM firmly in its sights when Apple significantly lowered the price of its new G-3 (3rd generation) iPhone on July 14, 2008. On that date, 21 countries, including Canada, sold 1 million of its iPhones in three days. The new iPhone has RIM and every other smart phone manufacturer clearly in its sights. We will now turn our attention to how RIM is meeting this challenge.

RIM's strategy is not to compete with the iPhone with just one phone, but with several, each of which offers different features and interfaces. For example, for people who like to type, there is the Blackberry Bold. The Blackberry Bold is a third generation smart phone that has the digital QWERTY keyboard for people with amazingly fast thumbs. A newer phone is the Blackberry Storm, which has a touch screen user interface similar to the iPhone. There is also the first Blackberry flip phone plus a new phone that should be out soon that is code named, the Blackberry Thunder, which is rumoured to have both the digital QWERTY keyboard and the touch screen user interface.

> *[I]t's hard to predict the future but one thing is certain. The discoveries made by today's researchers will change everything. An advanced education system will carry these breakthroughs to every corner of society, to every corner of the globe . . .*
> **Michael Lazaridis**

Michael Lazaridis is the co-president and CEO of RIM. He is a very busy guy, but he always makes time for the University of Waterloo. In his fall 2008 convocation address as Chancellor, Michael's passion for technology, innovation and higher education comes through loud and clear.

> [I]t's hard to predict the future but one thing is certain. The discoveries made by today's researchers will change everything. An advanced education system will carry these breakthroughs to every corner of society, to every corner of the globe . . .

> These days there is lots of talk of making universities more accountable for the relevance of their research. Technology transfer is the buzz word of today, especially in the circles that fund us and it usually means that we talk about patents, licenses and commercialization directly from the university. I don't ascribe to this view.

> To me convocation is the most significant form of technology transfer imaginable. It is a hundred times more important than all the patents, licenses and spin off companies combined. Real technology transfer happens when bright people, like you, armed with the latest knowledge, tools and inspiration from our research community enter the world with fresh insight and methods and take them to your places of work. Technology is transferred by people. You are a very powerful force, indeed you are the leaven for the bread we call the economy.

Michael's generosity at the UW also includes a donation of over $200 million to the Perimeter Institute for Theoretical Physics and the Institute for Quantum Computing in addition to Jim Balsillie's founding and continuing support for The Balsillie School of International Affairs, The Centre for International Governance Innovation and a founding donor for the Perimeter Institute.

Why the interest in theoretical physics and quantum computing? Michael believes that "Abstract knowledge never stays abstract for long. Basic research is a long-term investment that has always, always contributed to our success, well-being and financial security." Both Mike Lazaridis and Jim Balsillie have stepped up to the plate, not only in growing and developing one of Canada's best known high-tech companies, but also is their generosity in funding institutes like the Permiter Institute, the Institute for Quantum Computing and the Institute for Competitiveness & Prosperity that are helping to secure Canada's intellectual future. But securing Canada's intellectual future won't help us if we squander our environmental future. We need green leadership just as much as we need intellectual leadership. As you will discover in the next section green leadership also includes the fact that we are only as green as our supply chain.

The Big Impact of Small Changes

The third example of stepping up to the plate is Wal-Mart Canada. Wal-Mart is the world's largest corporation and Wal-Mart Canada began operating in 1994 when it purchased the Woolco chain of stores. During that time Wal-Mart has received some very good and not so good publicity. At the time of writing, there were 79,461 employees working in 312 Wal-Mart Stores, 255 Wal-Mart Discount Stores and 57 Supercenters in Canada. Wal-Mart Canada has only had two presidents and CEOs since beginning operations in Canada. Wal-Mart's Canada's current president and CEO is David Cheesewright.

The world of retail is undergoing a massive transition in Canada and Wal-Mart Canada is no exception. Wal-Mart probably isn't the first name you think of when it comes to environmental sustainability — but maybe it should be. Among the key features of Wal-Mart's green plan in Canada are:

➢ Hard targets for reductions in its carbon footprint and energy consumption

➢ A commitment to being Canada's largest consumer of renewable energy

➢ A $25-million fund to support the restoration of community green space over the next five years

> ➢ A sustained program to offer environmentally efficient products and educate consumers about their benefits

Wal-Mart is making great strides in being green. Because Wal-Mart is so big and because it buys products in such great volume – Wal-Mart has enormous influence when buying products from its suppliers. Four interesting examples of how Wal-Mart influenced its suppliers to be more environmentally sustainable follow.

1. Replacing short-lived cardboard boxes with plastic boxes that can be used 60 times, on average, before wearing out saving 1,400 tones of cardboard and driving out $4.5 million in cost the equivalent of saving 1.5 million trees.
2. 15% improvement in the efficiency of its truck fleet.
3. A 20% reduction in the size of the box for Hamburger Helper™ which is the equivalent of taking 500 distribution trucks off the road.
4. By getting Proctor and Gamble to change the formula for its liquid laundry detergent by doubling the concentration of soap and reducing the volume of water it will save 425 million gallons of water – equivalent to 100 million shower and will ultimately take 15,000 trucks off the road.

Excerpts with my interview with David Cheesewright follow.

B.M.   *How has going green been good for Wal-Mart?*

D.C.   *Being environmentally responsible is one of the things we talk a lot about and I usually summarize it into three relatively simple parts.*

1) I personally, and the leadership group here believe it is the right thing to do.

2) It makes good business sense, and this is one that a lot of people underestimate. I read a lot about this in the media and it really isn't new. Yes it is good for PR and reputation, but for us, it is not new. Eliminating waste, transport optimization and package reduction make good business sense – they have been part of the core of our being for a long, long time – we have been doing this literally since we started in business.

3) Being green is one of the few areas that is a unique competitive edge for us. As you know being one of the biggest companies in the world is a challenge for us because with that comes a lot of negativity — it varies from country to country — but generally people don't like big. So we have a number of challenges in how we manage our reputation in terms of our size, and sustainability. Quite frankly, size is another area where we have a competitive advantage because it allows us to do things that no one else can do because of the scale of the impact that we can have. On a corporate level, it makes a difference in the country where we operate and globally — because we are so big, we are uniquely positioned to make a difference.

B.M.   *Wal-Mart has just been held up as a good example of balancing economic and environmental sustainability by the David Suzuki Foundation. Can you tell me what that means to you and to Wal-Mart Canada?*

D.C.   *The impact is that it gives us enormous credibility to what we are doing because David Suzuki is known through out Canada and through out the world. For decades Suzuki has been talking about the link between business sustainability and environmental sustainability. I think he is gratified that a company like Wal-Mart is linking business sustainability to environmental sustainability.[4] We share his thinking; we don't have to make a choice between environment and economic success. David Suzuki said that with Wal-Mart's business model, the two go hand-in-hand. And when someone of David Suzuki's reputation and calibre on the environmental front praises what we are doing, it is very gratifying and humbling.*

One of the things that we will see even more of going forward is a change in approach from confrontation to collaboration. David Suzuki had taken the position that business is not the enemy, it is part of the solution to these things and by engaging and working with and putting in joint initiatives, this is a much better way to proceed. Now, I would also argue that this goes beyond the relationship between businesses and NGO, but also the relationships between businesses.

B.M.   *You have set some aggressive environmental targets for Wal-Mart Canada. What are they and how do you plan to go about achieving them?*

D.C.   *It is a topic our customers are very concerned about, but they don't particularly want to pay more money for it. That said, most of our targets operate on a global corporate level. The targets that were set in a speech on sustainability by Lee Scott, who is the president of Wal-Mart is that we want zero waste to landfill and our current target is 65% waste will be diverted by 2014, and in energy efficiency, we want 100% renewable energy. Our new stores for next year will be 30% more energy efficient, which will be mostly our Supercenters. We use the LEED Standards (Leadership in Environmental and Energy Design). We also have 300 stores that are not new and we are looking for initiatives that we can efficiently roll back into our existing chains, such as changing the wattage of our light bulbs, we turn the lighting down in the summer when it is brighter, we paint our roofs white so it better reflects the sunshine to reduce the cost of air conditioning, so by the end of this year, our existing stores will be 20% more efficient.*

Another small example is that all of the freezers in our new stores have motion sensors, so the lights are only on when someone is inside. This is a small thing, but all of the small things add up. Another example is that we have a meeting with Irving to reduce our disposable diapers by one-third by squeezing the air out. But one-third means that there will be reduction in transportation costs and they will need one-third less shelf space in our stores – and all of this contributes to increased sustainability. So there is a whole raft of initiatives in our new stores and in our existing stores. Also, at the moment Wal-Mart is the biggest purchaser of renewable energy in Canada.

B.M.   **A large percentage of your products come from China where the environmental regulations are lax to non-existent. The origin of pollution is critically important because Global Warming is a global issue. What is or what can Wal-Mart do to reduce pollution in countries where the products you sell are made?**

D.C.   *There are plenty of people who are producing things that are good for the environment but customers don't particularly want to pay more money for it, but that will change when we price products at their true cost, which includes taking care of the environment. Part of our principle* *role of that is to insure that the factories where we buy our products are audited for both their employment and environmental practices, and increasingly we are looking at who we source from. We use scorecards on such things as packaging and environment to actively selecting our partners who are doing the best job.*

We also have a much higher degree of vertical integration than most companies and we are not happy with some of the pollution in China and have stopped buying from certain companies because of it. We use score cards to make sure that the companies we buy from meet certain levels of sustainability – and because we are such a large customer – they usually comply. In fact, this fall Wal-Mart is hosting a global sustainability summit in Beijing, China, and it will bring together all of the leading organizations in China to see how we can address all of these issues.

What is a problem is the large number of goods that move around the world without the degree of monitoring and diligence that we employ because people are buying an item based on price only. We have to measure the true cost of producing, transporting and selling products, because as you know, if it is not measured, it doesn't change.

B.M.   *I understand that you often ride your bike to work.*

D.C.   *I bike to work as often as I can. It is about 17 miles each way and it takes me about 50 minutes to bike to work and 45 minutes to bike home because going home is more downhill. But I drove my car to work this morning with the bike inside and at the end of the day I will bike home and then bike in again the next morning. We have to be vigilant and do everything we can to protect the environment. I have three children who are counting on it.*

As the above three examples illustrate, leadership is indeed about stepping up to the plate, so leadership always at some point is about courage and that is the topic to which we next turn our attention.

Leadership and Courage

I had always assumed that there was a relationship between stepping up to the plate, leadership and courage; however, just what precisely that relationship was became clear to me when I read the book, *A Leaders' Legacy* by Kouzes and Posner.[5] More specifically, the authors talk about "Rosa Parks Moments." Rosa Parks is famous for being the mother of the civil rights movement in the United States. On December 1, 1955, Rosa Parks was ordered by a Montgomery, Alabama bus driver to give up her seat on the bus for a white person. She was told that if she did not move, she would be arrested. For Rosa Parks this was a

core value challenge and she took the initiative to remain sitting until she was removed from the bus. Rosa Parks chose to be arrested and stand up for her human rights rather than condoning the institutionalized racial inequality that existed at the time. In tribute to Rosa Parks, Kouzes and Posner called this type of courageous leadership a Rosa Parks Moment.

Being an ex-math major, I love it when social scientists use mathematical formulas to help us understand human behaviour. Kouzes and Posner did exactly that when they brilliantly defined a Rosa Parks Moment (RPM) with the following formula.

$$RPM = I \times (CVC)$$

In this equation, RPM stands for a Rosa Parks Moment, "I" stands for the initiative she took in refusing to move to the back of the bus and "CVC" stands for a Core Value Challenge that racial inequality was morally wrong, illustrating the relationship between leadership and courage. Core values are deeply held psychological beliefs that initiate our behaviour and guide our actions. Examples of core values are honesty, fairness, and loyalty. In the above examples, David Johnston's core value is achieving excellence in education while David Cheesewright's core value is attaining both economic and environmental sustainability.

Four personal examples of core values in action follow. The first example involves bullying in a high school in rural Nova Scotia. On the first day of the 2007-2008 school year, a Grade 9 student came to school wearing a pink polo shirt. Two Grade 12 students bullied him, threatened him, and called him a homosexual.

The good news is that two other Grade 12 students, David Shepherd and Travis Price, took the initiative to do something about it. That night they went to a discount clothing store and bought 50 used pink shirts. They then e-mailed their friends and their friends e-mailed their friends. The next day David and Travis wore their pink shirts to school and were surprised to find that over half of the students in the school were also wearing pink shirts. The bullies in question were never heard from again. To see the interview with David and Travis, enter the words "bullying" and "pink shirts" in the search box on YouTube.com.

Little did David and Travis know that they were about to start a movement. Shortly after the incident at their school, many students in other schools throughout the province went to school wearing pink shirts. Subsequently, the Government of Nova Scotia proclaimed the second Thursday at the start of each school year as Stand Up Against Bullying Day. In this case, David Shepherd's and Travis Price's core values about not being bullied were challenged and they had the initiative to create a RPM throughout Nova Scotia. Their action received media coverage throughout Canada and the United States. Even the premier of British Columbia and members of his cabinet wore pink shirts on anti-bullying day in British Columbia.

Exercise 2-1: Briefly summarize a Core Value Challenge that you acted upon. What helped you take the necessary initiative (I)?

What did you learn about leadership and about yourself from this experience?

Is there a Core Value Challenge currently in your life or in your community that is crying out for you to demonstrate leadership?

Who or what would stop you from taking initiative/responsibility?

Who or what would help you take initiative/responsibility?

Just as individuals face RPMs, so do teams and organizations. Therefore a fundamental question all leaders have to ask is, "Does our organization's culture encourage, support and reward individuals and teams for having the courage to face a Rosa Parks Moment, or does the culture discourage, put up road blocks and/or punish individuals and teams so that those individuals or teams will not have the courage to act on a Rosa Parks Moment?" Recognizing and acting on RPMs are two of the most important factors that help create Master Leaders.

In the rest of this chapter we will look at how Master Leaders use higher-order expectations, determination, initiative and commitment to get higher-order results. We will also see how Master Leaders use the concept of the Flywheel, discussed in Strategy 1, by starting with small wins and then increasing the momentum with additional wins until the organization develops the momentum necessary to carry it – not to – but past its goals.

Over and over again, I found that the Master Leaders I interviewed for this book came forward, stepped up to the plate, and took responsibility for getting the job done. Sometimes it was a difficult task at work and sometimes it was something that needed to be accomplished in a local, national or international community. Three examples of how people mustered their courage to step up to the plate – under some of the most dire circumstances that anyone would have to deal with – follow.

Finding a Cure for Huntington's Disease

Master Leaders have the unwavering courage to step up to the plate and lead, even when the personal costs can be astronomical. Some would rather be doing anything else, but their courage, combined with ability, dictates otherwise. A tragedy devastated Warren Evans' family when the youngest of his two step-daughters was diagnosed with juvenile Huntington's disease, which is a genetic degenerative brain disorder. Laura's greatest hope was that a treatment would be found before the disease could consume her older sister, Andrea, who had subsequently been diagnosed with the more common adult version of Huntington's. Laura died of the disease in October, 2001. Up until then there was no treatment for Huntington's and it always proved fatal.

Warren had been working with the Huntington's Society in the year prior to Laura's death. Warren recognizing that research was now bringing a cure within reach so he decided to honour Laura's wish by starting a new fund-raising campaign which he named "Laura's Hope." When the Canadian Association of Professional Speakers (CAPS), of which he is a member and past president, heard what he was doing, they insisted he tell his colleagues at their annual convention. Although Warren is an internationally recognized presenter, he is an intensely private person. Warren told me that his eight-minute presentation to CAPS in November, 2001 – where he first publicly told Laura's story and his vision for Laura's Hope – the most difficult and personal presentation he had ever made.

From the beginning, Laura's Hope was intended to be a five-year initiative, the purpose of which was to accelerate the clinical trial process to find a treatment for Huntington's. However, Laura's Hope was so successful that it will continue until a cure is found for Huntington's. None of the money raised goes towards administrative costs to manage Laura's Hope because all of the administrative work is done by Warren and other volunteers. As word spread of what Warren was doing, the professional speaker associations in Europe, Australia and New Zealand joined CAPS in designating Laura's Hope as their charity of choice. Warren has traveled to each of these countries multiple times, combining work with support of this initiative.

Based on the work of the Human Genome Project, scientists were able to *identify* all the approximately 20,000-25,000 genes in human DNA. Identifying and analyzing all of this material will help to eliminate or at least stop the advancement of many if not most genetic disorders. So far, there has been a great deal of progress. Kennedy disease, which works in much the same way as Huntington's, has been stopped 100% with pharmaceuticals. It is believed that a variation of the process that was used to stop Kennedy disease will be found to stop Huntington's, and that this research will also lead to treatments for Parkinson's, Alzheimer's, Lou Gehrig's and other degenerative brain disorders. The good news is that selected treatments have been able to reverse some of the damage in animals that have Huntington's disease. Hopefully future research will also help humans who are afflicted with Huntington's and/or help to prevent the progression of this disease. None of this progress would be possible without money to fund this research. Thanks to Warren's leadership and Laura's Hope, more of this research is taking place and more of it is taking place in Canada than would otherwise have been the case.

Creating the World's Largest Organization of Children Helping Children

FREE THE CHILDREN
children helping children through education

Craig Kielburger started Free the Children in 1995 when he was just 12 years old. Craig was deeply affected when he read about the death of a child who was advocating for positive reforms to stop abuse of young child workers in India. However, unlike most people who read a touching article, Craig decided to do something about it. This was the beginning of Free the Children, which is now the largest organization of children helping children in the world.

Craig's older bother Marc was also deeply involved in volunteer work at that time. In his senior year of high school, Marc volunteered to help troubled youth full-time while he was home-schooled by his mother. Marc graduated from Harvard Law School and subsequently studied law at Oxford University. However, instead of becoming a lawyer, Marc decided to become a humanitarian and activist. Marc is a gifted speaker. I had the wonderfully good fortune to hear Marc speak at the annual conference of the Canadian Association of Professional Speakers in 2005.

Marc Kielburger is the Executive Director of Free the Children. Free the Children's mandate is to help free children from poverty, exploitation and powerlessness and has helped over one million children in 45 countries since its inception. Free The Children works in the areas of education, alternative income, health care, water and sanitation provision, and peace building. It has built more than 500 primary schools, providing education to over 40,000 children. Free the Children has formed strategic partnerships with organizations such as the United Nations and Oprah's Angel Network, it has also been nominated for the Nobel Peace Prize three times.

Marc Kielburger is the co-founder of Leaders Today, which annually provides leadership training to more than 250,000 people. In 2004, Marc, who was 27, was chosen as the youngest ever Canadian "Top 40 leader under the age of 40." That is until in 2006, when his younger brother Craig, at age 23, was selected as one of Canada's "Top 40 under 40".[6]

When I spoke to Marc, he had just returned from the bush in Kenya, Africa. Free the Children has several initiatives in Kenya and Marc was very concerned about the recent violence in that country which stemmed from the contested presidential election of December, 2007. When I asked Marc how things were in Kenya he said much better, and the relief in his voice was palpable.

B.M.   *Your brother Craig was 12 years old when he gained national exposure for his efforts to stop child labour. What did you think of his doing that at the time?*

M.K.   *We were both socially involved at a very young age. When Craig was 12, he read about a child activist who was murdered for trying to improve the lives of child labourers in India. Craig wanted to go to India and see what was going on for himself. I was doing volunteer work in the slums of Thailand at the time and we talked it over. Craig made up his mind that he had to go to India and started negotiating with our parents. At first they said no, but Craig put together a plan to go with a chaperone.*

B.M.   *Why did you decide that you wanted to get involved with Free the Children?*

M.K.   *A couple of things. We were both accidental activists. By this I mean that we didn't chain ourselves to Gap stores. Both our parents were teachers and from a very early age we did volunteer work together in food banks and homeless shelters, and we read the paper together – it was a family tradition. We had to read an article, talk about it for 30 seconds and then say what we might do about it. Over the years this increased awareness and we could see we could do small things to make a difference.*

There are over 250 million children around the world who are involved in child labour. They lack even the most basic education – especially the girls — and they do not have health care. In some parts of the world, children have been forced to become child soldiers. They have been subjected to psychological warfare. In Sierra Leone, children were forced to shoot one of their parents or have their hand cut off.

B.M. *Why did you found Leaders Today?*

M.K. *We built 450 schools and saw the impact of that development — but we realized that we could never end poverty in Africa by building schools — it could only be changed by changing the mentality of people — how we shop, how we spend our resources, how we educate people and most importantly — what we value. It is from this experience that we became very keen on systemic change. We learned that we want to impact people and especially youth in a different way. This is one of the reasons we started Leaders Today. We offer one-of-a-kind local and international training experiences to more than 350,000 young Canadians every year through speeches, rock concerts and week-long workshops. We also have annual programs in Kuwait, Japan and China.*

B.M. *What are your plans to grow Free the Children and Leaders Today?*

M.K. *The next big thing for Free the Children, and I am very excited about this, is bringing Free the Children programming to the states. We are teaming up with Oprah to launch O Ambassadors in 2,000 schools. Our goal is to work directly and indirectly with one million kids in the United States. Our next big push is to develop volunteer centres in Kenya, China, India, Ecuador, Arizona, and Mexico. The volunteer centres are places where youth can volunteer to work in the slums — only we will make sure that they volunteer in a safe, productive, positive, proactive and happy environment.*

B.M. *You and your brother Craig's lives are about stepping up to the plate. What message do you have for other leaders?*

M.K. *Whatever you are doing that is good in the world — do 10% more. Mother Theresa said, "We can do no great things, but we can do small things with great love." So let's all do small things with great, great love and collectively we can change the world.*

If leadership is about bringing about and helping to influence others to bring about sustainable positive change for the future, then Warren Evans and Marc and Craig Kielburger are Master Leaders in every sense of those words. If leadership is about establishing metaphors for success, then Cath and Pete Moore, as profiled in "Strategy 1, Inspire by Vision/Fuel with Passion", are providing metaphors for success not only for individual Jamaicans, but for the entire country of Jamaica. They see the investment of their life savings as an investment in Jamaica, but it is also an investment in themselves, because they are learning and teaching invaluable lessons about leadership. Those lessons will stand them in good stead for the rest of their lives. There is one more example. I would like to end this chapter with an example of a woman who turned one of life's greatest personal tragedies into her life's work.

Teaching Peace-Making Schools in Canada and Around the World

Hetty van Gurp had to face a parent's worst nightmare when her 14-year-old son, Ben, was pushed by a school bully in the school's gymnasium, hit his head and died of internal bleeding. For many parents, their life ends when one of their children dies. Not Hetty. Although she was not able to prevent her son's death, she could help prevent bullying by helping schools teach positive social skills in addition to the traditional curriculum. As an elementary school teacher, she had a place to start with her own students. Hetty then went on to start the League of Peaceful Schools in the Halifax Regional School Board.

Peaceful Schools International

In May, 2001, Hetty started PSI, Peaceful Schools International. The purpose of PSI is to change the world one student at a time. PSI helps people change their outlook on violence by encouraging "schools to adopt a number of initiatives, including conflict resolution, peer mediation, co-operative teaching and student-based decision-making." One of Hetty's most cherished accomplishments was taking the PSI initiative to Serbia where she has helped train Serbian teachers. Serbia as a country has had more than its share of conflicts — including the break up of the former Yugoslavia and the worst type of civil war, ethnic cleansing and crimes against humanity took place amongst the Serbians, Croats, and Muslims. Against this background of ethnic hatred, Hetty taught teachers and students to role-play peaceful versus violent ways to resolve conflict. In 2003, the Government of Serbia implemented this program in every school in Serbia.[7]

Hetty's anti-violence work is multi-faceted. She has also helped organize a student exchange, known as Students for Teaching Peace, where Canadian high school students travel to Serbia to both learn about and help teach non-violence. She also helps run the Way to Peace Summer Camp, where students from war-torn countries spend part of their summers learning peace making. Perhaps Hetty's greatest legacy is a program that empowers both students and teachers to use peaceful means to settle disputes. This is also her greatest gift to her son Ben.

It is noteworthy that all of the Master Leaders I interviewed for this book had the ability to step up to the plate, no matter what the personal costs were. They took personal responsibility to do whatever needed to be done in order to make sure that crucial and important initiatives were started, taken seriously, supported, and were either completed or substantial progress was made. Warren Evans had to give the most difficult presentation of his life and put much of his personal career on hold, in order to successfully make Laura's Hope a reality; Mountain Equipment Co-op chose to locate its stores in the heart of many of the cities where it operates to help redevelop Canada's downtown areas, even though it could have proved more profitable to locate in big-box malls outside of the downtown areas, because it was the socially responsible thing to do; and Lieutenant-General Romeo Dallaire overcame a debilitating case of post-traumatic stress syndrome to write a best selling book and give riveting public lectures to help prevent future genocides.

Exercise 2-2: Can you think of a time in your own life when you stepped up to the plate?

If you answered yes to the above question, what did you learn about your character from this experience?

In summary, leadership is about character as much as it is about anything else. A good test of character is to see how we respond the next time we are given an opportunity to step up to the plate. However, stepping up to the plate is just as important with the small issues as it is with large issues as the following example illustrates.

Start with Small Wins

Master Leaders establish a reputation for getting things done very early in their leadership tenure. They then quickly turn the trust to do the small things into trust to do the big things right. An excellent example of this is Don Ford, former president and CEO of the Capital Health District, which includes the Queen Elizabeth II (QEII) Health Sciences Centre.[8]

Capital Health is the largest health region in Atlantic Canada. Like many health regions across the country it is faced with numerous challenges, from the need to reduce waiting periods, to the need to work within a tight budget, to a shortage of physicians, nurses and other health professionals (which only increases as many people in these professions approach retirement age), to trying to keep up with all the new medical treatments, procedures and technologies that increase the demand for and the price of health care. It is also true that many of these problems will take not years, but decades to resolve. Add to this a myriad of smaller problems such as aging buildings and equipment and the ever-increasing demand for program and service space and you have the definition of a next-to-impossible job.

Not so for Don Ford. One of the things that most impressed me about Don's leadership is that the word "problem" does not exist in his vocabulary. In Don's vocabulary, the word "problem" has been permanently replaced by the words "challenge" and "opportunity".

One of the mysterious challenges that Don faced was the case of the disappearing wheelchairs at the QEII Health Sciences Centre. When patients and families arrived for clinic visits or admission, there were no wheelchairs in the lobby areas to help with family transportation. This resulted in many unhappy patients who then took out their frustration on the admissions staff. So, who or what was responsible for the disappearing wheel chairs?

Don's investigation found out that when patients were discharged from the hospital, a significant number of the people who picked them up would take the patients to their cars and would then fold up the wheelchairs and put them in the trunk! The net loss to the hospital was approximately $30,000 per year — that amount, over a 10-year period was equal to $300,000, which would pay the salary of six entry-level nurses. In addition, there was the inconvenience for patients and families who were unable to find wheelchairs and the stress for the reception desk staff who took the brunt of the frustration expressed by these anxious family members.

Don's solution was to replace the folding wheelchairs with non-folding industrial strength wheelchairs, which were kept in the lobby areas in racks similar to those found in airports for luggage carts. These wheelchairs were available to be loaned to family members with the deposit of a loonie, which was refunded upon the wheelchair's return. The net result is that wheelchairs are always available, patients and families are not inconvenienced, and the reception desk staff is much happier.

In sum, Master Leaders establish a "can do" reputation very early in their leadership tenure. They then transform their individual "can do" reputation into a "we can do" reputation. Lastly they transform this reputation into a "we can do" culture. Much more will be said about cultural leadership in Strategy Six.

Exercise 2-3: List three small but significant wins that you have observed in other leaders.

1.

2.

3.

Next, list up to three small but significant wins that illustrate your own ability as a leader by illustrating your "can do" attitude.

1.

2.

3.

Finally, list up to three small but significant wins that will further enhance your own "can do" reputation.

1.

2.

3.

Higher-Order Resiliency

Willi Jolli states, "A set back is a set up for a come back." Never were those words more true than in the case of Master Leader Fred MacGillivray. Fred is the President of the World Trade Centre Limited in Halifax, Nova Scotia. His vision is to turn Halifax into one of North America's top 15 event destination centres in the next 15 years. This may sound like a tall order for anyone, but not if you are Fred MacGillivray. I came to appreciate how resilient Fred was when I learned how he handled the unsuccessful bid for the 1999 World Junior Hockey Championship.

> **Never confuse a single defeat with a final defeat.**
> **F. Scott Fitzgerald**

B.M.   *You must have been very disappointed when Halifax lost the bid to host the 1999 World Junior Hockey Championship. Especially, since many saw it as "Halifax's turn" to host a major event in Canada.*

F.M.   *Not at all. You have to be unsuccessful to be successful and I often look at the hockey bid I put forward for the 1999 World Junior Hockey Championships for Halifax. I still have the hat and jacket in my office, they hang there daily to remind me that when you think you're right,* *you're probably not, and you have to work harder. We didn't get that event because they said that we would not be able to sell enough tickets for it in Atlantic Canada.*

Instead of thinking that they were right and feeling sorry for myself, I said that we were going to get it right next time and we will take what we learned from our 1999 experience and use it to be successful for the 2001 bid.

We said were going to get it because it has never happened in Atlantic Canada and it's our turn. And we will be ready for this. We took what we learned from the 1999 bid experience and decided that we would come back the next time and have our business case 100 percent right.

B.M.   *How did you win the 2001 World Junior Hockey Championship?*

F.M.   *We got a group of interested people together and wrote on a blackboard all the things we had to do to be successful. I said I didn't care what the cost was and I didn't care what the dream was — but I needed to know from the team, on that day, what we needed to do to bring that championship to Halifax.*

The big idea that came out of that meeting for our 2001 bid, was to pre-sell the tickets and we subsequently sold 243,000 tickets in a 10-day period. We went on a public campaign and we sold 7,000 packages, which was an unprecedented number in any community.

Then we went to the bid presentation in Toronto. I could see the three decision makers in that room, I could see their eyes get larger, as I was making the presentation, I said to them not only are we committed to bring these championships to Halifax, we have already sold 7,000 packages or 150,000 tickets –they were amazed. Furthermore, I said, "We are so convinced that we would be successful, that we are going to guarantee $3 million. This event never made more than $1.8 million in the entire time it's been held around the world. We made a commitment of $3 million and we ended up making $4 million by the end of the actual event. We exceeded our expectations and certainly exceeded theirs, and there was no question we would have the championship awarded when one of the organizers said to me, "Do we get to keep the interest on that cheque?", I said "Certainly, it's yours, you can take it today" because

I felt so confident that we would win the contract to host the 2001 World Junior Hockey Championship in Halifax – and win it we did. Because we had pre-sold those tickets, they really had no choice but to award the games to Halifax.

Incidentally, under Fred's leadership and because the 2001 World Junior Hockey Championship had been such a resounding success, Halifax was successful in winning the bid to host the 2003 Woman's Hockey Championship. And of course, Fred was not content to rest until he was successful in winning a joint bid between Halifax and Quebec City to host the 2008 Men's World Hockey Championship. In hockey, scoring three goals is called a hat trick and that is exactly what Fred had accomplished, and of course, he has not stopped to rest. In 2006, Fred secured the Juno Awards and the Microcredit Summit and in 2007 he was instrumental in getting the Indoor Lacrosse Championship, and in 2009, the World Senior Canoe Championships. In other words, event-by-event, Fred MacGillivray is on his way to accomplishing his goal of making Halifax one of the world's premiere event destination sites.

Determination

> Nothing worthwhile can be accomplished without determination.... Good ideas are not adopted automatically. They must be driven into practice with courageous patience.
>
> **–Admiral Hyman Rickover**

When Admiral Hyman Rickover spoke these remarkable words, he was not thinking about Rick Hansen, but when I read them, I knew they applied perfectly to Rick.

Rick became a paraplegic at the age of 15 after being thrown out of the back of a pick-up truck in Williams Lake, British Columbia. Today he is described as having accomplished one of the greatest athletic achievements in the history of sport. Rick Hansen stroked his wheelchair 48,000 times a day for two years, two months and two days, through a 34-country, 40,000-kilometre journey around the world. His twin goals were fundraising for spinal cord research and consciousness-raising – among both the disabled and non-disabled – that if we focus on our abilities, anything is possible.

Rick's story is a testament to perseverance in the face of obstacles, which included everything from flat tires and injuries, to wheeling in both desert and blizzard conditions. For example, the following quote from Rick Hansen and Jim Taylor's book, *Rick Hansen: Man in Motion,* describes just some of the determination that was necessary to get through the first two days of the tour.

> All my training had been aimed at 23-mile wheeling sessions. Physically and psychologically that was what I'd programmed myself to do: three of those per day with regular short breaks during each wheel, and two-hour rest periods between sessions. Sticking to that schedule might not sound all that important, but if you've ever competed in any sport of endurance event you'll understand: to keep yourself going you have to establish goals-within-goals, carrots dangling out there in front of you to break the ordeal into mental and physical segments.[9]

> Don't look down the road, I told myself. You might scare yourself spitless — just wheel one session at a time, three hours and 23 miles per session, three sessions per day. Don't think about the 24,901.55 miles, think about the 23. Slice this thing into realistic, manageable sections or you'll go nuts.[10]

These were just the first two days; there were many more hurdles to overcome, from severe weather and painful injuries, to the lack of any progress in terms of fundraising. From the time that Rick left Vancouver and wheeled south to California and then all the way east to Florida, the tour had made a grand total of $6,000 dollars in the legacy fund. Still they continued. By the time they reached Melbourne, Australia, they were half-way through the tour. They had worn out one wheelchair, had been robbed four times, and Rick had completed approximately 7,180,800 strokes. By then the legacy fund had only reached $20,000. It would have been very easy for most people to quit, or at least fly back to Canada and

Nothing worthwhile can be accomplished without determination. . . . Good ideas are not adopted automatically. They must be driven into practice with courageous patience.
Admiral Hyman Rickover

hope that the fundraising would be better once Rick returned. But not Rick! He said, "As a matter of routine, I mentally split every wheeling challenge down the middle, because once I've done half, I can always tell myself I could do it again."[11]

When it was over, the Man in Motion tour raised more that $20 million for spinal cord injury (SCI) research. Today, the Rick Hansen Foundation is fundraising across Canada. "Half of the net proceeds are directed to improve the quality of life of people with SCI in event communities. The other half is directed to research that improves everyday life and ultimately leads to a cure."[12]

Rick Hansen needed a very strong internal leadership focus in order to accomplish his incredible feat. I asked Rick how he developed his internal leadership focus:

> *I started learning about leadership before my accident. In my younger years I was very active in sports and adventure. I learned to take control, to take initiative and be proactive in making something happen and I learned that I had to motivate others, not only myself. In sports, my coaches provided feedback that I could provide positive leadership, set goals and help others work effectively together.*
>
> *After my accident, I really had to learn about personal leadership. Eventually I learned to be an advocate, at first inwardly to myself, and then eventually outwardly for myself and others. I ultimately came to the realization that my disability was another barrier or obstacle that I had to face in my mind and out in the world. I finally came to realize that part of the way forward was to exercise personal leadership and to reframe my earlier reality and then to try to modify or remove barriers the same way I did in sports. I also became profoundly impacted by people who helped me and inspired me to want to help others. They taught me to have an incredibly deep respect and appreciation for people.*
>
> *I have always been focused in sports and it has been and continues to be an amazing metaphor to hone my focus and to achieve a particular outcome. The disability added a personal and human*

dimension to that growth through the lessons and challenges of life experiences. Every day I wake up and see that every day is a new opportunity.

I had the privilege of meeting Rick at a press conference on May 2, 2005. I noticed that when other speakers or dignitaries spoke or when people came up to meet Rick after the event, they all – and I mean all – had 100% of his attention. Since I had a copy of Rick's book, I joined the line so I could ask him to sign it. In talking with Rick, I found out that not only did he give me his total attention; he had an amazing sense of presence. In fact, I can't imagine that the Dali Lama has any more presence than Rick. Watching Rick meet people I had the privilege of watching a master at focus management in action. I asked Rick how he developed his incredible presence.

I'm not really sure how I developed my presence except by trying to live authentically and by being clear and present and congruent in my actions. I also know that when I am not clear and present it usually is because I am overextended and out of balance. For instance, if I am going to be out in public to work with people it is because of my mission and dream and trying to make a difference, then it is not so big a challenge. I work hard at knowing where my boundaries are and living a balanced life by making sure that I have time with family, and time for fitness and health.

Rick has been able to transform his incredible focus from sports and his world tour to his mission of helping both able bodied and people with disabilities, focus on their abilities. What makes his message so powerful is not that he says it, but that he lives it and encourages others to do so as well. In watching Rick interact with others who are physically challenged, I couldn't help but notice that after he talked with them, shook their hands or touched them on the shoulder that they looked more confident, because they were able to truly believe his message to focus on their abilities.

Rick is also a realist. He said that progress may take "10, 20 or even 50 years, but progress will be made." When I asked him how he developed his sense of patience, he replied:

My disability was one of the defining events that helped me to learn patience. I learned that some of the ways that I had learned to look at the world had fatal flaws. I learned how to change my reasoning and I learned that many things that I thought were not possible are possible. I learned to change my frame of reference. Here was an immovable obstacle that was thrust upon me and there were only two choices – depression, self-doubt and pity, or to live a full and vibrant life. At first, my disability was a grinding mill that was grinding me down. Then I learned how to ask questions differently. That is why I have a different appreciation of my disability today. At first it was the worst thing to ever happen to me. Today, it is one of the best things to ever have happened to me.

I ended the interview with Rick with a question that I had never thought of or ever intended to ask, but for some reason it just seemed to be the right thing to do. I asked Rick what he would say to Terry Fox if he were to meet him today.

As you know, Terry and I were very close friends. I would put my arms around him and give him a tremendous hug. I would ask him how he was doing and then I would tell him that I think of him often and I miss his friendship. Then I would tell him, "I am so proud of you that you can't ever imagine, that what you set out to achieve was absolutely phenomenal – it had a great impact on cancer, but it had an even greater impact on humanity.

Rick captured our imagination because of his determination, courageous patience, and because he touches people with his strong sense of presence. More importantly, he challenges people by his example that, "When you set your mind to it, anything is possible." In fact, Rick Hansen's story lies at the heart of this chapter because Rick had the courage to step up to the plate and achieve higher-order results.

In this chapter we have seen that leadership is about the courage to step up to the plate. In the next chapter we will examine how Master Leaders have learned how to assess their leadership style and learn where their style works for them and where improvements are necessary. You will also be provided with specially designed exercises to help you assess your own leadership style.

STRATEGY 3

Assess Your Leadership Style

Experience is knowing what happened. Learning is knowing why it happened.

— Edward Russo & Paul Schoemaker.

The *Harvard Business Review* published a seminal article in February, 2007, entitled "In Praise of the Incomplete Leader." The main point of the article is that, "No leader is perfect. The best ones don't try to be — they concentrate on honing their strengths and find others who can make up for their limitation." The article starts by stating that:

> We've come to expect a lot of our leaders. [They] . . . should have the intellectual capacity to make sense of unfathomably complex issues, the imaginative powers to paint a vision of the future that generates everyone's enthusiasm, the operational know-how to translate strategy into concrete plans, and the

interpersonal skills to foster commitment to undertakings that could cost people's jobs should they fail. Unfortunately, no single person can possibly live up to those standards.[1]

The authors describe four different types of leaders: Sensemaking, Relating, Visionary, and Inventing. Sensemaking leaders are valuable because they are able to make sense out of chaos – they see the world as it really is. Relating leaders have the ability to build the trusting relationships and use that synergy to achieve higher-order results. Visionary leaders see the world as it could or should be and then inspire others to achieve more than they thought possible. Inventing leaders move, "a business from the abstract world of ideas to the concrete world of implementation. In fact, inventing is similar to execution, but the label 'inventing' emphasizes that this process often requires creativity to help people figure out new ways of working together."

Organizations often need all four types of leadership. However, they are unlikely to get all four types of leadership in one person. As well, different times and different circumstances often necessitate more emphasis on one type of leadership to help that organization grow and/or survive.

In other words, we will need highly synergistic teams of leaders, at all levels in the organization to better understand and better solve today's and tomorrow's problems. If we add to this the work of Marcus Buckingham as outlined in his books: *First, Break All the Rules; Now, Discover Your Strengths*, and *The One Thing You Need to Know*, we have spent too much time trying to help leaders overcome their weaknesses rather than building on their strengths. The result of all of these efforts is that all we will achieve is developing improved weaknesses. Therefore, we should put most of our efforts and resources into improving our strengths. This is also in keeping with Jim Collins' dictum from *Good to Great* – get the right people on the bus, get the wrong people off the bus, and then get the right people in the right seats on the bus.

All of this means that as leaders, we have to know where our leadership style and strengths works for us and where they work against us and build leadership teams that have the right collection of competencies.

This chapter will help you identify and access some of your most important leadership competencies by examining two ground-breaking studies that differentiate Master Leaders from their average counterparts. You will then be given the opportunity to rate your ability on each of these critical competencies. We will then look at a process that will help you assess how others see your current abilities and highlight specific areas for improvement. Later, in Strategy 7, you will learn how to create a specific plan to develop and improve your leadership competencies.

Competency-Based Assessment

> Successful organizations do not just happen – and they do not just stay successful. Great organizations are made up of individually successful [leaders] who do the right things at the right time in the right circumstances.[2]
>
> **- Successful Manager's Handbook**

In the past 20 years, there has been a great deal of work done on competency-based assessment, competency-based training, competency-based compensation, and competency-based succession planning. For example, I was hired as a consultant by a large Canadian retail firm, which was in the position of retiring a number of its senior managers in three years' time. Managers below the senior level were invited to apply for these positions. All of the people who were accepted to apply for the positions underwent a thorough examination process composed of nine competencies, represented by 23 skills. These evaluations allowed the participants to look at their relative strengths and weaknesses as seen by themselves, their bosses, their peers, and their direct reports. With the retirement of the Baby Boom Generation, competency-based assessments will become even more essential.

Successful organizations choose, promote and train their employees based on the best set of competencies and skills for each particular job in the organization. A more specific description of this process can be found in the book *Competencies at Work*,[3] which describes different sets of competencies needed for various types of jobs. The authors describe how different types of competencies vary in the same job depending on the setting in which the job takes place, for example, a general manager for a research and development firm versus a general manager in a manufacturing firm. Although many of the competencies overlap, others are specific to one of the jobs or the other.

More recently, Daniel Goleman, author of *Working with Emotional Intelligence,*[4] has looked at the skills and competencies that make for effective team members and effective leaders. Goleman states that effective team members must have 60% of these skills and abilities to be an effective team member, and 90% of these skills and abilities to be an effective leader.

An excellent example of an organization that has a strong vision and has stepped up to the plate to develop its employees into high performers through its competency program is Pfizer Inc. To find out more on how this program works, I interviewed Rania Cassar-Awe, who is their Director of Learning and Development in Canada.

B.M.   *Please tell me about your competency program?*

R.CA.   *Learning in a global organization is critical to the success of our organization. In the past, we delivered country-customized solutions effectively, but this failed to capitalize on the globalization of corporate learning. We know now that for our organization to thrive and bring value to customers, we need to enable global capabilities. For example, our new global competency model replaces the local competencies we put in place a few years back. It has a laser-light focus on what Pfizer employees must do to continuously reinvent and enrich Pfizer's offering to customers and how individuals can apply their strengths to that process.*

Our new global core competencies are the foundation of Pfizer's global talent development strategy. They are based on over two decades of research and allow us to compare our proficiency and performance to other Fortune 500 companies. We are focused on building a high-performing, adaptive organization, and the development of leadership excellence through our competencies is key.

More specifically we have developed senior leader competencies, manager competencies and individual contributor competencies. For our senior leaders in particular, we're asking what strengths and talents make the difference between good and great, what experiences are needed to hone competencies and what behaviours may derail an otherwise capable leader. We know that leadership excellence can and will drive business growth at Pfizer.

B.M.   *You said that this is a part of your identity as a learning organization. Are there other parts?*

R.CA.   *In Canada, we have evolved the Canadian Campus of the University of Pfizer from a traditional corporate university offering structured courses in classrooms to a central gateway offering a multitude of*

learning opportunities and resources, within and outside Pfizer. Through the University of Pfizer, we offer a solid base of 'gold-standard' workshops, on-the-job learning activities and other learning resources as a foundation for performance.

All learning and development offerings of the University of Pfizer are grouped according to five major categories or "schools": Leadership, Management, Functional/Technical Learning, Brands and Core or Common Programs, such as Pfizer Values and business practices.

In sum, Learning and Development has to be front and centre as our business people face new opportunities and challenges every day which demand new ways of working. If people are uncomfortable or uncertain about how to learn and grow, old habits prevail. In a true learning organization, the focus is on continuous performance improvement.

At Pfizer we know that through rapid continuous real-time learning we stand the best chance of creating the business opportunities of the future.

The Four Factor Theory of Leadership

The Four Factor Theory of Leadership[5] is one of the most thorough studies of leadership ever undertaken. The authors, Bowers and Seashore, looked at the results of numerous studies to see what these studies had in common. Goal emphasis and work facilitation. The technique they used is called a meta-analysis and the results suggested that there are four primary factors that make up leadership. Two were social factors: support and interaction facilitation and two were work factors: goal emphasis and work facilitation.

The Social Factors

The first social factor is support, which refers to behaviour that enhances someone else's feelings of personal worth and importance. An excellent example of this in action is found in Moya Greene, President and CEO of Canada Post Corporation, as demonstrated in her speech to the Empire Club in Toronto on October 24, 2007:

> Nationally, a survey conducted earlier this year by a very respected polling firm, Strategic Counsel, found that Canada Post is in fact the most trusted federal institution in the country; more trusted than the federal Parliament, more trusted than the federal public service, more trusted than the Supreme Court of Canada, more trusted than our wonderful military. What a wonderful thing that is, to lead a company that is the most trusted federal institution in the country.

> Everybody was totally surprised, but I have to tell you I wasn't surprised ... because I have been across the country, I have met thousands, and thousands, and thousands of our wonderful people face-to-face, on every shift, in every town, in every city ... what I hear from them and from our customers are the great lengths that they go to every day to get the mail out, and they get the mail out in this country in all kinds of weather across ... one of the biggest geographic expanses in the world.

Another stellar example of a Master Leader who excelled in behaviour that supports someone else's feeling of personal worth and importance is General Rick Hillier, former Canadian Armed Forces Chief of the Defence Staff. Almost every time General Hillier gave a speech, he invited front line enlisted men and women to share the stage with him while he lavished praise on those individuals in particular and on the Canadian Forces personnel in general. It was also readily apparent that he knew of and very much appreciated each person's individual accomplishments. General Hillier acknowledged the Canadian Forces personnel every time he had the opportunity, whether being interviewed on television or radio or giving a speech. If you talk to anyone in the military, they will tell you that they loved him for it and that is not an overstatement.

The second social factor is interaction facilitation. Interaction facilitation is "behaviour that encourages all members of the group to develop close, mutually satisfying relationships." A unique example comes from my interview with David Cheesewright, President and CEO of Wal-Mart Canada.

D.C.   *Team work is one of the criteria of a good business. From the word go, one of the things that is a step-change for my team is that we move people around into different roles. The key partnerships in a retail store are the partnerships between the people who run the stores and the merchants who buy the products and if you spend any time in the retail business you will know that they both think the other are the cause of all of the problems. If you work in the office you think that life would be great if the stores just did what they are supposed to do and if you work in the stores you think that everything would be great if the office staff just did what they are supposed to do.*

I became the President and CEO of Wal-Mart Canada in February, 2008. At 8:30 a.m. on that morning, I restructured the business. One of the first things I did was swap the person who ran merchandising or the buying function with the person who manages all of the stores.

> **Successful companies had a culture in which people were deeply aware of an internalized mission, vision, and core values needed to execute the company's strategy. These companies strove for excellent leadership at all levels, leadership that could mobilize the organization toward it's strategy.**
> **Robert S. Kaplan and David P. Norton.**

B.M.   *Did they know ahead of time that you were going to do this?*

D.C.   *Yes. The change was very intentionally designed to promote teamwork and it was good timing because a week later both of them were going to be on stage in front of the whole business. So what you had was the person that all of the stores thought was the problem and visa-versa and immediately there was a very clear message about teamwork being important and immediately there was a very good understanding of what the other party's problems were. Both now have a very good bond and we are seeing a huge step-change in the partnership between those two teams and both are very happy with their new roles.*

When I worked at Mars Confectionary for 12 years in the UK, they were very good at cross-functional training and used cross-functional training as one of the ways to drive teamwork. So personally I am a very big fan of giving people the opportunity to see the business from a different perspective. I have been very lucky to have experienced a great deal of cross-training. I have worked across a lot of trade sectors from sales and marketing to running production lines. I have worked in retail and manufacturing and as long as you can execute on top of that breadth of knowledge, there is nothing better than knowing enough about those different areas and having the perspective of those different areas and being able to understand and empathize from that other person's point of view.

As a group of eight senior managers, we go through a five-year planning process, and spend a lot of time communicating through informal up-dating on what's going on. Also, every week we sit down as a broader group and go through the numbers, that flows out to the individual teams and is followed up with a conference call with the floor managers. There is a weekly rhythm of communication and flow that I don't think you will see in a lot of businesses and this promotes a high degree of teamwork. This type of communication plus cross-training have contributed significantly to team building and to our organizational success.

Another way to enhance team building is through social networking. Todd Kennedy, a Local Area Superintendent for the Canada Post Corporation in Fredericton, New Brunswick provides an excellent example. But first, you need to know that Todd is a gourmet cook. When his team received a perfect score in customer service, each team member and their spouse/partner were invited over for dinner at Todd's. The menu for the meal was:

- Amaretto Sautee Scallops on Spring Greens with raspberry vinaigrette
- Cream of Carrot Ginger soup with Wasabi Crème Fraiche
- Baked Atlantic Salmon wrapped Phyllo pastry stuffed with Scallop Mousse
- Phyllo Pastry cups filled with ice-cream and covered with flambé bananas

Consider any behaviour that helps the group to define itself, or see and feel itself as a team. Examples can be as varied as buying a lottery ticket together, working on a charity together, white water rafting, doing an "Outward Bound" type physical/adventure challenge together, or drawing a picture of the way the group currently works together versus the way the group would like to work together.

The Work Factors

There are also two work factors: goal emphasis and work facilitation. Goal emphasis is "behaviour that stimulates an enthusiasm for meeting the group's goal of excellent performance." Wal-Mart's David Cheesewright's comments on goal emphasis follow:

D.C. *Being the President of Wal-Mart Canada is like being the Prime Minister — only with a general election every day. We have 1 million customers in our stores every day and they will either vote for you or they won't, so there is an immediacy in retail which is why I love the industry. You try something, you put it in your store and you know by the next day if you have it right or wrong and you can then change it if it needs to be changed. So you have to be prepared to keep moving and keep changing. This type of relentless pressure creates an improvement* *loop. I can tell by four o'clock every day how we are doing on sales on that day, and if necessary, I can tell by the hour if changes need to be made. These types of automatic feedback loops will correct a business that is very goal focused.*

There are a few challenges and one of the challenges is to be very clear on what is important and what's not. In a retail business I could give you a thousand measures but what I have always tried to do is keep it very simple by using a pyramid of KPIs (Key Performance Indicators). You could have a fabulous scorecard of 40 things and someone might look like they are doing a fabulous job if 38 out of the 40 are green, but if you are in the retail business and the two out of 40, profits and sales, are in the red – then quite honestly – the other 38 don't matter. So we keep it very short and simple by tracking four key indicators:

Have we grown ourselves ahead of the market?

Are we improving our profitability?

Are we delivering price leadership?

How well are we managing our inventory?

The reason inventory is important in a retail store is that everything is proportional to inventory. If you have too much inventory, your efficiency and your profits go down. The other measures are important to know, but they are investigative, we can drill down to get more information when we need it, but overall they are supportive of the four I just mentioned.

I also spoke with Brian Warren. Brian is a CBC – Canadian by Choice. Brian is a former Canadian Hall of Fame football player who came to Canada to play football in the Canadian Football League (CFL) and stayed. Today, Brian is the President and CEO of Kidsfest and he is as passionate about Kidsfest and helping inner-city and disadvantaged children as he was about football.

Kidsfest is an organization that helps inner-city and disadvantaged children from Victoria to Halifax and from Toronto to the Northwest Territories[6]. Kidsfest is a combined exercise and reading program that helps inner-city children (Grade K to 6). There are a number of coaches who volunteer from the community to help organize and run the event. The children are divided into two groups. One group does various fun exercises to increase their level of fitness — always in at least groups of two so they can encourage each other before they run out of steam. The other group runs, after which both groups switch activities. Then the children take a break and are given a healthy snack. After their break, they read with a partner/coach who helps the students develop their reading skills. Each week the number of miles run is tabulated and added to the number of miles they've already run. The total is displayed on a map of Canada so the participants can see their collective progress. On the day I visited the Halifax program, I could see how the combined distances run by all the students had brought them as far as The Pas, Manitoba from their start in Halifax. I was able to see how the program emphasizes setting individual and group goals and if that isn't an important lesson, I don't know what is.

The second work factor is work facilitation. Work facilitation is "behaviour that helps achieve goal attainment by such activities as scheduling, coordinating, providing resources, materials, and technical knowledge." Two excellent examples of Master Canadian Leaders who excel at work facilitation are General Rick Hillier and Brian Warren.

At the time that General Hillier became the Chief of Defence Staff, the Canadian Military was very demoralized. For years the military budget had been cut and the military was and to a certain extent still is working with substandard equipment — the four ill-fated used British submarines being a case in point. Rick Hillier made it his mission to refurbish the Canadian military and spoke about it often as the following excerpt from his presentation on January 10, 2008, at Pier 21 points out.

> *We are growing the Canadian Forces for the first time in 30 years. We are adding 1,000 to 1,100 outstanding men and women per year. We are making 100 to 110 percent of our objectives. We are revolutionizing how we attract, recruit, train, develop, support and sustain our members. In fact, we offer training in 115 different types of jobs. We are also working very hard to support the families of those who are deployed. We have a duty to support the Moms and Dads, husbands and wives and children.*

We are also re-equipping the Canadian Military. A great deal of our equipment was on its last legs. For example, in the last year we purchased four C17's so we could better support our operations domestically and around the world. We are also rebuilding the Navy. We are refurbishing our frigates so they will be the best frigates in the world. We have the best equipped military on the ground in Afghanistan. Our men and women have confidence in their equipment. They have ballistic glasses and without those ballistic glasses the personnel would have died or been blind because of a shrapnel injury to the eye. Now there is a dent on their glasses.

You may know that we have a Tim Horton's in Kandahar. Some of our troops think that a double-double is a part of their uniform. We have a ball hockey rink in front of the Tim Horton's so you see we have our own little Canada in Kandahar. The real measure of morale is measured in the recruiting numbers, the reenlistment numbers, and talking with the troops. I would encourage all Canadians to support our troops and their families as much as possible.

It is easy to see how General Hillier used the concept of work facilitation by working to provide the Canadian Forces with the equipment and wherewithal they need to do their jobs. It is also apparent from the above example that General Hillier also excelled in the other three factors. That is, behaviour that supported our military personnel on an individual and team level, in addition to goal emphasis.

An equally interesting example of work facilitation can be found in the Kidsfest program which was described earlier. At the start of the program, each child receives a backpack and a new pair of Brooks' running shoes. When they need a second pair of running shoes, they can purchase them for five dollars. This is another excellent example of work facilitation: providing people with what they need to get the job done.

In the exercise below, you will be able to rate yourself on each of these four factors. It is an excellent idea to give an example that describes – as specifically as possible – how you applied each of these four factors.

Exercise 3-1: Rate yourself on each of the four factors where 1 is low and 7 is high. Briefly summarize an example that shows how you demonstrated using each of the factors

SOCIAL FACTORS

1. **Support**: Behaviour that enhances someone else's feelings of personal worth and importance.

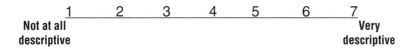

Not at all descriptive

Very descriptive

My personal example is:

2. **Interaction Facilitation**: Behaviour that encourages all members of the group to develop close, mutually satisfying relationships.

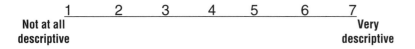

Not at all descriptive

Very descriptive

My personal example is:

WORK FACTORS

3. <u>**Goal Emphasis**</u>: Behaviour that stimulates an enthusiasm for meeting the group's goal of excellent performance.

```
      1       2       3       4       5       6       7
 Not at all                                         Very
 descriptive                                 descriptive
```

My personal example is:

4. <u>**Work Facilitation**</u>: Behaviour that helps achieve goal attainment by such activities as scheduling, coordinating, providing resources, materials, and technical knowledge.

```
      1       2       3       4       5       6       7
 Not at all                                         Very
 descriptive                                 descriptive
```

My personal example is:

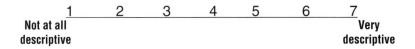

It is important to note that this doesn't mean that each and every leader must be high on each of these four scales. For example, one person in the group may be high on the social factors and another person in the group may be high on the work factors. As long as these two leaders work together synergistically and support each other, the group or organization will have the leadership it needs.

There was another ground-breaking study that examined eight essential differences between effective senior managers and their average counterparts. I will describe this study in some detail because it tells us much of what we need to know in order to become more effective leaders, as well as more effective influencers, problem-solvers and negotiators.

Eight Essential Differences

In general, there is a strong positive relationship between intelligence as measured by intelligence tests and performance in school. However, there is only a small positive relationship between intelligence test scores and competency on the job at the senior management level; accounting for an average of approximately 4% of the variance in on-the-job performance. One explanation for this low level of correlation is that by the time people become successful enough to gain and maintain a job at this level, their less intelligent counterparts have been weeded out. The result is that 96% of most leaders' and managers' success at this level can be attributed to competencies not measured by standard, academically oriented intelligence tests.

One question that researchers have been asking themselves is whether there is another method that could help define and measure these other factors. The people who study "practical intelligence" or "competencies," as opposed to academic intelligence, believe there is. The key is to find methods to identify and measure this practical intelligence. For example, a study by Klemp and McClelland[7] examined the attributes that distinguished successful senior managers from their less successful counterparts. The senior managers in the study were drawn from diverse types of organizations including Fortune 100 companies, volunteer organizations, the military and universities.

The method of identifying the top performers involved both objective performance measures and nominations by others in the organization. For example, one of the objective performance measures used was greatest financial growth. In order to be selected as a successful senior manager, the subjects also had to be nominated by their peers and by their president and/or CEO. To be listed as a top performer, the candidate also had to demonstrate excellent financial results. People who were not on any of the lists were listed as average performers.

The results of the study indicated that there were eight competencies that differentiated top senior managers from their average counterparts and each of the eight competencies were grouped into three distinct categories:

The Intellectual Competencies are:

      1) Planning/Causal Thinking;

      2) Diagnostic Information Seeking, and

      3) Conceptualization/Synthetic Thinking,

The Influence Competencies are:

      4) A Concern for Influence;

      5) Direct Influence;

      6) Collaborative Influence, and

      7) Symbolic Influence,

And the last competence is:

      8) Self-confidence.

The Intellectual Competencies

1. Planning/Causal Thinking.

This competency enables effective senior managers to "see distant consequences of today's activities and to design sound implementation strategies for their business or operations." The skills that make up this competency are: anticipating problems or opportunities, identifying multiple implications of an action or event, accurately predicting outcomes of activities or events, taking action to avoid problems that are foreseen, identifying cause-and-effect relationships, anticipating future opportunities and requirements, stating implications of events and behavior, and stating thoughts in a causal sequence ("If X, then Y").[8]

The best way to describe this competency is strategic thinking. All of the Master Leaders who are profiled in this book apply this competency exceptionally well. One such leader is Clive Beddoe who guided WestJet from a small regional carrier to become Canada's second largest airline. There are numerous examples of how Clive used causal or strategic thinking, some well known and some less well known. Among the best known are selling WestJet shares at a discount to WestJet employees. With 80% of the employees as shareholder/owners there is a strong sense of pride that translates into legendary customer service.

Somewhat less well known is the fact that WestJet flies only one type of airplane which means only knowing how to maintain and fly one type of plane which also makes substituting one plane for another in case of maintenance or weather-related issues timely and efficient. Also, WestJet entered the charter business, which "gives us incremental use of our aircraft ... and better utilization of our crews. It's very profitable for us to do the charter work. And it's a very good way to expose people to WestJet who wouldn't otherwise fly [with] us.[9]

Less well known is the fact that WestJet has invested in one of the newest and most fuel-efficient fleet of aircraft of any airline in the world. Also less well known are WestJet's innovative hiring and monitoring practices. "Rather than having [a] supervisor monitor customer [telephone] calls for quality, peers review and rate them, knowing that their own calls will be monitored too ... The team-play approach is integral in hiring new WestJet Pilots. Candidates have to be recommended by pilots on staff ... [Keeping] in mind the top attributes that we look for in a WestJetter: Courteous, Friendly, Outgoing, Pleasant, Cooperative, Team Player with a CanDo Attitude.'"[10]

The second example of exemplary strategic thinking is Louise Arbour in her role as Chief Prosecutor for war crimes in the former Yugoslavia and Rwanda. CBC journalist and author, Carol Off, describes Louise Arbour as one of the most strategic individuals she has ever seen because Arbour was 17 steps ahead of everyone else.[11] Among Arbour's first decisions – and against the wishes of all of the NATO countries – was to select a Russian as her full-time assistant. Russia had been a staunch ally of Serbia during the civil war in Bosnia and Herzegovina. However, in order to issue the indictment against, Slobodan Milosevic, the President of the former Yugoslavia, for crimes against humanity, Arbour had to get all of the NATO allies as well as Russia on-side. Having a Russian as her assistant in the end helped her to get Russia to go along with the indictment. What Louise Arbour did, as chief prosecutor for war crimes in the former Yugoslavia and Rwanda, was to set one of the most important and powerful precedents in the history of international law. By doing so, all leaders of all countries can now be held responsible for what they do while in office.

The third example of an exceptional strategic thinker is Mayor Hazel McCallion. Mayor McCallion is Mississauga Ontario's first and so far only mayor. She was first elected Mayor in 1979 and at the time of this writing, this remarkable woman is 88 years old and finishes her current term as mayor in 2010.

Because 80% of Canadians now live in cities, cities are one of our main "economic engines that generate wealth and stimulate creativity. They are centres of opportunity that attract people and business from across the nation and around the world."[12] Mayor McCallion has taken this advice to heart. When she was first elected as mayor, Mississauga was a bedroom community. Based on her vision and her execution of that vision, today 80,000 to 90,000 people commute *to* Mississauga to work. As of July, 2008, 40 of Canada's top 500 companies and 59 of Fortune 500 corporations have offices in Mississauga.

Excerpts from my interview with Mayor McCallion illustrate her strategies for developing the city of Mississauga.

B.M.   *Harvard's Michael Porter focuses on how urban regions can build a competitive advantage and develop competitive strategy through a process he calls clustering. I understand that Mississauga has done exactly that.*

H.M.   *We began with a single bio company in the 1960's and today Mississauga has the third largest bio cluster in Canada. One of the reasons for this is that we have a large and well-educated workforce. Mississauga is surrounded by some of the finest, post-secondary institutions in the world. More specifically, The University of Toronto at Mississauga offers one of the few Masters in Biotechnology programs in Canada.*

Mississauga is also part of the Greater Toronto Area (GTA), and hence, part of one of North America's largest centres of biomedical activity. The GTA is home to more than 300 biomedical companies, world class teaching hospitals and research facilities.

We also champion initiatives to support innovation and scientific breakthrough such as information technology, which is an important infrastructure for the biotechnology industry. The Mississauga Information and Communication Technologies Cluster consist of 3,912 technology-based companies with more than 37,000 employees.

We also have one of the world's busiest and most modern airports and we are currently going through a visioning process where we want to plan for the future of Mississauga and the GTA. We need to take a million cars off the road in the Greater Toronto Area. One way we can do that is by building a fixed link [high speed rapid transit] from the Pearson International Airport to downtown Toronto and Mississauga. We are also working on integrating all of the transportation networks in the GTA.

B.M.   *How are you communicating all of your efforts with your constituents?*

H.M.   *Through town hall meetings. We have also partnered with Roger's Television to record some of our meetings and re-broadcast them on their cable networks so people who were not able to attend the meetings in person can still be part of the process. In addition, so far at least one of these programs is available on the Internet. Our goal is that this process is as inclusive as possible.*

2. Diagnostic Information Seeking.

Benjamin Disraeli said, "As a general rule, the most successful people in the world are those who have the best information." Some of the specific skills that make up the competency of diagnostic information seeking are: "pushing for concrete information in ambiguous situations, seeking multiple sources to clarify a situation, using high-yield questions to identify the specifics of a problem or situation."[13]

In a similar vein, business executive John Reh states, "You can't manage what you don't measure. ... Unless you measure something you don't know if it is getting better or worse. You can't manage for improvement if you don't measure to see what is getting better and what isn't."[14] Following the same reasoning, Michael Wolfson, Assistant Chief Statistician at Statistics Canada, states that, "We really need a different kind of statistical indicator – not to replace the GDP, but to complement it." There is a groundbreaking initiative to do just this. It is called the Canadian Index of Wellbeing (CIW). To find out more about this critically important initiative, I interviewed one of Canada's most respected politicians and social activists, the former Saskatchewan premier and Chair of the 2002 Royal Commission on the Future of Health Care in Canada, the Honourable Roy Romanow.

Just as David Johnston of the University of Waterloo has a compelling vision for higher education in Canada, Roy Romanow has a compelling vision for the future for a healthy Canadian Society and his vision is more inclusive and holistic than anything that currently exists in the world. An important part of his strategy to get there is the Canadian Index of Wellbeing and Roy Romanow is currently the chair of its board of directors and its chief spokesperson.

B.M.   *What is the Canadian Index of Wellbeing?*

R.R.   *The purpose of the CIW is to develop a national system of indicators that links economic realities with social, health, and environmental conditions that define the wellbeing of Canadians. Too often, we gauge our society's wellbeing according to a narrow set of strict economic indicators. The CIW is a transformational initiative that will report on the wellbeing of Canadians in specific areas that directly relate to their wellbeing and health based upon 64 specific measurable indicators in the following eight domains:*

- *Health Populations,*
- *Living Standards,*
- *Ecosystem Health,*
- *Time Use,*
- *Educated Populace,*
- *Community Vitality,*
- *Civic Engagement, and*
- *Arts, Culture and Recreation.*

All of these domains will be aggregated into a single index of wellbeing, similar to the GDP (Gross Domestic Product), which would be readily understandable by Canadians.

B.M.   ***The Canadian Index of Wellbeing is much more holistic than any of the other initiatives that you have been involved with. Why do you think that this is a better way for you to use your time and the leadership capital that you have worked so hard to attain, rather than to continue to work on the single issue of health care?***

R.R.   *I was honoured to see the response of Canadians to my work as Commissioner on the Future of Health Care in Canada. I was especially gratified to see the way it galvanized opinion and sparked action for change. But I feel as if my work is just beginning. A health care system, even the best in the world, can only take us part of the way to ensure that Canadians are the healthiest people in the world. There are broader determinants of health related to our social and economic structures and the environment that have a profound impact on the health of individuals and communities. Some of the factors included in an adequate standard of living for all Canadians are: nutrition, affordable housing, early learning and childcare, social inclusion, and a healthy environment where the water we drink and the air we breathe are safe and sustainable.*

B.M.   ***How will the CIW work?***

R.R.   *When we establish all the indicators, we will have a specific and measurable index that will be a barometer of the social, health and* *environment to compliment the economic measurement of GDP. A more holistic measure is important because GDP measures good things and bad. For example, the 1998 ice storm in Ontario and Quebec was the biggest single event in Canadian history to boost the GDP (due to increased construction after the storm), and at the same time the devastation to local businesses and people's lives was really not measured or counted. Likewise, at the present time, our GDP is high but the number of Canadians living in poverty and the obesity rates in both children and adults are skyrocketing. Therefore we need a more holistic measure. The CIW will give us better information to make better social policy decisions – locally, nationally and internationally. We can then take a real and specific look at where we are improving and where we need to improve.*

Another Master Leader who excels at diagnostic information seeking is David Johnson, President of the University of Waterloo.

If you take the public universities in Canada and you exclude the private universities in the States, such as Harvard, Stanford, Yale, Princeton, etc., and you compare the public universities in Canada with the public universities in the states, you will find that Canadian universities are funded at 60% of the level of the public universities in the States. This is why our Canadian universities have larger classes and more multiple choice exams. It also shows up in NSSE, the National Student Survey of Engagement where [in which] the US scores higher than Canada and the ability to teach in Canada is less concentrated because there are more students per professor. The final thing I say when talking to my university friends is that it is instructive to compare UW to MIT and the University of Michigan because we want to be their Canadian equivalents. At the UW the faculty student ratio is 27 to 1, at the University of Michigan, it is 10 to 1, and at MIT it is 4 to 1. If you compare dollars from tuition fees, operating grants and private income, the UW is funded at $11,000 per student per year, Michigan gets $27,000 and MIT $100,000. As I tell *my friends in business, imagine yourself selling your product or services and your competition has 10 times the resources you do.*

The good side of that story is that UW is already the equal to the University of Michigan and MIT in many of our programs. That means that we are being as efficient as possible with what we have. Therefore, even a small incremental investment in us is very appealing because it has a very good ROI (Return on Investment) so every additional dollar spent on higher education would go a long way.

This excerpt illustrates the types of pertinent questions David asks, both of himself and others to benchmark the UW. He then uses the answers to those questions to develop credibility as a leader and to make a strong case for bringing his vision that Canada should be a world leader in higher education, innovation and research by 2020.

Roy Romanow, Hazel McCallion, David Johnston and all of the Master Leaders who were profiled in this book developed the skill of asking the right questions, at the right time and in the right way. They also kept on asking until they got the information they needed (diagnostic information seeking) long after their average counterparts would have given up.

It is easy to see how the first two competencies, strategic thinking and diagnostic information seeking, work hand-in-hand. We can all be more strategic when we have the very best information available. Likewise, having the very best information leads to innovative insights that helps us to be more strategic in our thinking. We now turn to the last of the three intellectual competencies: conceptualization/synthetic thinking.

3. Conceptualization/Synthetic Thinking.

The specific skills that make up this competency are understanding "how different parts, needs, or functions of the organization fit together, identifying patterns, interpreting a series of events, identifying the most important issues in a complex situation, using unusual analogies to understand or explain the essence of a situation.[15]

An excellent example of the crucial importance of conceptualization/synthetic thinking is how Steve Jobs and Apple changed the way we purchase, listen to and play music with the iPod. What made the iPod such a phenomenal success was the integration of software, hardware and design into a revolutionary product that did not exist before. A Canadian example of conceptualization is Research In Motion (RIM). RIM is the company that developed the ubiquitous Blackberry and is one of the most successful high-tech companies in the world. In fact, RIM is referred to as one of the "Four Horsemen on Nasdaq." The three others are Google, Amazon and Apple.

The original Blackberry was designed to be a wireless device for sending and receiving e-mails. However, when RIM added phone capabilities to the Blackberry — sales doubled. As of October, 2007, the number of BlackBerry subscribers had reached 8 million. As of September 25, 2008, that number had reached 19 million. The ability to conceptualize is critical because as Deal and Kennedy state, "The ability to conceptualize allows executives to create a strong sense of mission and to mold the corporate culture to fit an adopted agenda."[16]

High tech organizations that work on or with the Internet will either prosper or meet their demise, depending on whether they conceptualize changes in the next generation of Internet evolution as threats or as opportunities. Much of the innovation is and will be based on convergence and minimization. The companies and organizations that conceptualize and bring to market devices that we have not even dreamed of, and who make their products smaller; more user friendly, portable and powerful, will be the true winners in tomorrow's economy.

Klemp and McClelland point out that these three intellectual competencies do not work in isolation — they work together and for Master Leaders, they work together as synergistically as possible. "Planning/causal thinking is essentially hypothesis generation, because it involves seeing either the potential implications of events or the likely consequences of a situation, based on what has usually happened in the past. By contrast, conceptualization/synthetic thinking is essentially theory building to account for consistent patterns in recurring events or for connections between seemingly unrelated pieces of information. Both are enhanced by diagnostic information-seeking."[17]

An example of how these three strategies interact is the contest between Apple and RIM for supremacy of the multi-function smart phone market. RIM is not pursuing *one* strategy against the iPhone – but *four* separate and distinct strategies simultaneously. The Blackberry Bold is a tactile device, meaning the user types on the little keys with his or her thumbs and runs on the faster G3 interface. Typing with the keys is often the preferred format for people who receive a lot of e-mails. For users who use the PDAs primarily for entertainment, there is the Blackberry Thunder which uses a touch screen interface similar to the iPhone. There is also the new Blackberry flip-phone and there are rumours that there will be another new Blackberry that will have both the tactical and the touch screen interface. RIM also announced that Blackberries would run Facebook, the popular social networking software, have full GPS capabilities and be compatible with one of the world's most popular database management systems – SAP. The new software, and there will be more to come, will increase the functionality of Blackberry.

In the meantime Apple is not sitting still. You may remember that Apple introduced the replacement of their first iPod when the old model was still sold out. Apple just announced that the new iPhone and iPod will be significantly more environmentally friendly and you can be sure that Apple is working on future improvements. So stay tuned. RIM is now the world's largest and second largest supplier of devices that also include a cell phone. This is a contest that will be well worth watching. Also interesting to watch will be how the traditional makers of cell phones, Nokia, Motorola, LG, and Samsung will respond.

The three intellectual competencies have traditionally been taught in courses on management and leadership development and in MBA programs using the case study method. They are also taught on the job in terms of developmental assignments. More will be said about the critical importance of developmental assignments when we talk about the lessons of experience in Strategy 4. The second major skill set – the influencing skills, have only recently been taught in the more experiential courses in leadership and negotiating and influencing courses.

The Influence Competencies

The four influence competencies identified in the Klemp and McClelland study are:

4. Concern for influence.

This includes "an alertness to the potentialities for influencing people".[18] Master Leaders start to develop their concern for influence early in life and take on roles where they learn how to and how not to influence others. This concern for influence continues to develop both at work and in non-work settings, for example, becoming the president of the local PTA, fundraising, coaching a sport or becoming president or being on the executive of a volunteer organization. You can then take on more and more challenging developmental assignments, both at work and outside of work.

An excellent example of concern for influence is Sheila Watt-Cloutier. Sheila Watt-Cloutier grew up in Northern Quebec and lived "a traditional Inuit life until she attended school in Nova Scotia at age 10."[19] She studied psychology and sociology at McGill University and subsequently became increasingly concerned about the effect climate change was having on Arctic communities and the threats it presented to the Inuit's cultural survival. Sheila travels extensively, speaking out about climate change as an early warning system of worse things to come if we don't mend our wasteful ways and start taking care of the planet.

In 2007, Shelia-Watt Cloutier received the Mahbub ul Haq Human Development Award, from the United Nations and was nominated for the Nobel Peace Prize along with Al Gore. Sheila resides in Iqaluit, Nunavut and is the past Chair of the Inuit Circumpolar Council (ICC), which represents 155,000 Inuit. I have reproduced the text of Sheila Watt-Courtier's speech, "This I Believe", below.[20]

> I believe that how we deal with the losses in our lives can help us realize our potential as human beings. Everything that happens to us is interconnected — with other people, with nature and with each stage of our journey through life.

For most of the first ten years of my life, my family and I travelled near our Arctic home by dog team. I bonded with the ice, snow and cold during those journeys just as I bonded with my family and community. The bounty from the ice and snow represented life and nurturance to me in the best of ways. At the end of a day of hunting and fishing there was always a delicious meal prepared from the land and sea.

Government officials thought I had potential and convinced my family to send me to school in the south at this early age of ten. I lost a large part of my language and culture and through my own family the chance to learn all the lessons that my rich traditional way of life would have taught me.

As a young adult I returned to the Arctic. And over time I began rebuilding my connection with my roots through my community work and later on global environmental issues. I knew from my early childhood that we are irrefutably connected to nature. And I came to learn and believe that the dramatic changes in the Arctic environment are an early warning for the rest of the world. And as these changes affect the every day lives of people living in the Arctic now, so too will they affect lives in southern climates in profound ways very soon.

It was a second cycle of loss in my adult life that made me see how much I needed the skills I had missed acquiring as a teenager in order to live my life to its fullest potential. My life defining and greatest personal test started in February 1999 when my beloved and only sister died suddenly of a massive heart attack at the age of 48. My entire world stopped. For a very long time I could not let her go. Over the next five consecutive years, still grieving deeply over her death, life continued to test my resolve. I lost four more close family members — my Aunt, my mother, a young cousin and a young niece. I thought I would never stop grieving. I wept literally for years — in foreign countries, in strange hotels, in airports — whenever the waves of sadness would overcome me.

In those places of deep grief I deepened my personal journey. Each loss held me in a place I needed to be until I gained insight and clarity. I could eventually translate my new perspectives into powerful opportunities for personal change and growth. I came to see in a vivid way that all things are interconnected and that all things happen for a greater cause. I came to know trust in the life process. I came to know courage, tenacity and commitment. I needed these character skills in order to survive my grief. As it turned out, I also needed them to strengthen and raise the volume of my own voice on the global stage. There were many times I thought I could not carry on. But I learned that true commitment really begins when we reach a point of not knowing how we can possibly go on — and then somehow find the strength to go on anyway.

I used my commitment and the potent lessons I learned to pioneer the work of connecting climate change to human rights on the global stage. I now honour my losses by turning the energy of dealing with loss to protection — protection of this wise hunting culture upon which I began my life with my small and close knit family. And trust me when I say, this work requires much trust, boldness, courage and commitment.

There is no question that leadership is about influence and Master Leaders have a strong concern for and ability to influence others. However, they also had to choose the right method or methods of influence and use those methods with the right people, at the right time and in the right place. We will now look at three influencing methods and see how the Master Leaders profiled in this book used them.

5. Direct influence.

This includes "using one's personal authority or expert power to make sure that something gets done. This competency typically appears in a person's telling someone to do something, and [getting them to do it]."[21]

6. Collaborative influence.

This competency is based on working to meet the needs and to satisfy the interests of all parties. Collaborative influence is covered in much more depth in *The Seven Strategies of Master Negotiators*.[22] However, I would like to give a discerning example of the seasoned judgment that Master Leaders and Master Negotiators must possess. It illustrates that just as it is important to know when to collaborate, it is equally important to know when not to.

Research on negotiation style listed "cooperative" as one of the two primary negotiation styles, with "competition" being the other. Furthermore, negotiators who are effective cooperative negotiators have learned that they have to be *strategically* cooperative. In other words, they have to know when to cooperate and when not to. Effective cooperative negotiators are not afraid to use power or force if necessary and they have learned how to disagree without being disagreeable. I asked National Chief of the Assembly of First Nations Phil Fontaine how he applied these three characteristics of effective negotiators during the historic negotiations that led to the defeat of the Meech Lake Accord.

P.F.   *The Meech Lake Accord was defeated because the process was flawed. The accord only recognized the English and French as the two founding peoples of Canada. Because the First Nations People were not recognized along with the French and English as a founding people of Canada, on principle, it had to be defeated. Elijah Harper was our voice in the Manitoba Legislature. We, the Assembly of Manitoba First Nations, where I was the Grand Chief, designed the strategy that enabled Elijah Harper to say "No". We retained legal council and set out the entire strategy. Elijah became our voice — he is a hero without question.*

B.M.   *Is there anything that could have been done to make Meech Lake work? If they would have reworded it to state that there were three founding people, would that have made Meech Lake work?*

P.F. *Absolutely, because that would have been true! That would have been an accurate description of Canada's history and an accurate picture of the place of the indigenous people in the founding of Canada.*

B.M. *That is not asking a lot. Why didn't they do that?*

P.F. *The Mulroney government's position was consistent with the way successive governments have always treated our people – that we just have to wait our turn – we will deal with your interests and your issues later. So their decision to try to sell this to us was not entirely surprising or unusual. All the same it was extremely disappointing because they hadn't learned from their past mistakes.*

B.M. *So that's all they would have had to do?*

P.F. *They would have had to describe Canada as having three founding nations, and the integrity of our languages, our cultures and our history and at the same time describing our people as possessing unique characteristics that made up Canada – and of course, all of that was absent in the Meech Lake Accord – and that is why we opposed it.*

B.M. *You were under a lot of pressure. They were saying that Quebec would separate and the country would fall apart if Meech Lake Accord wasn't passed – but you stood firm.*

P.F. *We never thought that Quebec would separate and our position was not anti-Quebec. We are definitely not against the French language or culture or their unique values and traditions and history. We just wanted to be treated fairly – and we conveyed that language consistently throughout all of the Meech Lake process.*

B.M. *Do you think they have learned? Do you think next time they would recognize the three founding peoples?*

P.F. *I'm not sure if they have learned that lesson. There was a First Ministers meeting on January 16, 2009 to deal with the stimulus package in the January 27 budget and we were not invited to be at the table. We had a dinner the night before the First Ministers' meeting – to have us at the table as an equal partner in the Canadian Federation would be too much of a concession for this government.*

B.M.   *One of the other Master Leaders I interviewed for this book is Brian Warren, the President and CEO of Kidsfest. Brian speaks about ROI in terms of Return on Inclusiveness. It looks like you are saying that we haven't learned that lesson when it comes to Canada's indigenous people, at least not yet.*

P.F.   *No, and we haven't learned that as a country because there are some people, and I am referring specifically to us, who are seen as less than the rest and our culture and the way that is done is to deny us the integrity of our languages and culture and our rights to self-determination, the right to our land, and the respect and recognition of our treaties and aboriginal rights. There are people in the central government who see the Assembly of First Nations as an outsider organization, which means that we don't represent a legitimate government with unique rights.*

B.M.   *I understand that you are a big fan of Gandhi and Martin Luther King, Jr., you have chosen the path of non-violence. Why?*

P.F.   *I am a big fan of the peaceful approach to the peaceful transformation of society. I believe the most positive way to achieve the transformation of society is through negotiations even though I recognize that there are moments when the most effective response to denial is taking to the streets through peaceful demonstrations and occupation of government buildings – as we did in Manitoba in 1989 when the federal government unilaterally and arbitrarily decreed that the treaty right to education only extended to Grade 12 and anything beyond that, meaning university and community college education, was not covered. This is completely contrary to anything and everything we have always believed about the treaty right to education. And, up until that point, the federal government never challenged that understanding. So this was a huge betrayal and there were 300 of us who were charged and arrested.*

I also did things that went completely against the grain. We have a huge problem with the proliferation of gangs and many of our young people are drawn to the gang lifestyle. So I hired the most senior ranking gang member in Manitoba to come and work with me so we could learn directly from the source what it is that draws our young people to gangs and what to do about it. And I came under severe criticism for that.

B.M.   *You describe yourself as non-threatening, non-intimidating, soft-spoken, quiet, reserved, non-charismatic and not an orator. You then add that you didn't think anyone should be fooled by that. What exactly do you mean?*

P.F.   *The point I was making is to look back and see my track record when I was chief at a very young age in my community. We were the first First Nations community to establish local control of Indian Education. We were one of the first to have a First Nation's child welfare agency that maintained the historical relationship with the federal government, meaning that we didn't accept provincial jurisdiction. And then we established the first alcohol and drug addiction treatment centre on a reserve in Canada. I only served four years as chief and throughout that term we achieved some significant accomplishments for us as a community. And as Grand Chief in Manitoba where I served for three consecutive terms, we negotiated the Framework Agreement Initiative, which is still the most progressive self-government agreement in Canada even though it has not been fully implemented. We also negotiated the Statement of Reconciliation, the Truth and Reconciliation Commission and now the apology. And all of this has been achieved, not necessarily through great speeches or aggressive actions, but through negotiations.*

You can also observe these influencing skills in many of the stories about the Master Leaders who are profiled in this book. There is also one additional area that warrants more in-depth explanation at this point and that area is symbolic influence.

7. Symbolic influence.

This competency is "indicated by a use of symbols to influence how people act in the organization. A senior manager with this competency can, by personal example or a statement of mission, create a sense of purpose for the whole organization, which engenders individuals' loyalty and commitment to it." [23]

Master Leaders fully understand the importance of symbolic influence, on both the individual and the organizational level. Poor leaders underestimate the power of symbolic influence as the following example points out. A university was facing a substantial shortfall due to provincial funding cuts. The new president informed every department on campus that they would face budget cuts of 10 to 15% for the coming academic year. The following day, however, it was announced in a local paper that the president had just spent $100,000 on new china for the presidential mansion. What happened to this new president's credibility? It was severely damaged.

A second example concerns symbolic influence in a merger. The research on acquisitions and mergers indicates that two-thirds of mergers and acquisitions fail due in part to a war between the two cultures from their previous institutions. After the war, there is usually a winner and a loser. Many of the best and brightest people on the losing side eventually look for work elsewhere. The new organization loses one of its best assets and much of the value that could have resulted from the merger or acquisition.

But what about the other one third where the acquisition or merger worked? One of the best examples of a successful merger was due in large part to the symbolic leadership of Norman Augustine, who became the CEO of the combined companies of Lockheed and Martin Marietta. Augustine came into his job at a time when the U.S. defense industry had decreased procurement by more than 60% as a result of the end of the Cold War. Consequently, 15 major companies were downsized and merged into four. Norman Augustine used 12 essential steps that led Lockheed through this difficult time and on to phenomenal success. The following quotation illustrates symbolic influence:[24]

> ... when we combined Lockheed's and Martin Marietta's headquarters in a building previously occupied by Martin Marietta, we moved everyone out and reassigned offices from scratch to avoid the impression that anyone had been bumped or that some people were more important than others. That action was critical from a social standpoint, and it is for that reason that we at Lockheed Martin try to treat acquisitions as mergers of equals. The attitude "we bought you" is a corporate cancer.

The third example took place in Montreal a number of years ago. It was reported in all of the Quebec newspapers that the president of the Quebec Federation of Teachers had been caught shoplifting a pair of gloves at Eaton's.

The president very much wanted to keep her job in spite of the humiliating revelation. However, the directors of the Quebec Federation of Teachers fired her on the spot. How long did it take her to develop the type of reputation that would allow her to be elected to the job of president of the Quebec Federation of Teachers? Twenty to 30 years. How long did it take to lose her reputation? A matter of seconds. Object lesson: A leader must nurture and guard his or her reputation with their life.

The fourth example is from WestJet. When Clive Beddoe, who started WestJet, was asked how he typically spends his time when he flies, he answered:

> On a WestJet flight, I usually wait until the last hour or half-hour of the trip, and then I introduce myself to the passengers. I thank them for flying with us, encourage them to fly with us again, tell them about our future plans and ask them to give a round of applause to our employees. Then I schmooze with the passengers and help our flight attendants pick up garbage[25]

Clive Beddoe could have sent out millions of pamphlets telling the employees and customers of WestJet that they were valued by the company, and it would not have had nearly the effect that this story has in exemplifying WestJet's values and culture.

The Master Leaders I interviewed have developed an influencing style that works for them. Although they may have a preferred style, they are flexible enough to choose from each of the four styles listed above and/or to select the correct combinations of styles in order to work effectively with a number of different types of people in a number of different types of situations.

The last competency, and certainly not the least, is self-confidence.

8. Competency of self-confidence.

This important competency might well have been listed first, because we found it to be so prevalent among the outstanding senior managers. These people, although recognizing difficulties, never expressed any doubt that they would ultimately succeed. In the behavioural interviews, they displayed strong self-presentation skills and came across as very much in charge: they acted to make the interviewer feel comfortable, and they responded quickly and confidently to the request for key situations. By contrast, the average senior managers were more tentative, saying such things as, "To this day I don't know whether I made the right decision." Moreover, the outstanding managers expressed self-confidence by being stimulated by crises and other problems, rather than distressed or overwhelmed by them.[26]

The Interaction of the Competencies

These eight competencies do not work independently; rather it is the interaction among these competencies that make a leader effective and successful. Therefore, training has to be developed and delivered that helps all leaders and potential leaders develop not only individual competencies but also groups of functionally-related competencies.

The model of training that we developed in our course "Become a Master Leader" teaches competencies in all eight of the critical domains listed in this research study. By becoming a better problem solver and improving our influencing skills, our sense of self-confidence, the eighth competency, is also built up. As our sense of self-confidence goes up, we take on more difficult problems and challenges, which in turn help us to become better problem solvers and influencers.

The principle of modeling suggests that if we want to become more like Master Leaders we need to develop a similar set of leadership competencies. The following exercises have been developed to help you hone your leadership competencies to the highest degree possible.

Exercise 3-2: The following competency survey will help alert you to the areas in which your leadership skills are strong and where they most need to be developed and/or to work with someone who has the competency in question well developed. Rate yourself with an "X" on the following 10-point scales; in which "1" is indicative of a low level of skill development and "10" is indicative of a high level of skill development. It is also an excellent idea to document in writing how you use each of these competencies with personal examples. By looking at your examples, you can see your progress over time.

1. Planning/Causal Thinking: "Planning/causal thinking is essentially hypothesis generation. It involves seeing either the potential implication of events or the likely consequences of a situation based on what has usually happened in the past."

I do not enjoy nor am I good at developing hypotheses and seeing the consequences for a situation based on what has happened in the past	I enjoy and I am good at developing hypotheses and seeing the consequences for a situation based on past events

| 1 | 2 | 3 | 4 | 5 | 6 | 7 | 8 | 9 | 10 |

2. Diagnostic Information-Seeking: "Diagnostic information-seeking is pushing for concrete data in all sorts of ways, using a variety of sources to get as much information as possible to help with solving a particular problem. People who are good at diagnostic information-seeking are naturally curious and they ask questions to help them get the most data/information possible."

I do not typically ask very many questions nor am I seen by others to engage in a great deal of diagnostic information-seeking	I typically ask a great many questions. Others see me engaging in a great deal of diagnostic information-seeking

| 1 | 2 | 3 | 4 | 5 | 6 | 7 | 8 | 9 | 10 |

3. Conceptualization/Synthetic Thinking: "Conceptualization/synthetic thinking is theory-building in order to account for consistent patterns in recurring events or for connections between seemingly unrelated pieces of information. It is enhanced by diagnostic information-seeking."

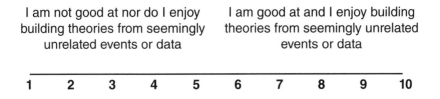

I am not good at nor do I enjoy building theories from seemingly unrelated events or data	I am good at and I enjoy building theories from seemingly unrelated events or data

1	2	3	4	5	6	7	8	9	10

4. The Need or Desire to Influence Others: "The need for influence is an alertness to the potentialities for influencing others. Concern for influence appears in such statements as, 'When I walked into that meeting, I was trying to figure out how to persuade them to agree to my proposal.'

I do not have a strong need or desire to influence others	I have a strong need or desire to influence others

1	2	3	4	5	6	7	8	9	10

5. Directive Influence: Directive influence measures the ability to "confront people directly when problems occur, [to] tell people to do things the way [you want] them done."

I am not comfortable using my personal authority or expert power to make sure that something gets done	I am comfortable using my personal authority or expert power to make sure that something gets done

1	2	3	4	5	6	7	8	9	10

6. Collaborative Influence: Collaborative influence measures the ability to "operate effectively with groups to influence outcomes and get cooperation, to build 'ownership' ... among key subordinates by involving them in decision-making."

I need improvement in building relationships for the good of both parties	I am good at building relationships for the good of both parties

1	2	3	4	5	6	7	8	9	10

7. Symbolic Influence: Symbolic influence "is indicated by a use of symbols to influence how people act in the organization. A senior manager with this competency can, by personal example or a statement of mission, create a sense of purpose for the whole organization, which engenders individuals' loyalty and commitment to it." Symbolic is also related to "walking the talk".

I have difficulty leading others by enrolling them with a sense of mission	I can easily lead others by enrolling them with a sense of mission

1	2	3	4	5	6	7	8	9	10

8. Self-Confidence: Leaders with strength in this competency, although recognizing difficulties, never expressed any doubt that they would ultimately succeed. In behavioural interviews, they display strong self-presentation skills and come across as very much in charge. They act to make others feel comfortable, and they respond quickly and confidently to requests in key situations. By contrast, the average senior managers are more tentative. Moreover, the outstanding managers expressed self-confidence by being stimulated by crises and other problems, rather than distressed or overwhelmed by them.

I have a low degree of self-confidence	I have a high degree of self-confidence

1	2	3	4	5	6	7	8	9	10

An excellent book on how self-confidence plays out in business and organizational settings is *Confidence: How winning streaks and losing streaks begin and end*[27] by Rosabeth Moss Kanter.

My Results of the Eight Competencies:

1. Planning/Causal Thinking:	
2. Diagnostic Information-Seeking:	
3. Conceptualization/Synthetic Thinking:	
4. The Need or Desire to Influence Others:	
5. Directive Influence:	
6. Collaborative Influence:	
7. Symbolic Influence:	
8. Self-Confidence:	

Based on your self-ratings of the above competencies, and knowing that competencies are made up of skill sets and that the whole is only as strong as the weakest link, which three competencies do you most need to work on? As an example, Martha found that others rated her higher on directive influence and lower on collaborative influence than she rated herself, it turned out that they thought she was so forceful and focused, that even when she thought she was being collaborative, others thought she was being directive or as one person said, "Sometimes when Martha is excited or passionate about something, she comes across as too directive, too focused and even a bit dictatorial. I have known Martha for a long time and I know I can stand up to her, but some members of the team are intimidated by her and this is not good for Martha or the team."

Once Martha processed this feedback, she made a distinct effort to be more collaborative. After talking with her mentor, they created a development plan to be and to be perceived to be more collaborative. Part of Martha's development plan was to use more neutral phrases such as, "I am curious about how you think this would work?" or "How do you see the pros and cons of this approach?" And "How would this approach affect you and your colleagues?" Martha also asked her peers and direct reports to let her know when they thought she was being too directive by reminding her of her commitment to be more collaborative.

Eight months later, Martha asked her HR department to re-administer the questionnaire on the eight competencies. Much to her credit, her peers and direct reports noted that there was a noticeable improvement in Martha's ability to collaborate.

The Skills Identification, which appears below, has been designed to help you in this important task. State the skills/strategies as specifically as you can and develop benchmarks that will demonstrate progressive levels of proficiency. Then ask yourself: are there books or articles you should read?; would it be beneficial to have a coach or mentor?; or are there any courses, seminars or conferences that would be advantageous for me to attend?

Exercise 3-3: Skills Identification

The three skills/strategies/competencies that I will develop further are.

1. _____

2. _____

3. _____

You will create your plan to develop these critically important skills/strategies/competencies at the end of this chapter and in Strategy 7. After you have carried out your development plan, it is also an excellent idea to reassess yourself on the eight competencies in three to six months' time.

Harvest Feedback on Your Leadership Style

Master Leaders are masters at harvesting feedback on their leadership style. Master Leaders know that there is always a built-in bias when they rate themselves. In this section I will present three leadership feedback methods. In order for these techniques to be effective, you must select people who know you well, who have observed your leadership style in action and who will tell you honestly how they perceive your leadership style.

The following example illustrates the power of harvesting feedback from others. Over 25 years ago, I was asked to do an assessment on all of the senior managers in a regional sales department of a large national broadcasting organization. This is when I first developed The Leadership/Managerial Evaluation Form (Appendix A). In this case, we will assume that the person being evaluated is Sally. At this point, I would like to draw your attention to the following two items on the Manager/Leader Evaluation Form.

I receive feedback from Sally:

Infrequently						Frequently NA
1	2	3	4	5	6	7

I receive feedback Sally that is:

Vague						Specific NA
1	2	3	4	5	6	7

It is important to note that the feedback from these two questions allow us to do a differential diagnosis just like the swimmer in the Introduction to this book was able to assess the percentage of the forward motion that was due to her arms and the percentage of forward motion that was due to her legs. In this case, the first question asks about the frequency of feedback that the respondent receives from his or her leader and the second question asks about the specificity that the respondent receives from his or her leader/ manager/supervisor.

The answers to these two questions give us four possible combinations. Sally could be deficient in that both the frequency and the specificity of the feedback is poor. Or it could be that the frequency of Sally's feedback is fine, but the specificity is not. Conversely, it could be that the specificity of Sally's feedback is fine but there is a problem because it is not frequent enough. Lastly, it could be that Sally is a star in this area and both the frequency and the specificity are excellent.

In this case the feedback will tell Sally if she needs to develop a plan and/or get coaching/mentoring to improve her performance in both areas (frequency and specificity), in one of the areas (specificity is fine but there is a problem with frequency or frequency is fine but there is a problem in that she is not specific enough), or both areas are excellent and she will need to look at another area in order to identify an objective for development/improvement.

This story illustrates two things. Salient feedback is very powerful. Secondly, we live in a feedback-rich world; however, to actually improve our leadership, we must make more of an effort to obtain that feedback. It is important to have a sense of what we do well. Everyone needs and can benefit from positive feedback. Positive feedback also increases the likelihood that we will do the things that were positively reinforced or encouraged. However, not only do we need feedback on what we do well, we also need feedback on what we need to improve.

Since there is always built-in bias when we rate ourselves, social scientists have developed a technique called 360-degree feedback. In 360-degree feedback, the person being rated rates herself, and she is also rated by her boss, manager or supervisor, her peers, her direct reports and/or by her customers. All of the rating forms for these eight competencies for managers or supervisors, peers, direct reports and/or customers are displayed in Appendix B. You may want to consider asking someone in human resources or some other independent third party to collect this information for you as the information will tend to be less biased and more honest if it is collected by a neutral third party. If you cannot get all of the traditional ratings in a 360-degree feedback, try to get as many different perspectives as possible. Research has demonstrated that each level or type of response adds to the overall validity of the assessment.

There are three additional factors that should be considered when you analyze your feedback. Sometimes, extreme scores, both positive and negative, can bias the results of the feedback. If there are extreme scores that come from one individual, an alternative is to use Olympic Scoring. In Olympic Scoring both the top and bottom scores are discarded and this may give you a more accurate picture of your true competencies. Secondly, in addition to computing the average score for each competency, you or the independent scorer can list the range. For example, an average score of 4 with a range of 3 to 5 shows less variation in the way you were scored than an average score of 4 with a range of 1 to 7. Lastly, the written results are summarized, to questions such as "What can Sally do to improve her leadership/managerial performance?" Remember, it is a good idea to change any unique wording so that the person giving the feedback will not be readily identified.

Table 3.1
Comparison of My Ratings on the Eight Competencies

	Self	Direct Reports	Peers	Boss/ Manager
1. Planning/Causal Thinking:				
2. Diagnostic Information-Seeking:				
3. Conceptualization/ Synthetic Thinking:				
4. The Need or Desire to Influence Others:				
5. Directive Influence:				
6. Collaborative Influence:				
7. Symbolic Influence:				
8. Self-Confidence:				

After you have filled in your results in the above table, it is worth noting that there are three common patterns when you compare your results with the ratings of others. The first pattern to look for is people who are known as over-raters. Over-raters tend to see their own skills and competencies much more positively than others rate them. Over-raters are at risk of derailing. Research at the Center of Creative Leadership in Greensboro, North Carolina has demonstrated that approximately 35% of executives, leaders and managers will derail at some point in their career. As the old adage states, "An ounce of prevention is worth a pound of cure." Therefore it is better to identify any potential problems early and work to overcome them before they become larger, and subsequently harder to resolve. Good mentors and/or coaches have proven to be very beneficial in helping to rectify any problems that have been identified – you can read more about the value of coaching and mentoring in Strategy 4, "Become a Purposeful Learner", and in Strategy 7, "Transform Competence to Mastery".

The second pattern that is less than optimal is found in respondents who consistently under-rate their skills and abilities as compared to their bosses, supervisors, mentors, peers, customers and/or direct reports. Known as under-raters, these people see themselves as less talented than they really are. The problem is that they do not volunteer for developmental assignments that would help them further develop their careers. Others may see their lack of confidence and as a result assume that they either can't or don't want to take on the very assignments needed to continue to develop increasingly advanced levels of responsibility within their organizations. In other words, their low levels of self-confidence act as a self-fulfilling prophecy. The results from their 360-degree feedback may open the door to having more realistic conversations, with the result that all parties can make better and more informed decisions about further developing the talents of these under-rated individuals whose careers may have prematurely stopped progressing – both to the detriment of these individuals and their organizations.

The last group is made up of those individuals who more or less see themselves as others see them. However, there may be cases where one of the stakeholder groups and/or a specific individual sees that person differently. For example, Sally's peers, direct reports and Sally all see Sally as very competent on each of the eight scales. However, in the area of being strategic, William, Sally's boss, sees Sally as significantly below the ratings that Sally, her direct reports and her peers see her performance. There could be several different reasons for discrepancies in Sally's ratings. It could be that William isn't seeing Sally accurately and may have to look more closely at her level of performance in this area. Likewise, it may be William is in a better position than everyone else to see what Sally's true performance level is. However, without these different ratings, it is quite likely that the problem, if it exists, will not be properly diagnosed.

There are two other forms you can use to harvest feedback from others. These forms can be easier to administer and it is also true that different forms will give you different feedback. The first is to ask three people who know you well to give you written feedback, using the form in Exercise 3-4, below. The form asks them to list three things that you do well as a leader and to list three objectives for improvement. This exercise works best when you choose for your respondents insightful people who know you well, who will be honest with you, and who will give you unbiased feedback. For instance, if you are on your way to the divorce court with your spouse, this is probably not the right person or the right time to ask for unbiased feedback.

Exercise 3-4: The Three-By-Three Leadership Feedback Form.

Please list three things that you like about _____'s leadership style. Please be as specific as possible. Simply saying, "John is a good communicator" is not specific enough. It should be so specific that John will know exactly what he should do more of in the future. For example, a specific comment would be: "John is very good at listening to our concerns, helping us develop creative options and only then offering any creative options he might have to help us solve our most difficult problems."

1.

2.

3.

Please list three specific targets for improving _____'s leadership.

1.

2.

3.

THANK YOU.

The exercise works well only if the feedback is specific. Once the forms are filled out and returned to you, carefully examine all the feedback you received. Were there any inconsistencies in the comments? It may be that the respondents see you differently because you behave differently in diverse situations. Or, it may be that the respondents are telling you more about themselves than about you. Or it may be that the respondents see you more accurately than you see yourself.

The leadership memo in Exercise 3-5 is a confidential form whereby the leader asks his or her followers to list one thing that the leader does that helps that particular person do his or her job, and one thing that the leader does that interferes with that particular person doing his or her job. Anyone who uses any of the feedback forms must reassure his or her staff that feedback will be taken in good faith with no repercussions/penalties for negative feedback. One way to insure that this is done is to ask a neutral third party, such as someone in HR or Personnel, to collect the feedback. As well, any unique wording that could potentially identify who said what should be removed.

You can re-administer or have someone else re-administer the forms on your behalf in six to eight months' time to track the progress that has been made.

Exercise 3-5: The Leadership Memo

What is one thing that I do as a leader that helps you do your job? What is one thing that I do that interferes with you in doing your job well. This form is confidential, so please do not sign it and please be honest.

Thank You

Exercise 3-6: INTEGRATED ASSESSMENT.

In this chapter you have evaluated your leadership style using three instruments: "Rating yourself on the Eight Competencies," "The Three-By-Three Leadership Feedback Form," and "The Leadership Memo." From these three instruments:

What are three areas these instruments agree on in relation to your leadership style?

a.

b.

c.

What are three areas these feedback forms agree on for improvement in your leadership style?

a.

b.

c.

Were there any questions raised about your leadership style that need further clarification, understanding, and/or more information/data before you can improve them?

Based on the ratings of the eight competencies, from yourself, your managers or supervisors, peers, direct reports and/or customers a Skill Development Plan can be created to further develop your leadership skills. A sample development plan appears below followed by Exercise 3-7 where you can start to work on your own development plan.

A sample development plan for Mr. Smith, President and CEO of a retail firm based on feedback using The Manager/Leader Evaluation Form is summarized below. In this case the feedback was from the people who reported directly to the president and by the board of directors. The feedback was collated and summarized by an independent third party and any unique wording was changed to help insure confidentiality and anonymity.

Developmental Plan for Mr. Smith

Executive Summary:

Many areas of strength were identified. Smith was seen to be extraordinarily personal, visionary, a superb networker, conscientious and very hard working. Smith is seen as having personal integrity and always worked hard to give back to the community. Many of the respondents said that they would always do the best job they could and that loyalty in this organization is a two-way street. They reported Smith has always supported his staff when they needed it, for example having to stay home with a sick child. The respondents also appreciated that Smith puts a high emphasis on staff training and development.

The major areas where improvement was noted was in Smith's organization and time management skills: especially in the areas of delegation, setting priorities and sticking to them and in having staff meetings that were planned, purposeful and productive. In regard to delegation, staff suggested a written form because at times Smith would delegate the same responsibility to more than one person and had a tendency to micro-manage.

A small number of respondents suggested that Smith was so nice that problems that needed to be confronted were not and/or they were confronted too late. Lastly, and most importantly, the respondents thought that Smith spent too much time managing and not enough time leading. They suggested hiring and/or promoting an existing staff member into the role of 2IC (Second in Command), which would free up Smith to lead the company and do an even better job of marketing/selling the company and its products. Five specific and actionable area that were identified for Mr. Smith's development are outlined below.

Organization/Time Management Skills

The President and CEO of this company is currently doing the work of three former managers. Some of this work could/should be delegated or other staff trained/hired to do some of this work. He can also try out the Time Management = Results Management Program and read and implement some of the concepts from the book *Prioritize/Organize: The Art of Getting It Done*. Another book for the future is Stephen Covey's *First Things First*. A specifically tailored Organization/Time Management/Prioritization/Delegation program can be developed and implemented one step at a time. A copy of the Delegation Form appears in Appendix C.

Staff Meetings

Schedule and evaluate staff meetings using the attached Meeting Improvement Form. Have preset agendas with time estimates and decide if there will be a permanent chair, rotating chair, note-taker, and time keeper. View the film by John Clease "Meetings Bloody Meetings." A copy of the Meeting Improvement Form appears in Appendix D.

Manager/Supervisor/Staff Training

1. Develop a specific short, medium and long-term manager/supervisor/staff training program.
2. Conduct a needs analysis for managers, supervisors and staff.
3. All staff should read *Good to Great* and decide how to implement the leadership principles from this book in their organization.
4. Bring in trainers/consultant for supervisory and sales training.
5. Any further goals should be established with the managers/supervisors/staff.

Suggested Reading:

Larson, C. E. and LaFasto, F.M. *Teamwork: What must go right/What can go wrong*, Thousand Oaks, CA: Sage Publications, 1989.

Larson, C. E. and LaFasto, F.M. *When teams work best: 6,000 team members and leaders tell what it takes to succeed*, Thousand Oaks, CA: Sage Publications, 2001.

Negotiation/Conflict Resolution

Look into taking a course on negotiation, conflict resolution and/or managing workplace conflict. Another option is to hire a trainer to do an in-house session so that all the staff will benefit.

A partial list of suggested readings follows:

Ferraro, V.L. & Adams, S.A. "Interdepartmental Conflict: Practical Ways to Prevent and Reduce It," Personnel. July-August, 1984, 12-23.

Fisher, R. & Ury, W. *Getting to yes: Negotiating agreement without giving in*, NY: Penguin Books, 1981.

McRae, B. *The seven strategies of master negotiators*. Northbridge Publishing, Toronto, ON, 2005.

Ury, W. *Getting past no: Dealing with difficult people*, NY: Bantam Books, 1991.

Leadership

Every once in a while a business book comes along that revolutionizes our thinking. *Good to Great* is just such a book.[28] Mr. Smith and his executive team can read the book and then use the Good to Great Diagnostic Tool to assess how well Mr. Smith and the team demonstrate the characteristics outlined in *Good to Great*. The Good to Great Diagnostic Tool can be downloaded free of charge from Jim Collins' website at www.jimcollins.com. An additional suggested reading is:

Covey, S. *The seven habits of highly effective people*, NY: Simon & Schuster, 1989.

Exercise 3-7: Skill Development Plan.

The one to three skills/strategies that I will develop further are:

Development Plan:

In this chapter, we looked at ways in which you could assess your leadership style. You should now have a better sense of your current style and you will have developed several specific targets for improvement that will help you become more like the Master Leaders. In Strategy 4 we will look at how just the right type of seminal experiences and learning opportunities can help you become a Master Leader.

STRATEGY 4

Become a Purposeful Learner

Love not what you are but only what you may become.
— Miguel de Cervantes

Groundbreaking research at the Center of Creative Leadership[1] investigated how leaders actually develop. What makes this study so fascinating is that they were able to quantify the sources of that developmental learning. The authors demonstrated that 50% of what leaders and executives learn is learned from experience. The authors call this "trial by fire" which means that:

➢ Job challenge and specifically difficult assignments are indeed the best teachers, and

➢ The essence of development is that diversity and adversity beat repetition every time.

Twenty percent of what managers and executives learn is learned from good, bad and flawed bosses/mentors. From the good bosses/mentors one can learn what to do, from the bad bosses/mentors one can learn what not to do, and from the flawed bosses/mentors one can learn that everyone has weaknesses or flaws. If a leader does not keep his or her weaknesses and flaws under control, they will lead to that leader's downfall. Twenty percent of what a leader learns is learned from failure and hardship. This category includes failures at work or a personal crisis or hardship that leads to lessons that could not have been learned in any other way. The last 10% of what is learned stems from formal education. Although this only accounts for 10%, it can be an incredibly important percentage if the education relates to the overall learning goals and objectives of the individuals, teams, departments and/or organization in question.

Lessons from Experience

You can't learn anything from experiences you're not having.
– Louis L'Amour

Research from the Center of Creative Leadership concluded that we need the right experience to transform potential talent into actual talent. It is often through this type of trial-by-fire that leaders come to fully understand the importance of initiative and decisiveness as well as that of being held accountable and responsible for their own efforts, in addition to the efforts of others. Experience and overcoming adversity are also confidence builders. It is important to note that we are not talking about isolated experiences, although an isolated experience can be life changing. Developing one's leadership skills and abilities to the point where one becomes a Master Leader takes, not years, but decades. An excellent example of how someone used her diverse experiences to help her become a Master Leader is Moya Greene.

Moya Greene is the President and CEO of Canada Post and she is a stellar example of a Master Leader and purposeful learner as the following overview of her resume illustrates.

> ➤ Strong public sector background spanning 17 years in seven different ministries of the federal public service;

> ➤ Senior officer of three of Canada's largest multinational companies: TD Securities, CIBC and Bombardier; and

> ➤ Named as one of Canada's top 40 female corporate executives by the Ivey School of Business for her "strong track record in strategic planning, complex negotiations and relationship building."[2]

Although Moya has had a great deal of experience in both the public and private sector, she did not have any direct familiarity with Crown corporations or postal operations. However, Moya decided to rectify that in her first six months as President and CEO of Canada Post. During that time, she worked in numerous roles within the corporation from letter carrier, to operations clerk to retail clerk. This type of cross-training was invaluable in helping Moya understand how to lead such a complex organization where over a billion pieces of mail are moved every day in a country that is as large and sparsely populated as Canada — with our very challenging weather conditions.

Exercise 4-1: Describe a personal leadership experience that taught you a great deal about becoming a leader. This could be from childhood, volunteer, work and/or family experience.

What did you learn from this experience?

Please estimate how much, on this 10-point scale, this experience taught you:

Very Little   A Great Amount

| 1 | 2 | 3 | 4 | 5 | 6 | 7 | 8 | 9 | 10 |

Please estimate how many in-class or formal course hours this would have taken:

Two common mistakes short-circuit the lessons of experience. The first is leaving high-potential people in jobs where they are no longer learning. The second common mistake is to move the "fast trackers" too quickly, so they never see the impact, both good and bad, from their leadership interventions. Thus, they never know if what they did was successful, partially successful or not successful at all. If they don't know the results, it makes it almost impossible to learn from the experience. Psychologists have a name for this problem and it is called "The Halo Effect." Because a person performs well in one area, there is a tendency to assume that he or she will perform well in most if not all areas.

An equally damaging mistake is to leave people in the same job for two long after they have stopped learning and stopped growing. Even when there is no position higher in the hierarchy and/or if the person in question is not ready to move up in the hierarchy, lateral transfers and cross-training can still lead to accelerated growth, learning and career advancement.

The lesson is clear: to develop our leadership and executive talent, carefully designed developmental assignments are a key factor, and these key developmental assignments must be pushed for by the job incumbent or his or her boss or mentor. At this point, it is a good idea to ask yourself if your own personal growth as a leader would be best served by gaining new and different experiences or slowing down and learning more from your current experience, or some combination of the two.

Cross-training is a valuable and usually inexpensive developmental assignment that can be used to gain the lessons of experience. People who are cross-trained not only have a better idea of how different parts of the organization work, they can also look at problems from other people's points of view. In other words, they can act as a linking pin to increase understanding and decrease unnecessary and often destructive conflict that occurs at the boundaries between departments, divisions and different professions within an organization. For example, the sales department "calls" the credit department "The Non-Sales Department." However, if the credit department did not do its job, invoices would not be paid or credit would be extended to untrustworthy clients, which would result in there being no money left in the budget for product development, paying suppliers, and/or making goods to sell.

Exercises 4-2: Have you ever experienced cross-training? If so, did you find it helpful to you and/or your organization?

If you answered yes, how was cross-training beneficial?

Is cross-training something that you and/or your organization should use more often?

I also think we underestimate the important value that early life experiences can have in developing our character and core values and how both character and core values affect our subsequent development in becoming a Master Leader. This is illustrated with what I learned from my interviews with Annette Verschuren, Ruth Goldbloom and Phil Fontaine.

Annette's family were Dutch immigrant farmers. Annette's life changed drastically when she was 10; her father had a debilitating heart attack. Annette's parents decided not to sell the family farm, but to run it. Annette's mother, Annette and her siblings not only took on a great deal of responsibility, but they succeeded against all odds and were able to earn a livelihood. Annette had the following to say about her mother and father.

> **They were a great team. Mom, Dad and the family held board meetings around the kitchen table. Together, the family made the farm work.**
> **Annette Verschuren**

A.V.   *My father had a heart attack when I was 10. I had four siblings, the oldest of whom was 13. We had no choice — we had to work and we took on a great deal of responsibility. We had to learn to milk cows, drive a tractor, pull a calf out, and breed bulls — so we absolutely had to work together as a team. Dad gave guidance and he was a very wise, innovative and creative man. Mom was very efficient, pragmatic and very organized. They were a great team. Mom, Dad and the family held board meetings around the kitchen table. Together, the family made the farm work.*

So at the age of 10, Annette not only learned a great deal about responsibility, she also learned first-hand about the value of teamwork.

Early life experiences also played an important part in Ruth Goldbloom's development as a leader. Ruth's father died when he was 32. At the time her mother had five children and was pregnant with her sixth.

R.G.   *My father died in August and my youngest brother was born in February. My mother had a vision for her six children. And that vision was, no matter what happens to you in life there is one thing that no one can take away from you — your education — and I have never, never forgotten that. It was my mother's belief that if you can give that to your children, you have given them the greatest gift that they could hope to have. And my mother was able to put all six children through university. She also gave us a strong sense of community and taught us that we should give back to our communities and to our country. For example, this morning, I got up at 5:30 [a.m.] for a fundraiser called,*

"Raise a Reader," and I stood on the corner of Barrington and Sackville, from 6:30 to 9:00, and I sold newspapers with all of the proceeds going to literacy.

B.M.   *How was your mother able to put six children through university?*

R.G.   *My father had a haberdashery store. My mother knew nothing about business. She didn't even know the combination to the safe, so after my father died, she had to have the safe blasted open.*

At the time she knew nothing about running a business because she was so busy having children and raising the family. So she walked down the street to the T. Eaton Company Limited. Their best salesperson was Mr. Carmen Hughes. She asked Mr. Hughes how much he made and he said $15 per week. My mother offered him $19 per week provided he would start work on the following Monday.

Mr. Hughes accepted and worked in and managed our family's store for 40 years. When he retired, my mother gave Carmen and his wife a trip to the UK as one of the ways she showed her appreciation. I should also tell you that my brother Irving worked in the store. When he was 14, she sent him on a buying trip to Montreal to buy furniture to sell in the store. About a month later, the furniture arrived by train. Irving suggested that we sell the furniture right out of the railway cars and that way we wouldn't have to pay to have the furniture trucked to our store. My mother immediately agreed. If it worked, it would demonstrate that it was a great idea; if it didn't work, my brother would learn a valuable lesson. All of us adored my mother. Rose Schwartz was a wise and remarkable women and I was very fortunate to have her as my mother and role model.

What did Annette and Ruth have in common? They had extraordinarily courageous mothers, who made decisions that were very much out of the norm for their times. I asked Annette and Ruth to tell me how much of their success they would attribute to having mothers who were such strong role models. Annette said, "I never see gender as liability, in fact, it's been an advantage all of my life. I learned my planning and organizational skills at an early age and they have served me very well ever since. I also learned how to multitask and how to get teams producing at the highest level."

Ruth said, "It's hard to assess a percentage of my success attributed to my mother – but I would have to say 85-100%. As I slowly mature, I recognize her wisdom, strength, honesty and determination as the most influential factors." Similarly, National Chief of the Assembly of First Nations spoke eloquently about his mother, Agnes Fontaine.

> *My earliest role model would have been my mother, Agnes Fontaine, and although she is deceased, she still inspires me. She was the first woman to be elected as a band counsellor in Canada. She was elected to band council 1952 because this was the first time women were allowed to run for elected office due to revisions in the Indian Act. The headline in the Winnipeg Tribune commented, "Indian Squaw Elected to Band Council".*

> *My mother had 12 children, 10 boys and 2 girls and I was the youngest boy. My father died when I was seven. I spent 10 years in residential school as did all of my 11 siblings, my mother and her father as well as my grandmother on my father's side. My mother was an incredible force, very determined and a fierce fighter for her family. She didn't take a back seat to anyone. She was truly amazing – a true protector of our family and probably the best cook on the reserve. Once my father passed away and the insurance ran out – we became a poor family or maybe I should say another poor reserve family. She was tenaciously hardworking and wasn't about to let her family fall apart. so she worked multiple jobs and learned how to make do with very little.*

B.M.   *Did you get your fighting spirit from her?*

P.F.   *It rubbed off – but I am not as tough as she was and I don't think there is anyone in my family who is as tough as she was. She was a wonderful woman and a wonderful person.*

In the next section we will look at the importance of having role models and mentors at work.

Lessons from Mentors

As stated in the book, *Lessons from Experience*, 20% of what we learn comes from bosses and mentors. Mentors can show us the way by example, by making suggestions, asking profound questions and opening doors that ordinarily would not have been opened to us. Part of a mentor's role is to spot raw talent and help polish that talent and make it shine. Mentors also plant ideas that may take years to come to fruition.

When I met Ken Boyce, he was the Vice-President of Sales at ATV (Atlantic Television).[3] The first thing about Ken that impressed me was his gracious manner. He also had an incisive vision for his department. Ken ran the sales group as if it were a department of continuing education. I found this out when Ken hired me to teach a series of courses on effective management and team building. He said he was looking for in-depth transfer of training rather than short motivational lectures. This was quite early in my career as a trainer and consultant, and I was not sure that I was up to the job. However, Ken was an educator in the true sense of the word; he was also an exceptional talent scout and developer of people.

After I had done the training, Ken suggested that we have breakfast on a monthly basis, and those breakfast meetings changed my life. First, Ken asked extremely incisive questions about how I saw my teaching style and how I planned to develop it further. Since I knew next to nothing about sales and marketing, he also became my sales and marketing coach. Lastly, he became my career counsellor, and was in fact the person who first suggested that I go into business for myself. At first I thought the suggestion was ludicrous. After all, I did not consider myself an entrepreneur and no one in my family or circle of acquaintances had ever owned their own business. Secondly, I was accustomed to having a stable and predictable pay cheque. Yet sure enough, four years later, I took the plunge and it was one of the best decisions I ever made.

A further example of Ken's ability as a talent scout and mentor was hiring a Victorian scholar. Linda Law was in the process of finishing her Ph.D. in Victorian literature. Although Linda loved to teach, she did not want to live in the publish or perish world of university teaching, and outside of university teaching, there was not much of a market for Victorian scholars. In addition to that, Linda had developed an interest in business. However, if there was one thing that Ken was good at – it was spotting raw talent. Ken was in the process of setting up a demographic and psychographic research department to help support his sales staff. Ken figured that Linda knew enough about research and was hard working enough to allow her to master what she needed to learn in very short order. So this is how a non-television owning, former Victorian scholar started her career in the business world. In the following interview Linda Law describes what it was like to have Ken Boyce as a mentor.

L.L.   *I was very insecure moving from an academic world to an industry where advanced university degrees were regarded with suspicion. While other people told me over and over what a shame it was that I was no longer "using my degree", Ken understood that my educational experiences made me uniquely qualified for my job by developing my overall research and communication skills, my presentation and teaching skills and, perhaps most importantly of all, my independent learning style.*

B.M.   **How did Ken help you develop your skills and abilities on the job?**

L.L.   *When Ken hired me at ATV it was to develop the marketing department. He gave me a huge budget for training and development and essentially told me to do what I needed to do such as buy the books and take the courses I needed to take to learn what I needed to learn. It was a very growthful experience for me because I had always been an independent learner, and have always thrived in that atmosphere of freedom. At the same time I always knew Ken was my champion, and that if I needed support in any way he was there for me.*

Another purposeful learner who speaks candidly about the mentors who helped her achieve much of her success, is Canada Post's President Moya Greene.

B.M.   *Paul Tellier was the former President and CEO of Canadian National Railroad. He was also one of the Master Negotiators I interviewed for my book, The Seven Strategies of Master Negotiators. I understand that he was one of your mentors. Can you tell me what you learned working with Paul?*

M.G.   *Paul is a great executive and he is very focused, disciplined, and quite driven. During his tenure at CN, most of CN's employees actually became owners. Until recently, this was the most successful IPO (Initial Public Offering) in Canadian history. It would be an understatement to say that Paul orchestrated a sea change in the culture at CN.*

I know Paul because we both worked for the Federal Civil Service in Ottawa and I worked on the opposite side of the table from Paul during the privatization of CN. When Paul took on the responsibilities as President and CEO of Bombardier, he recruited me and I worked directly for Paul.

B.M.   *It sounds like Paul Tellier is an amazing talent scout.*

M.G.   *Paul is an amazing everything.*

B.M.   *Who were your female mentors and role models?*

M.G.   *My mother was a school teacher who taught kids who had to struggle to learn because they were learning disabled. Her attitude was that since her own children were born capable of learning — it was up to us to use it. I can't remember her ever helping us with our homework.*

I have also had the opportunity to work with some exceptionally talented leaders and a few of them became my mentors. At the top of the list is Huguette Labelle. Huguette was the Secretary of State during the patriation of the Canadian Constitution. She then became Deputy Minister of Transport and she recruited me to work there. At that time she became and still is a mentor and I still talk to her after all of these years. She now runs Transparency International[*] and she is very much at the top of her game. Transparency International rates countries as to how transparent or corrupt they are. This is very important in today's globalized world.

B. M.   *Did you find your mentors or did they find you?*

M.G.   *Most of my mentors have been my bosses — so pick your bosses well! Do your due diligence on the organization you are joining, but do more on your potential boss. I've kept in contact with my mentors and former bosses along the way.*

Most of my mentors
have been my bosses
– so pick your bosses
well!

Moya Greene

Very few people get to the top without support from strong mentoring relationships. And the higher you go, the more important these relationships are, and the more likely it will be that those influence mentors will be men.

I think mentorship is hard to force. You work for someone who sees the talent and energy you bring to them. They see your potential and they want that potential to be realized. Therefore, try as much as possible to pick your boss – you only have one life and there are so many talented people. Read about people who are extraordinary and find out what makes them extraordinary. Then try to work close enough to see them in action and let them see you in action. Without even noticing it is happening, a mentoring relationship is likely to start.

B.M.   *We also have a major problem, which is also a major opportunity in the upcoming "war for talent." Only 2% of CEOs in Canada and the US are women. Do you have any special advice for women?*

M.G.   *My advice is don't be afraid of your ambition. Ambition is not a four letter word. You have to be credible and you have to prepare yourself. If you are a woman moving up to the executive level, you will have to move out of your comfort zone. Work in areas that are very important to the organization you are working for. Taking risks and moving outside of your comfort zone is of paramount importance.*

Don't be surprised or knocked off your game by setbacks. Setbacks occur because the boss or the organization changes its mission; the person who was your champion or benefactor is no longer there; the project you are working on gets changed or dropped. Setbacks tell you who is on your team and in your camp, they're inevitable – everyone has them.

The final thing that people don't pay attention to is that part of it is luck. Sometimes people have developed and honed their talents and shown that they are very capable and still don't get offered the top job. The reason they don't is very complex, Anna Fels' research demonstrated both men and women undervalue what women bring to their work.[5]

Getting selected for the top job is complex and most of the people doing the selecting are men. However, we are going to see more women being selected for the top job as more women become CEOs. It should also be noted that although you can make a huge contribution being a CEO, it is not a crowning glory. I know lots of professional women who have chosen, for very good reasons, to put more emphasis elsewhere and we are seeing that with more and more men as well.

B.M.   *Do you have any final advice on mentoring?*

M.G.   *A person who becomes known for always giving his or her best is by definition a role model and a leader. Of all of your assets, your reputation is the most important asset you will ever build — and the best way to build a great reputation is by always giving your best!*

My mentors, both men and women were committed to my success and I owe them a huge debt of gratitude.

Exercise 4-3: Think of one of the best bosses, mentors, supervisors, or managers you have had. What was the most important lesson you learned from that person?

Think of one of the worst bosses, supervisors, or managers that you have had. Briefly describe the most important lesson you learned from this experience.

Lessons from Flawed Bosses

Often, our most important learning comes from flawed bosses. Flawed bosses are those who do most things well, but have a fatal flaw that makes them much less effective than they could or should be. For example, Mike was a visionary, hardworking and determined leader; however, he micromanaged to the point where his best people looked for work elsewhere. Flawed bosses teach us about the complexity of leading and managing and the need to examine our own character for flaws that make us less effective than we could be.

> *A talented, successful person can see first hand how another talented and successful person can do himself or herself in.[6]*
> *- McCall, Lombardo, and Morrison*

Another example of a flawed boss is Lynn. Her employees feel that she is so cold, aloof and distant that they don't seek out her advice even when they know they should. Flawed leaders have a blind spot or Achilles heel that prevents them from being all that they could be.

Exercise 4-4: Think of a flawed boss and describe an important lesson that you learned from this experience.

We all know the importance of Aristotle's statement – "Know Thyself." At the Center of Creative Leadership, their research showed that approximately 35% of managers'/leaders' careers come off the rails at some point. This research identified 10 fatal flaws that are listed below.[6] Look at this list very carefully and check any flaws that you consider the most likely to cause you to derail. Another option is to ask a trusted friend and/or colleague to list the flaw or flaws that would most likely do you in and find out the reasoning behind their choice.

THE TEN FATAL FLAWS

1. Specific performance problems with the business:

A series of performance problems sometimes emerges in which a manager runs into profit problems, gets lazy, or demonstrates that he can't handle certain kinds of jobs (usually new ventures or jobs requiring lots of persuasion). More important, by failing to admit the problem, covering it up, and trying to blame it on others, the manager shows that he can't change.

2. Insensitivity to others: an abrasive, intimidating, bullying style:

The most frequent cause for derailment was insensitivity to others. This often shows when managers are under stress.

3. Cold, aloof, arrogant:

Some managers are so brilliant that they become arrogant, intimidating others with their knowledge. This remark is descriptive of such managers [leaders]: "He made others feel stupid . . . wouldn't listen, had all the answers, wouldn't give you the time of day unless you were brilliant, too."

4. Betrayal of trust:

In an incredibly complex and confusing job, being able to trust others absolutely is a necessity. Some managers commit what is perhaps management's only unforgivable sin — they betray a trust. This rarely has anything to do with honesty (which was a given in almost all the cases); rather, it is a one-upping of others or a failure to follow through on promises, which wreak havoc on organizational efficiency.

5. Overmanaging: failing to delegate or build a team:

After a certain point, managers cease to do the work themselves and become executives who see that it is done. Some never make this transition, never learning to delegate or build a team beneath them. Although overmanaging is irritating at any level, at the executive level it can be fatal because of the difference in one's subordinates.

6. Overly ambitious: thinking of the next job, playing politics:
Some, like Cassius, are overly ambitious. They always seem to be thinking of their next job, bruising people in their haste, and spending too much time trying to please upper management.

7. Failing to staff effectively:
Some managers get along with their staff but simply pick the wrong people – staffing in their own image with technical specialists, or picking people who later fail.

8. Inability to think strategically:
Preoccupation with detail and a miring in technical problems keep some executives from grasping the bigger picture. They simply can't go from being doers to being planners.

9. Unable to adapt appears as a conflict of style:
Failure to adapt appears as a conflict of style with a new boss. Although successful managers have the same problem, they don't get into wars over it, [instead they] fight problems with facts and rarely let the issues get personal.

10. Overdependence on a mentor or advocate:
Sometimes managers stay with a single advocate or mentor too long. When the mentor falls from favour, so do they. Even if the mentor remains in power, people question the executive's ability to make independent judgments. Can he stand alone, or does he need a mentor for a crutch?

Exercise 4-5: In the space below, please outline how you will control the one flaw that you listed rather than have that flaw control you.

Since 20% of what we learn comes from bosses, mentors and supervisors, organizations need to do a better job of taking this into account both when promoting and when assigning their staff to new positions. For example, if the person in question is a brilliant strategist and a driven, hard-working employee who can be too abrasive or demanding and doesn't do a good enough job of acknowledging other people's contributions, that person can be paired with a boss who can both model and teach getting things done in a more relaxed manner, being polite and respectful and acknowledging others. Exposure to a variety of bosses and mentors can help us learn these important lessons because one of the ways we learn best is by observing, comparing and contrasting styles. Remember that you don't have to learn all these valuable lessons at work. Volunteering for challenging assignments — both at work and away from work — will also increase your exposure to a number of different role models while maximizing the lessons you need to master in adapting to different styles.

Lessons from Failure and Hardship

It is not the critic who counts; not the man who points out how the strong man stumbles, or where the doer of deeds could have done them better. The credit belongs to the man who is actually in the arena, whose face is marred by dust and sweat and blood; who strives valiantly; who errs, who comes short again and again, because there is no effort without error and shortcoming; but who does actually strive to do the deeds; who knows great enthusiasms, the great devotions; who spends himself in a worthy cause; who at the best knows in the end triumph of high achievement, and who at the worst, if he fails, at least fails while daring greatly, so that his place shall never be with those cold and timid souls who neither know victory nor defeat.

— **Theodore Roosevelt**

Failure and hardship are some of the most difficult things we can experience and are often the most difficult to learn from because our pride has been wounded. Consequently, we often experience self-doubt or we feel a sense of shame, which will lessen or even prevent us from learning. However, learn from them we must if we want to become Master Leaders. In this section we will see how Master Leaders learned from failure and then see how they learned from hardship.

Learning from Mistakes and Failure

The Master Leaders I interviewed have made one very fundamental decision – to learn from their mistakes and failures. In fact, for Master Leaders, there are no mistakes, only lessons to be learned, as the following example from my interview with Master Leader David Rathbun attests.

B.M.   *Tell me about one of the most important mistakes or failures you experienced in your career and what you learned from it.*

D.R.   *I had just graduated with my MBA with an undergrad in science. The economy was growing rapidly at the time and I was soon hired by a great organization, Shell Canada.*

In my first job at Shell, I was assigned to operations and I had supervisory responsibility for three or four people who had 20 to 30 years experience. I was a kid who had just graduated with an MBA and no experience in the petroleum industry. Why did they put me in that role when I did not have any experience in operations? I believe the reason was – an MBA. I was taught a very valuable lesson by that small group of dedicated people at Shell.

My first task was a minor rudimentary issue that the plant manager asked me to address. I wanted to use this as an opportunity to impress the boss. I brought my whole team together with a few people from other departments and we walked through the issue. There was more talking than listening on my part. There was a lot of head nodding, we had agreement and drafted an action plan.

The group came back together a week later and not one thing had progressed since that first meeting. What they were essentially telling me was; we don't care that you have an MBA, you are not able to relate to us therefore we are not advancing tasks under your direction. They were a great group of people. At the subsequent meeting, I did more listening than talking and the problem was solved within days.

The most important lesson that I learned and it has stood me in good stead for my entire career is if you cannot form relationships, you are dead in the water. If you cannot build relationships you will not be successful. Period! Full Stop!

David then became a Territory Manager for Shell in Atlantic Canada. He then went to work for Maritime Life and over time to become Comptroller and then senior leader Human Resources. David was headhunted, in 1997, in a North American wide competition to become the Vice President of Human Resources at Aliant where he worked on the merger of four Atlantic Canadian telephone and telecommunications companies.

In 2007, David was selected to be the President of xwave, an Information Technology Company. One of the first things he did in this new role, after getting to know his leadership team, was to help develop a new strategic direction. At the time he became President, xwave had 25 products/services. The next year, David worked with the company to identify its strategic bias and list the top five choices for a strategic direction. The following year they choose their strategic direction and focused on a select few products/services.

I chose this example so that you could see how David learned from a mistake he made on his first week in a new job. I would also like to point out how David's time horizon has changed. At his first job with Shell, David's time horizon was measured in weeks. Today his time horizon spans three years or more. Learning from failure and the ability to take a long term perspective was one of the most important competencies that differentiated the Master Leaders in this book from their less masterful counterparts.

Exercise 4-6: Summarize a mistake you made and the important learning that resulted from that mistake.

Is there a mistake that you made that you haven't fully forgiven yourself for? Is there some way you can learn from that mistake and move forward?

For most of us, there is a big difference between how we react to a mistake and how we react to a failure. When we make a mistake, the consequences are usually not as big, and we usually attribute the mistake to not knowing or not perceiving something in the external world. When we use the word failure, we usually attribute it to something inside us like a flaw in our character. It is for this reason that we experience a "failure" as something much more severe and much more personal in nature than we would a mistake. Consequently, "failure" is much harder to learn from, because we take it so personally. It is worth noting, however, that Master Leaders view both types of experiences as learning experiences. Richard Norris developed the following anagram to help us remember this important lesson:[7]

F	ocused
A	nd
I	nsightful
L	earning
U	sing
R	eal
E	xperience

Some of my favourite quotations about learning from failure follow.

There are no mistakes. The events we bring upon ourselves, no matter how unpleasant, are necessary in order to learn what we need to learn; whatever steps we take, they're necessary to reach the places we've chosen to go. — **Richard David Bach**

Anyone who has never made a mistake has never tried anything new. — **Albert Einstein**

It's impossible to live without failing at something, unless you live so cautiously that you might as well not have lived at all — in which case, you fail by default. — **J.K. Rowling**

Failure is success if we learn from it. — **Malcolm Forbes**

When you make a mistake, write down what you've learned before a week passes. The process of writing it and reading it can help you avoid repeating it. — **Michael Levine**

We either make ourselves miserable, or we make ourselves strong. The amount of work is the same. — **Carlos Castaneda**

Dismal failure is if you had an idea, you didn't plan it very well, you executed it really poorly, and after you failed, you felt sorry for yourself. Noble failure is if you had an idea, you planned it well, you executed it well, it failed. And then you said, "What can we learn from this?" — **David Pottruck**

Exercise 4-7: Learning from Failure. In the space below, briefly describe an experience where you experienced failure, but in retrospect helped you learn a valuable lesson that you may not have learned in any other way.

Learning from Hardship

The most difficult thing any parent can experience is the death of a child. The toll this can take on a family is so enormous that only 10% of marriages survive after a child has died. Many people who have experienced the death of a child never recover. Therefore, one of the most difficult struggles that grieving parents face is fighting to re-establish meaning in their lives.

However, there are some amazing people who have been able, not only to re-establish meaning in their lives, but to transform their personal tragedy into a leadership opportunity to help make the world a better place. Mothers Against Drunk Driving (MADD) was founded in 1980 by Candy Lightner after her daughter was tragically killed by a drunk driver who was a repeat offender. Despite having to face the most terrible circumstances a parent can find herself in, Candy used her pain and suffering to help others.

Similarly, Phil Fontaine has dedicated his life to the advancement of First Nations people. He was first elected into public office at the age of 28, and is currently serving his third term as the National Chief of the Assembly of First Nations. As an activist leader, Phil Fontaine helped to expose the shocking abuses that existed within the residential school system when he courageously revealed that he had been abused. He became a role model which made it easier for other victims of physical, sexual and emotional abuse to come forward.

Another moving example of learning from hardship is Lieutenant-General Roméo Dallaire. Dallaire was the head of UNIMAR, the United Nations Peacekeeping operation in Rwanda between 1993 and 1994. However, instead of keeping the peace, he witnessed a genocide where 800,000 men, women and children lost their lives and 3 million people became refugees. Tragically, even after countless heroic efforts, Dallaire could not get the United Nations or any developed countries to intervene.

Even though Dallaire is credited with helping to save over 200,000 Tutsis and Hutu moderates by setting up "safe areas," he returned to Canada a broken man, suffering from PTSD (Post Traumatic Stress Disorder). The images from the genocide haunted him. He turned to alcohol, hit rock bottom and even considered suicide.

However, Dallaire did not give up because he found a new mission. Although he could not do anything to prevent the genocide that had taken place in Rwanda, he could, by the very fact that he witnessed these horrific crimes against humanity, do everything in his power to make sure that a similar tragedy would not be allowed to occur. He held the United Nations and the world's powers accountable for passively sitting back and letting the genocide take place. His book, *Shake Hands with the Devil: The Failure of Humanity in Rwanda,*[8] is an account of what took place in Rwanda. He concludes his book with the following plea for action:[9]

> Though I too can criticize the effectiveness of the UN, the only solution to this unacceptable apathy and selective attention is a revitalized and reformed international institution charged with maintaining the world's peace and security, supported by the international community and guided by the founding principles of its Charter and the Universal Declaration of Human Rights.

Dallaire firmly believes that Canada is a model for the world, and at the same time Canada is "screaming for a mission, a vision, a calling." The question Dallaire asks is "How deep are our convictions?" Are some human beings' lives worth more than others? How can we be so generous and altruistic in help-

ing the victims of the tsunami and do so little to help the innocent victims in
Darfur? How is it that we help some countries in the world develop a civil society, and not others? Dallaire states, "Engraved still in my brain is the judgment
of a small group of bureaucrats who came to 'assess' the situation in the first
weeks of the genocide: 'We will recommend to our government not to intervene as the risks are high and all that is here are humans.'"[10]

In the December 6, 2003 *National Post*, Mark Gallant states that,

> If there is a Canadian identity, Roméo Dallaire may have much
> to teach us about it. If our ideals are about equitable use of
> power, about consensus, about compassion, about confronting
> racism and about just doing our somewhat insecure community-
> minded best, no matter what, then Dallaire may embody our
> nation more than any other Canadian today.

I would like to add to Mark Gallant's comments, I have seen Roméo Dallaire
speak twice and there is no doubt that he is a master presenter. His energy and
commitment to a number of human-rights issues is inspiring. Although he has
painfully come to accept that he was unable to prevent the genocide in Rwanda,
he has made it his mission to do everything in his power to prevent future genocides and he works to prevent children from being turned into child soldiers.
He has become an outspoken advocate for mental health and has taken the issue
of PSTD out from under the carpet where it had been swept – and asserted that
it is a mental health issue of which no one should be ashamed and for which
proper treatment should be put into place. He exemplifies leadership, heroism
and resiliency in action by overcoming his own demons and turning hardship
into empowerment.

Exercise 4-8: Have you used hardship to help you become a more effective leader in either your personal or professional life? For example, many divorced or separated parents have used this experience to learn to become a better parent. People who have been fired from their jobs, either fairly or unfairly, have used the experience to make themselves "un-fireable" or have started their own businesses.

Lessons from Formal Education

Sometimes books and formal courses influence our thinking in such a way that we perceive the world in a richer and more complex fashion than we did before. For example, I first read *Getting to Yes* when I was a representative on the board for the Dalhousie Faculty Association. We were preparing to go into collective bargaining with management and both sides were reading *Getting to Yes*. I was so impressed with the book and the method that I decided to switch my focus from teaching stress management to teaching effective negotiating and influencing skills. In truth, this book changed the course of my life. I subsequently took all of the negotiation courses offered at the Harvard Program on Negotiation.

My experience with the books *Getting to Yes* and *Getting Past No* and the courses I have taken at the Harvard Program on Negotiation have given me a mental model in the area of effective negotiating that is more effective than the model I grew up with. This was much more than the learning of a new set of skills; it was a paradigm shift both in my way of thinking about negotiating and in the way I behave while negotiating. Both of these lessons have been invaluable both personally and professionally. In fact, I would say that most of my success has resulted from learning to be a purposeful learner. I first learned this from my father, and it was reinforced by two of my mentors, Henry Peterson, who was my psychology professor and who employed me as a teaching assistant and Ken Boyce who first hired me to work in private industry.

Another purposeful learner is Jamie Baillie. Jamie is the President and CEO of Credit Union Atlantic and he provides us with another example of the transformational effects of the right type of formal education. Excerpts from my interview with Jamie follow.

B.M.   *What is the best formal educational experience you have had?*

J.B.   *Actually there were two. One is the Bill Black Leadership Seminar and the other is the High Potentials Leadership Program at Harvard.*

The Bill Black Leadership Seminar I attended is just for CEOs and there were 14 or 15 of us and we met over a two and a half day period in an executive retreat setting. However, the experience was much more intensive than the two and a half days because we received a binder full of prework — and the binders were two or three inches thick, in addition to a reading list, like Jim Collins' Good to Great, that we had to read before the seminar. Our prework included everything from plays, to the classics, to textbook chapters. On the surface, you would have no idea why you were reading the material. But we soon realized that each reading and topic had deeply critical questions that we had to contemplate. For example, one of the plays was The Visit, which is all about morality and how through a thousand little compromises you can end up justifying just about anything.

We started the seminar by making a chart on how we allocated our time. We had to estimate the percentage of time we spent during a typical week on various tasks such as responding to e-mail, preparing reports, looking at financial reports, etc. Then we looked at the great moral and ethical issues that a CEO has to deal with rather than transactional ones. We had to concentrate for 8 to 10 hours a day — and Bill has a lot of stamina — he doesn't let up. We would have two-hour intense discussions and then move instantly on to the next issue. It was total and full immersion. At the end of the course we then had to look at how we were going to allocate our time when we returned to work and the difference was astonishing. I remember driving home invigorated.

Bill Black has another program for senior executives who are not CEOs. We have had someone at every Bill Black program except one. So far three of our VPs and Directors have taken his leadership course for senior executives. We are sending our senior staff one person at a time and at this time we have three more who will take Bill's Senior Management course.

B.M.   *Tell me about your experience at the Harvard High Potentials Leadership Program.*

J.B.   *The five-day program at Harvard was also a total immersion experience. We spent four days working on intriguing case studies in work groups of eight. However, it was a double total immersion program in the sense that all eight of us were from different countries and hence difference cultures. For example, I was the only Canadian in my group. The other seven members of my pod were from Belgium, Hong Kong, France, England, the US, and Australia.*

It was also a total immersion experience in a third sense, since we all came from different professional backgrounds: finance, accounting, operations, HR, manufacturing, etc. What I loved is that even at the end of a case study, we had to figure out the questions we had to answer and, as leaders, one of the most important things we have to do is figure out what are the right questions to ask. Since our group was cross-disciplinary and from different countries we had to think, at a very deep level, how to solve very real world examples from vastly different perspectives.

It was also very interesting that we took one full day not doing case studies. During this day we worked with a group of professional actors to work on our communication and creative thinking skills. For example we had to act out scenes from scripts and then we received feedback on how well we communicated. We also had exercises which tested our ability to speak extemporaneously. The whole premise of this day is that for leaders doing is only half the equation — the other half is communicating what you are doing.

This just reinforced something I had already learned. If you are not talking about something you are passionate about — do not talk about it. When I am passionate about something, I can talk about it all day. When I was in government, I was used to being hammered over programs that I knew were right and I learned to communicate until they got it. I learned that you have to spend as much time communicating it as designing it.

Exercise 4-9: In the space below, please describe a formal educational experience and/or book that has been especially helpful to you.

What was it about the course or book that made it so helpful?

How has this course or book contributed to you being a purposeful learner on this subject?

How might you identify similarly helpful educational experiences in the future?

Motivation and Learning

How well and how much you learn will depend on your motivation to do so. Social scientists have long endeavoured to better understand motivation. The work of Hackman and Oldham on developing the job components model adds much insight into the psychology of motivation of peak performers. Hackman and Oldham postulated that there are five major components to every job. An individual's score on each of the components is entered into a mathematical formula to determine that individual's motivational potential score (MPS). The MPS is one way to determine how close that particular individual comes to being a peak performer. MPS can also help you to make decisions about career choices and more clearly see when it is time to make a change, for example, seeking increased responsibilities, applying for a lateral transfer, looking for a promotion, or leaving your current position and moving on.

Determining Your Motivational Potential Score

The MPS is made up of the following components: Skill Variety, Task Identity, Task Significance, Autonomy and Feedback. Each of the components is scored from a low of zero (0) to a high of seven (7).

Skill Variety. Skill Variety (SV) is a subjective score of the richness of the variety of skills you currently use on your job. For example, think of an assistant who types all day long and does not even have the luxury of changing his or her duties, he or she would probably give himself or herself a very low score. A leader who has to define the scope of an operation, hire, fire, supervise, motivate, plan and budget would probably have a very high score (closer to seven). The reason I use the word "probably" is that your score depends on your current perception of the "richness" of the variety of skills you see yourself using on your present job. For example, five years ago you may have felt that your job was relatively rich in skill variety, whereas today you may feel that it is more in the middle ground for variety of skills.

Skill Variety

Low
Repetitive and
routine

High
Many new tasks
New learning
required

| 0 | 1 | 2 | 3 | 4 | 5 | 6 | 7 |

The score that you would give yourself for Skill Variety on your present job is

_____.

Task Identity (TI). "...[t]he job must include a sufficiently whole piece of work to allow the worker to perceive that he has produced or accomplished something of consequence. This would be expected when a job is high on task identity." Jobs high on task identity are characterized by a very clear cycle of perceived closure, that is, the job provides a distinct sense of a beginning and ending of a project. For example, an engineer feels good when he has completed the design of a new product, just as an artist feels good when he completes a painting, because they identify with what they have helped create.

Task Identity

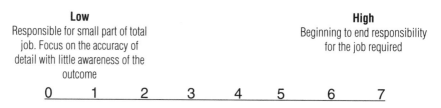

Low
Responsible for small part of total
job. Focus on the accuracy of
detail with little awareness of the
outcome

High
Beginning to end responsibility
for the job required

| 0 | 1 | 2 | 3 | 4 | 5 | 6 | 7 |

The score that you would give yourself for Task Identity is _____.

Task Significance. The score you give yourself on Task Significance (TS) depends on how personally meaningful you find the work that you currently do. For example, you probably have heard the story of the three bricklayers. When asked what they did, the first one said that he was laying bricks; the second one said that he was helping to build a church, and the third one said that he was building a house of worship for the Lord. Each person had the same job title and job description, yet the quantity and quality of their work differed because of how each viewed the importance of his or her job.

Task Significance

The score you would give yourself for Task Significance is _____.

Autonomy. Autonomy (A) has to do with how you are supervised on the job. Most people have had a job where they were so closely supervised that their morale and motivation suffered greatly. Under these circumstances, people rate themselves nearer to the zero end of the continuum. On the other hand, most of us have had bosses or supervisors who gave us both the responsibility and the authority to get the job done. Under these circumstances, the rating would be nearer the seven end of the continuum.

Autonomy

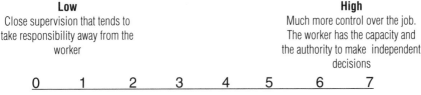

The score you would give yourself for Autonomy is _____.

Job Feedback. The Job Feedback (F) score is a global score reflecting the richness of the feedback one receives. Typically, poorly motivated individuals live in a feedback-impoverished world, while peak performers live in a feedback-rich environment. People who score near the zero end of the continuum are often ignored, living in a feedback vacuum, or receive vague feedback – usually negative, but sometimes positive, e.g., "That-a-boy, you did a good job." This type of feedback is often insincere; the person giving the feedback did not make the effort to find out specifically what the employee did to make a difference. People who live at the high end of the continuum live in a feedback-rich environment – receiving clear, direct, strong feedback from all directions: above, below, sideways, diagonally, and from themselves. To learn more about how to give constructive feedback see the article *Praised Reappraised* in the Harvard Business Review.[11]

Job Feedback

Low	**High**
Feedback tends to be unrelated to a worker's performance, or worker receives only one-sided feedback (either all positive or negative)	Worker receives direct, clear feedback from all directions, i.e., from above, below, and sideways

0	1	2	3	4	5	6	7

The score you would give yourself for Job Feedback is _____.

You can now calculate your own motivational potential score using the formula below:

$$MPS = [(SV + TI + TS)]/3 \times A \times F$$
$$= [(\_\_\_ + \_\_\_ + \_\_\_)]/3 \times \_\_\_ \times \_\_\_$$
$$= \_\_\_$$

Now that you have figured out your own score, what is the lowest possible score you could have, and what is the highest possible score? Figuring out the lowest and highest possible scores will give you more insight into how motivation affects the maintenance of peak performance.

Summary	
Components	**Score**
Skill Variety (SV)	
Task Identity (TI)	
Task Significance (TS)	
Autonomy (A)	
Job Feedback (F)	

Exercise 4-10: To get a fuller appreciation for the power of the Motivational Potential Score, try doing the following comparisons: compare the ratings for the worst job you ever had to the best job you ever had; or the worst job you ever had with your present job; or your present job with the job you held before your present job.[12]

It is interesting to note that the MPS can also be very useful when you are considering a job change. A participant in my seminar was having difficulty deciding whether or not she would give up her own small business, which she found rewarding but not terribly financially secure, and take a "secure" job with a prestigious national consulting firm. When she figured out her MPS scores for her current job and the job with the national firm, she found that she would lose 70 points on her MPS score by moving to the national firm, due to loss of autonomy. This helped her make her decision and get on with the job of building up her own company.

In teaching courses on peak performance, I have found that the MPS is one of the most powerful diagnostic tools we have for identifying what is working well and what needs course correction in order to develop and maintain peak performance. Wise use of this formula will help you more consciously and consistently stay in the zone of peak performance. I have also used the MPS to better understand the level of motivation in particular teams and/or departments and in organizations as a whole.

The next point to consider is that compound learning works just like compound interest. Almost everyone wishes to maximize his or her short-term learning and to compound his or her long-term learning. Most of us do this; however, much of our learning takes place in a hit-or-miss fashion. In this chapter we examined how Master Leaders applied these lessons to accelerate their development through purposeful learning. We also identified how much of that learning was dependent on experience, mentors, failure and hardship, and formal education. Lastly, we used the Motivational Potential Score as a diagnostic instrument to help you determine how motivated you are and to look at specific factors that you can change to increase your own motivation and the motivation of those who work with you.

In the Strategy 5, we will examine how Master Leaders are Master Decision Makers and you will learn eight methods that are guaranteed to improve your own decision making.

STRATEGY 5

Become a Master
Decision Maker

One of the dominant themes from our research, is that breakthrough results come about by a series of good decisions, diligently executed and accumulated one on top of another.

– Jim Collins

All of the Master Leaders I interviewed for this book were inspired with vision, fueled by passion and had the courage to step up to the plate. They knew how to make their leadership style work and they were purposeful learners. There is a critical additional competency that enabled them to be Master Leaders and that competency is judgement. In their book, *Judgment: How Winning Leaders Make Great Calls*, Noel Tichy and Warren Bennis state:

> The single most important thing that leaders do is make good judgement calls. In the face of ambiguity, uncertainty, and conflicting demands, often under great time pressure, leaders must make decisions and take effective actions to assure the survival and success of their organizations.[1]

Any act of leadership starts with a single decision. It has also been said that who we are today is the sum total of all of our decisions. In spite of this, many of us do not pay enough attention to how we make decisions nor do we do a good enough job of harvesting the necessary feedback that will help us become better decision makers. Reading this chapter will sharpen your understanding of how accurate and viable decision-making paid off for the Master Leaders who are profiled in this book. Doing the exercises provided in the chapter will help you become a more masterful decision maker in your own right. Following is an enlightening example of how astute decision-making helped Annette Verschuren become a Master Leader.

Annette Verschuren is President of The Home Depot Canada and Asia. When Annette became the president of The Home Depot Canada in 1996, she was relatively young (39) and knew nothing about the hardware business. At that time, The Home Depot had 19 stores in Canada and the company had set a goal of 50 stores. Annette thought they could do better: "I remember saying to our CEO, Arthur Blank, that we could open 100 stores in Canada." Annette Verschuren has proven to be an extraordinarily capable leader. As of September 2009, Home Depot had 179 stores across Canada.

In September, 2006, Annette was asked to become head of Home Depot China. China is a market worth $50 billion and growing by a compounded 20% each year. In August, 2007 Home Depot opened 12 stores in China. In my interview with Annette Verschuren I was particularly interested in finding out more on how decision-making affected her career, her life and her ability as a leader.

B.M.   *Did Home Depot consider anyone else for the position of Home Depot Asia?*

A.V.   *I don't think so. Frank Blake was responsible for business development and he said, "If we go into China, I want Annette to head up our efforts because she is the strongest candidate."*

B.M.   *Why do you think they offered this assignment to you?*

A.V.   *The reason we were given the assignment is that the Home Depot Canadian leadership team is very creative, and we successfully adjusted Home Depot to the Canadian environment. My success has everything to do with the people who support me. I am not threatened by people who are smarter than I am because it makes our team and our results stronger. I work hard to keep my ego in check, and out of my judgments.*

B.M.   *How did you decide to take it?*

A.V.   *The offer was extremely complementary and I was intrigued with the international opportunity. I said yes I'm interested; I just want to speak to my family. That was on Friday and on Monday I said yes. It was also a great way to develop my Canadian team by giving them international experience and that experience in terms of our team's development is priceless.*

B.M.   *What did you think the challenges would be?*

A.V.   *The challenge is how do we transfer some of the culture and the values of Home Depot into a culture that is very different and at the same time respect the Chinese market and working environment. For example, I learned a little about this when we opened our first store in Quebec; we had to learn how to operate in a different language and culture. People in Quebec don't have the same level of home ownership; there are more renters, so we sell a different product mix. The experience in Quebec helped us when we went into China.*

I am a retailer at heart and at Home Depot we do a lot of walking around our stores and talking with our customers and staff. For example, very early in my visits to China, I was walking down an aisle and I suggested a change and before I got to the end of the aisle, the change had been made. This was a big realization for me. They are used to taking direction so getting them to work independently is not something that comes naturally to them.

B.M.   *What advantages does Home Depot have in China?*

A.V.   *We have to be attuned to what the Chinese customer needs and wants in order to grow the business. That's why we brought Yves Chen on as President for China Retail Operations. Yves is from Beijing but studied* *in France, and has worked for a multi-national. Growing up he was part of the Cultural Revolution and was forced to work on farms in the countryside. He is an extraordinary leader and has extraordinary experience.*

The other advantage is that in China, the market includes 60 B&Q stores and 26 Orient Home stores. All of these stores were designed on a Western concept of home ownership. We (at Home Depot) don't impose our Western ideas as to how a Chinese customer should buy or how a Chinese manager should lead. Yves will bring invaluable insight to our operations and growth strategy.

B.M.   *How are you building your team in China?*

A.V.   *We have developed a strong indigenous team in China and are working on a model that we are in the process of executing. In the past year, we have been rebuilding the stores we purchased in China. For example, we upgraded our merchandising department, refurbished the bathrooms and training areas. It was really tough in the beginning and now the momentum is there, the team is coming into place, our performance is improving. We have a team of 3,000 people who work for us in China and they will build the Home Depot brand in China.*

B.M.   *How much time do you spend there?*

A.V.   *I go to China every five or six weeks and stay for 5 or 6 days. I work with Yves to make sure he has the resources necessary to help him get the right team in place and to help drive the business — but I am not going to run it. And I tell my people here that their job is the same. Both my team in Canada and in China are really quite independent.*

B.M.   *How is branding and marketing different in China than North America?*

A.V.   *In China, product branding is everywhere. You can't go down a commercial street without seeing a lot of US, Japanese, and Korean product signage. For example, GE was a major sponsor of the 2008 Olympics and they had neon brand signage everywhere.*

China is also a society that is developing disposable income so people are buying more and more. At the same time I think China will advance faster than anyone thinks. In China speed is critical – it is a fast moving place. In China our customers have a different mind set from our North American customers. The Chinese people who shop at Home Depot are not do-it-yourselfers – they get things done for them because the price of labour is so inexpensive. So just as Home Depot had to adjust to the Canadian, Mexican, and even the Quebec culture, we are adjusting to the Chinese culture.

B.M.   *Are you in any other Asian countries?*

A.V.   *We want to get our 12 stores in China right and then expand and develop a model to go forward, but we are not going to make stupid decisions. We started with seven stores in Canada and now we have 179. We started with four stores in Mexico and now we have 65.*

B.M.   *What is the best decision you made in your career?*

A.V.   *When I switched from arts to business in 1976 at Saint Francis Xavier University, it was at the beginning of my second year and I was taking courses to become a teacher, but it really wasn't working for me. I met several women who were taking business – there were not many women in business at that time and they intrigued me. I talked to the dean of the business school and he was very encouraging. I told him that I loved solving problems. The dean encouraged me and he genuinely listened. One of the other professors I talked to thought I should become a secretary because I didn't know anything about accounting, but that only made me more determined. So in October, I changed my major to business.*

B.M.   *What is the most difficult decision you have had to make in your career?*

A.V.   *Leaving Cape Breton – I miss it every day. I love nature I feel very centred there. I can get away from everything – so I go there often. I left 18 months after my father had died. My mother thought I was crazy. It was 1986 and I was making $56,000 a year – the most amount of money of any woman in Cape Breton and my mother couldn't* *understand it. But I always wanted to get ahead and become a VP and I knew my future wasn't there.*

B.M.   *How would you describe your leadership style?*

A.V.   *Too many people see leadership in silos. Leadership is actually much more holistic than people usually think it is. Leadership is more than inspiration; it takes vision, strategy, planning, and execution. My style is that I am an inclusive leader and I am very curious, I love to try something new and I am very pragmatic. I can be tough when I need to be tough. I am a very positive person. I always see the cup more than half full. That has been a big plus for me. I am a person who will find another way up the mountain if I cannot get up one way.*

Negative thinking sucks energy out of everything. With negative thinking there is no way out. My position has always been to focus on the issue not the personality. I work with people I love, with people I like, with people I dislike and with people I can't stand. I have learned to always strive to bring people on side to fix things.   I learned that when I was very young. As children, my siblings and I, had to learn to milk cows, drive a tractor, pull a calf out, and breed bulls.

After graduating from university, I was one of the first women to work in the coal mines in Cape Breton. Between the ages of 20 and 29, I worked in planning and eventually became Director of Planning at DEVCO.[2] I was involved in the 26 Colliery explosion. Being a woman working in the coal mine was a very challenging experience, but just like on the farm, I learned a lot because I had to. I learned to be creative, innovative and forward thinking and to execute well and increase productivity. Today, I still draw upon the good and bad experiences I had on the farm and at DEVCO.

As Annette Verschuren so aptly demonstrates, decision-making is one of your most important leadership activities. Not only must you make good decisions, those decisions must be made in a timely manner especially as the world becomes more complex. When I had my first job, the telephone only came in one colour — black — and all I had to know was that I had to dial "9" to get an outside line. A lot has changed in the days since the one-colour telephone.

In addition, our timeline for making decisions has shortened significantly; so many decisions have to be made in a shorter time period[3].

Fortunately, there are many excellent methods that you can use to make better and more timely decisions. In the remainder of this chapter we will look at eight of the best. They are:

1. The Weighted Averages Method

2. The 70% Rule

3. Do A Double Pro/Con Analysis

4. Determine Readiness for Change

5. Consult Your Inner and Outer Circles

6. Bill Black's Question

7. The Power of Mantras

8. Audit Your Decision-Making Process

The Weighted Averages Method

Michael Useem states, "Time and again during the interviews [for his book on decision-making], I would ask people to name their most difficult decision, and as often as not, the answer would be deciding to accept a new position with amplified responsibilities."[4]

I would like to demonstrate how the Weighted Averages Method can help you make employment and other important decisions. Research has demonstrated that when decision-making reaches a certain level of complexity, it becomes increasingly difficult to make a decision. The reason is that most of us can only keep a certain number of variables in our minds at any one time. The psychological research shows a steep decline in our ability to make decisions once the number of variables exceeds 14. However, there is an excellent method that can help called the Weighted Averages Method. I will illustrate this with a decision that one of the Master Leaders I interviewed had to make when she was asked to become the president of a new organization. You can try the method yourself on either a personal or professional case. Once you see how helpful this method is, it will become one of your most valuable decision-making tools.

For reasons of confidentiality, we will call our leader Megan. Megan has had a stellar career and is now a senior vice-president with her current organization.

> *The single most important thing that leaders do is make good judgement calls. In the face of ambiguity, uncertainty, and conflicting demands, often under great time pressure, leaders must make decisions and take effective actions to assure the survival and success of their organizations.*
>
> **Noel Tichy and Warren Bennis**

Over the past several years Megan has been headhunted on a fairly regular basis. Recently, the calls became more and more frequent and the offers more and more enticing. Given her age, and the fact that her husband Ted had just retired, Megan knew that this would most likely be her final working assignment before she retired, so there was even more pressure on Megan to make the right decision. In particular, there were three offers on the table that were very tempting. However, Megan and Ted felt very comfortable in their home and in the community within which they lived, so staying put was also a viable option. As Megan's husband said, "You just don't pack up and go at our age and expect to be able to develop the type of friendship network that we had developed over the past 20 years."

They began the process by listing the factors that were important in making the decision, such as type of city, income, learning opportunities, legacy, distance from their children and most importantly for Megan and Ted, distance from their grandchildren. The next task was to rank each factor as to its importance. The only caveat was that all of the rankings must add up to 1.0. For example, the reputation of the possible new organization could rank at .25, income could rank .3, and Megan's opportunity for growth and development in her career could be .2. It often takes several tries to get the combined ratings to equal 1.0 and the process of giving the weightings to each factor can itself be very illuminating. In the case of Megan and Ted, living in a city with easy access to a first class airport so they could easily visit with their grandchildren was an important issue that they wanted to consider very carefully.

When you do your own rankings, you will notice that just by trying out the various weighting you will get a better sense of how each factor should be rated and also if some factors should be combined or removed or whether additional factors should be added. Coming up with the right categories or factors and then giving each of those factors just the right ranking is much like adding salt and other spices to homemade soup – with the homemade soup, you taste and correct as you go along. It is the same type of feeling you will get as you work your way through this exercise and make corrections in order to come up with the best listing and weighting of the factors possible. For example, in Megan and Ted's case when other factors became apparent – such as contribution to society/legacy – some of the factors changed as well as the weightings of some of the other factors. In other words, coming up with the right weights is an iterative process. Using a spreadsheet makes it easier to try out different factors and weightings until you get it so that it feels just right.

The next task was to list the potential positions and Megan's current position across the top of the page. Megan then did research to better understand the ramifications of choosing each of the positions before rating them with a score from 1 to 10 to reflect how closely each position satisfies the requirement listed in the column on the left (See Table 5-1 below). For example, she rated position number one as a 6 on income and position number three as a 7 on income.

Then, for each factor, she multiplied the ranking for each possible position times the weighting she had given each criteria. The next step was to add up all of the numbers in each column and multiply the sum by 10, which gave the ranking of each position.

By using a computerized spreadsheet you can enter formulas that automatically give you the total number of points each position scores. You can also change the numbers as you discover additional information that might reflect the value of the criteria as it relates to each position in question. Table 5-1 demonstrates the rankings for Megan and Ted for each of the three possible new positions and for her current position.

Table 5-1
Megan's Ratings for Each of the Four Positions

Selection Criteria	Weight of Each Criteria	Position Number 1	Position Number 2	Position Number 3	Current Position
Control over what Megan does with her time	0.15	5	5	5	7
Income	0.25	6	6	7	6
Contribution to society/legacy	0.2	4	4	7	6
Opportunity for Megan's growth and development	0.2	6	6	8	6
Easy access to grandchildren	0.2	2	7	5	8
Total Score	1.00	46.5	56.5	66.5	65.5

As you can see, number three comes out as the top rated position, however, the difference between number three and Megan's current position is just too close to call. Therefore, Megan and Ted will have to do some further work in order to make the best decision possible. One option is to add some additional criteria and see if that makes a substantial enough difference so that a clear decision can be made. For example, one category could be the cost of moving and decorating a new house if Megan was to take a new position. In other words, by introducing additional criteria, giving each additional criteria a weighting and then recalibrating and re-ranking all of the options, might make Megan's and Ted's decision easier to make. However, because the top two scores are so close, Megan and Ted might be better off using a different decision-making method such as the 70% Rule.

The 70% Rule

In times of war, decisions have to be made quickly, but the consequences of a wrong decision can be fatal. It is also true that you will never have 100% of the information needed to make a decision. Therefore, to better enable its soldiers to make the right decision more often, the United States Marine Corps developed "The 70% Rule." This Rule states that if you have 70% of the data and have completed 70% of the analysis and if 70% of your gut feeling or instinct is in agreement with the first two, then go ahead and make your decision. In other words, you have a greater likelihood of making the best decision by using the 70% Rule than you would have had, if you had not used the 70% Rule.

When Megan and Ted added "The 70% Rule" to their decision-making process, the results were very helpful. In terms of the data and the analysis part of the 70% Rule it was a virtual tie (see Table 5-1). However, in terms of "gut feel" there was a significant difference between position number 3 and Megan's current position. Ted was equally content moving or staying put. However, when Megan thought of staying in her current position, it just didn't feel right. It turned out that she wanted a new challenge more than she thought she did. Since they lived near a university, they could rent their current house to visiting professors and rent a condo in their new location. This would give them the opportunity to try out condo living and see if they wanted to buy a condo or return to their home when they both retired. This example points out the benefits of using more than one decision-making technique.

Exercise 5-1: Can you think of a time when you used "The 70% Rule", even if you were not conscious that you were using it? How did the decision turn out? Alternatively, you can try the 70% Rule with an important current decision and see how it turns out.

Then grade yourself using A (Very Good) through F (Very Poor) in each of the three areas from the 70% Rule:

Information Gathering _____

Analysis _____

Gut Instinct _____

What proof do you have that would validate the grade you gave yourself in each area?

What proof do you have that invalidates or does not substantiate the grade you gave yourself?

Ask several peers, colleagues and/or friends to rate you on the three areas.

Information Gathering _____   _____   _____

Analysis _____   _____   _____

Gut Instinct _____   _____   _____

Do their ratings substantiate the ratings that you gave yourself?

Where do their ratings not substantiate the ratings you gave yourself?

What additional information or data analysis do you need to improve the accuracy of how you rate yourself?

Next, think about another situation where you could or should apply the 70% Rule.

Research into decision-making has determined that most of us put too much emphasis on gut instinct. The Double Pro/Con Analysis will help you do a better job at information gathering and analyzing so you can find the most creative solution(s) possible.

Double Pro/Con Analysis

A variation on the old pros and cons analysis is the Double Pro/Con Analysis. Once you have seen how powerful and easy-to-use this technique is, you will find many uses for it in both your professional and personal life — and you will be able to create better and more creative solutions.

Let me give an example of a decision that my daughter had to make. She very much wanted to complete her Grade 10 piano exam but also wanted to go to Jamaica with me over March break. The deadline for applying to take the exam was March 4. This resulted in Katie having to make a decision because she had only completed one-third of the work needed to successfully take the Grade 10 exam. In order to take her Grade 10 exam, Katie needed to practice for two hours a day. However she was in the last four months of her senior year of high school and was already involved in many extracurricular activities, including the high school musical which meant that a great deal of her time was already committed. On the other hand, if she did not complete her Grade 10 piano at this time, it was unlikely that she would be able to work on it when she entered university. Figure 5-1 lists the pros and cons of working on piano over March break and the pros and cons of going to Jamaica over March break.

Figure 5-1
Pros and Cons of Working to Complete the Grade 10 Piano Exam

<u>Pros</u>	<u>Cons</u>
I almost always complete what I start	I would be disappointed if I didn't get to go to Jamaica
Feeling of satisfaction from completing my Grade 10 piano	I missed out on the last trip with my father to Africa when I had mono
Keeps my options for music open	I deserve a vacation
I don't want to disappoint my Mom or my piano teacher	I won't have time to do other things I would like to do in the four months left of my Grade 12 year
If I don't get my Grade 10 now, it will be very likely that I will never get it because I won't have the time or interest to work on it when I start university	

Pros and Cons of Going to Jamaica over March Break

Pros	Cons
I need a break	I need practice time for Grade 10 piano
I could spend quality time with my Dad	I would like to see if I could pass Grade 10 piano after all the work I have done
I have always wanted to travel south	My mother would be disappointed
I like learning about new cultures and seeing/visiting new places	I am too tired right now to make a decision so doing nothing is the easiest thing to do
My Dad knows a lot of neat people in Jamaica	I'm not comfortable flying
I'm tired of working all the time	There will be other times in the future when I can travel with my Dad and I am sure that he will be doing volunteer work in Jamaica for years to come

At this point, the person doing this analysis crosses out a pro and con of equal value in both columns for each of the pro and con analyses. In the above case if "I need a break" in the pro column is equal to the "I'm not comfortable flying" in the con column, then they are both crossed off. However, if the weightings are not equal and Katie were really terrified of flying, then she might have to cross off two or more of the pros, for example, cross off both "I'm tired of working all the time" and "I need a break" to be able to cross off the con "I'm not comfortable flying."

When you have finished crossing off the pros and cons to the best of your ability for both analyses, you may see that there is a clear preference for one of the options. In the above case, when Katie considered everything, she decided to work on her Grade 10 piano and travel with me in the future.

However, in the process of doing this analysis it became clear to me that there was another option that we had not considered and that option was to see if Katie could spend some time practicing her piano in Jamaica. I called around to various hotels and found out that some of the hotels did not have a piano. One hotel had a piano but they would not let anyone except their resident pianist use their piano. I called the music department at a performing arts school and that was a possibility, however, when I talked to the sales department at the Jamaican Pegasus Hotel I hit gold. They had two pianos. There was no problem if Katie wanted to practice for two hours a day. If the piano was in a room or near a room where there was a conference going on, they would move the piano to somewhere where Katie could practice. I held my breath and then asked what the charge would be — the answer: "No Charge". And the Pegasus is one of the nicest hotels with one of the largest and most beautiful swimming pools on the island. The idea of Katie being able to practice the piano in Jamaica would never have occurred to me if we had not done the double pro/con analysis.

We have looked at three methods that will help you make better decisions, The Weighted Averages Method, the 70% Rule and The Double Pros/Cons Analysis. Shakespeare said "Ripeness is all," which means that timing is everything. Therefore, we now turn our attention to readiness for change because Master Leaders know that leadership is about change — and the timing of any change is crucial to its success or failure.

Determine Readiness for Change

> We're all in the business of change, not maintaining the status
> quo. Whatever we're doing, by whatever means, will be wrong
> in the future. So we must continually shed our past practices
> and grow into a new form, with new behavior, if we are to meet
> the future. – William B. Werther, Jr.

Leadership is about change and, like any change, it can be for better or worse. However, the timing for the change must be right. Although almost all leaders have a mandate to bring about change, not enough leaders pay enough attention to their organization's readiness for change.

The two basic mistakes with regard to the timing of change are too much too soon, and too little too late. Too much too soon translates into the staff being overwhelmed, burning out, or simply paying lip service to the change because they believe "this too shall pass". Too little too late translates into apathy, weakened organizations, downward spirals, inability to compete, and at its worst, the failure of individual organizations or of entire industries.

There is another factor that is even more neglected than the speed of change – and that factor is the complexity of the change. The Readiness for Change Diagnostic Tool measures both the speed of change and the complexity of change. Measuring both is a much better indication of readiness for change than is either alone. An apt analogy is that, "Half of any cure is an accurate diagnosis". The Readiness for Change Diagnostic Tool will help you better analyze your organization's readiness for change.

The Readiness for Change Diagnostic Tool can help you and your organization make the right changes at the right time. It is composed of the following two questions:

1. On a scale from 1 to 10, where 1 is slow and 10 is fast; rate the speed of change in your organization. _____.

2. On a scale from 1 to 10, where 1 is minor and 10 is major; rate the complexity of change in your organization. _____.

When the employees of an organization are surveyed using these two questions, their answers can be plotted on a two-by-two grid, see Figure 5-2. Depending on how the majority of employees respond, their average response will end up in one of four quadrants. In Quadrant I, both the speed and complexity of the change are low and the net result is that the change is almost unnoticed. In Quadrant II, the complexity of the change is high and the speed of change is slow. This results in a change that is highly planned and evolutionary. In Quadrant III, both the complexity and the speed of change are high. This results in a change that is traumatic and revolutionary. And in Quadrant IV, the speed is high and the complexity is low, which results in a change that is perceived as relatively quick adaptation.

Figure 5-2: Complexity vs. Speed

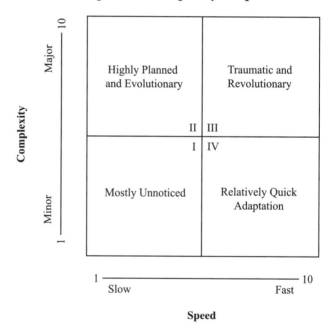

Although the average score for an organization can be very helpful, Master Leaders make finer and finer diagnoses with respect to readiness for change. For example, senior leadership in an organization may be ready to embrace more change, but middle management may not be, or senior and middle management may be ready for more change, but line workers are not; or employees who work in Department X are ready to embrace change, but employees who work in Department Y are not. How can you know where your organization is ready to change and where it is not ready to change? The answer is the Readiness for Change Diagnostic Tool.

Mergers, acquisitions and amalgamations are often much more difficult than anyone could have imagined. This is often due to false assumptions about the degree and magnitude of the uncertainty associated with the change and overly optimistic expectations as to how long it takes for the changes to work their way through the system and become accepted. Also common are clashes, and sometimes wars, between the organization's cultures. In fact, the research literature suggests somewhere between 50% and 70% of mergers, acquisitions and amalgamations fail.[5]

An example of how the Readiness for Change Diagnostic Tool helped in the amalgamation of five hospitals into one health sciences centre follows. With such a large scale integration, virtually every department in all of the hospitals would be integrated and new department heads would have to be selected. New policies and procedures would have to be developed and approved and there would be multiple contracts that would have to be ratified. There were an equally large number of changes in that 14 unions would be amalgamated into five and new policies and procedures for management/union negotiations would have to be developed.

In this case the average rating for senior management on the speed of change was 3.2 and the average rating for the complexity of change for the senior management was 5.7. This indicated that senior management saw the change as highly planned and evolutionary. The average rating for staff on the speed of change was 6.7 and the average rating for the complexity of change for the staff was 7.8 indicating that the staff saw the change as traumatic and revolutionary. Without this data, senior management would have assumed that this was a good time to introduce more change. However, with the complete set of data, senior management was able to see that this was not the ideal time to implement additional change.

Senior management wisely waited until the staff was comfortable with the current changes rather than overloading them with more changes. Unfortunately, there are too many instances where leaders assume that the rest of the organization has already adjusted to change and has the capacity to take on more change. Master Leaders do not assume. They monitor staff reactions knowing that people adjust better when they feel they have more control over the rate of change, while their more ineffective counterparts plow on, regardless of their staff's readiness for change.

Consult Your Inner and Outer Circles

Generally, most of us have an inner circle of people we consult with on a regular basis. We also have an outer circle of people we consult with much more sporadically. For example, if you were unemployed and looking for a job, who would be more helpful to you when it comes to leads: your closest friends or your more distant contacts? The answer, in most cases, is not your inner network but your outer network. The reason is that there is a greater degree of overlap in information about leads within your inner network, while your outer network is much more likely to be tapped into other networks of people and consequently there would be many more new leads.

For example, while I was writing this book, I needed to get the names of a broad cross-section of contemporary Master Canadian Leaders. Therefore, I got into the habit of asking everyone I knew for the names of leaders that they thought I should interview for the book. One day I had lunch with a colleague that I usually see once a year. Most of my close colleagues came up with the same list I did. However my colleague Kevin, whom I see once a year, came up with a substantially different list.

Exercise 5-2: Who is in your outer circle?

Describe an experience when your outer circle helped you make an important decision by providing you with information that you previously did not have access to and/or with options that enriched your decision-making.

Is there a current decision or a decision you will need to make in the near future where consulting your outer circle would be beneficial?

How do you determine when to use your inner or outer circle?

Bill Black's Question

> Leadership is as much about genetic and moral propensity as it is about intellect, communication and craft . . . It is a little like making chicken soup . . . if you start with a bad chicken, all the nourishment from the vegetables can't protect it.
>
> — Roger Velik

Bill Black, former President of Maritime Life Assurance Company, currently lectures and conducts seminars, keynotes and workshops on leadership. I was very fortunate in being able to see him present to the Canadian Centre for

Ethics in Public Affairs. Bill started his presentation by asking how many people in the audience had seen the musical *Les Miz* or had read Victor Hugo's book *Les Misérables*. A majority of the people in the audience raised their hands. Bill then described a scene that was in the play and the book in great detail. In the scene, Jean Valjean has been released from prison. His crime was stealing a loaf of bread to feed his sister's family. As an itinerant ex-prisoner, Jean Valjean is unable to get work or support himself. He desperately seeks shelter for the night and the Bishop of Digne takes Jean Valjean in. Jean Valjean leaves early the next morning, after stealing a silver plate from the Bishop's home.

Jean Valjean is caught by the police, who take him back to the Bishop's house so they can return the silver plate. Surprisingly, the Bishop says that it has not been stolen — and there was another gift, which Jean Valjean had left behind. He then gives Jean Valjean his only remaining possessions of value — the silver candlesticks that match the silver plate — and in so doing he claims Jean Valjean's life for God.

Then Bill asked one of the most thought-provoking questions I have ever heard — *"When did the Bishop make the decision to pardon Jean Valjean? Was it at the time when Jean Valjean was brought back to face the man he stole from? Or was it when he studied religion as a younger man? Or was it based on values he learned as a child?"*

The more I thought about this and several other similar cases, the more certain I became that the Bishop's decision was based on his innate core values that he had been developing throughout his entire life. The incident with Jean Valjean just became another point in time where the Bishop, like the Master Leaders I interviewed in this book, were able to put their core values into action. At this time, their core values are precursors to the decision-making process. However, over time, they become conscious guides that aid the decision-making process by becoming mantras that guide their lives.

A personal example of how core values influence the decision-making process will help to illustrate these points. I grew up in a very frugal household just north of San Francisco. My mother, bless her heart, was particularly thrifty. My friends used to tease me by saying that my house was the only house they knew of where they could come for lunch to lose weight. Needless to say, I grew up to be very frugal as well.

In 2005 I started doing volunteer work in Jamaica. I teach seminars at the University College of the Caribbean on leadership, negotiation and presentation skills and the money I make, over-and-above my expenses, is used to help children from the inner-city learn to swim through SwimJamaica. In 2005 we had three instructors teaching 50 children at the National Stadium Pool. At last count we had 25 instructors teaching 1,500 children at 10 pools and the program has been an overwhelming success for the children, for our instructors and for the communities where the pools are located. The only problem was that we had run out of swimming pools where the instructors could teach children to swim.

One morning in late September, 2007, John Eyre, head of the Amateur Swimming Association in Jamaica, which includes SwimJamaica, asked me if we could meet with Chris Evans, president of the Kingston Rotary Club. Chris explained that the major project for the Rotary Club of Kingston for 2005 to 2007 was the refurbishment and re-opening of the Bournemouth Bath Pool. The Bournemouth Bath Pool was a derelict swimming pool that had seen better days. The major problem was lack of funding. In the two years that the Rotary Club of Kingston had been fundraising for the pool, they had only raised half of the money necessary in order to get the matching J$10 million that had been promised by the Jamaican Ministry of Health. To make matters more challenging, the matching funds from the Ministry of Health would disappear as of November 3, 2007, which meant that they only had two months to raise the additional funding that they needed to secure the J$10 million.

After the meeting, John asked me if I wanted to see the Bournemouth Bath Pool. "Certainly", I said, and off we went. Although the pool and surrounding buildings were in desperate shape, in my mind's eye, I was able to see this pool refurbished and re-opened and at that point, I committed myself to raising as much money in Canada as I could.

In spite of my commitment, there were three major problems. The first was that there was little time and I needed to get a Canadian Rotary Club on side so people could donate and have their donations considered tax deductible. Secondly, I had very little free time since this was a very busy time for me at work. Thirdly, there was a battle inside me that seemed to go on for days between my core value of altruism and my core value of frugality.

In the end, I decided that I would donate the rest of the necessary funding if we could get a Rotary Club in Canada to work with us so that the funding could be tax deductible. Although I struggled with the decision to spend that much of my own money, I think I really made the decision the moment I saw the pool. The opportunity of helping to refurbish and re-open the pool fit perfectly with my core values of helping others and altruism. Answering Bill Black's question helped me to more clearly see my core values. Translating our core values into mantras provides a shortcut to both remember them and teach them to others.

The Power of Mantras

As I was doing the interviews for this book, I found that many, if not most, of the Master Leaders I spoke with had mantras that they had developed. Mantra comes from the Hindu language and means a sacred verbal formula that one repeats to oneself. The mantras that were used by the Master Leaders were tied to their deep value structure and helped these leaders focus their energies, make tough decisions, persevere in the face of resistance, overcome obstacles and recover from set-backs. As one of the Master Leaders I interviewed stated, "[Mantras are based on] values that are here now and will be here 100 years from now." These values in action are frequently found in stories that are told and retold within the organization. The first person I interviewed for this book was Fred MacGillivray. Fred is the President and CEO of Trade Centres Limited, which provides the settings for many of the entertainment, cultural, conferences, commercial and sporting events that come to Halifax.

B.M.   *Many, if not most, of the Master Leaders I interviewed had mantras that guide them in their professional and personal lives. Do you have one?*

F.M.   *No question. My mantra is "Think Forward." That is I always think of what I want five to ten years in the future. I am very committed that if it is the right thing to do we will find a way. All I have to do is put successful people around me. Building a strong management team is what makes every CEO successful. I also learned to never dwell on the obstacles. Remove any and all of the barriers and you will achieve your goal.*

Annette Verschuren in particular uses two mantras that I have taken to heart. The first is, "*The glass is always* more *than half full*" and the second is "*There is always more than one path up the mountain.*" I found myself repeating Annette's mantras to myself and became more and more conscious that they were great tools. In the past I would often ruminate, for far too long, on things that didn't go the way I wanted. Now I remind myself that the glass is always more than half full and/or that there is another path up the side of the mountain. The mantra saves me a great deal of time and grief, plus I can use my time and energy much more productively.

I began to realize that many of the Master Leaders I interviewed had translated their core values into mantras that guided their decision-making. Their mantras helped them make higher-order decisions and made it easier for them to both remember and operationalize their core values and teach them to others. A stellar example of how one of the Master Leaders I interviewed learned to use his core values to help create a transformational difference is Ray Ivany. Ray was President of the Nova Scotia Community College (NSCC) between 1998 and 2005.

To best describe how this transformational change came about, I need to first describe a bit of the background. Nova Scotia has an excellent university system. In fact, there are more universities per capita in Nova Scotia than in any other province. However, the community college system in Nova Scotia had been woefully neglected and under-funded. Ray Ivany was chosen to radically change NSCC. In listening to Ray talk about these changes it was impossible not to hear the energy, excitement, enthusiasm, commitment and determination in his voice.

B.M.   *How did you get government onside?*

R.I.   *This was really fascinating. I never thought of it as getting government onside. Both the government and the community college knew that a massive transformation was needed. However, in 1999 when Premier Hamm first formed a government, he inherited a large deficit and there was the on-going health care crisis, so we had to be patient. Those of us who are proponents in a public policy environment have to realize there is a plethora of needs. There is only enough funding for two or three out* *of 50 proposals, all of which are well-thought-out and have a broad-based need. I learned that you get a lot of No's on the way to Yes. I also learned two other important things: first, the No's are not absolute No's, and second, many proponents tire and go away. It's the tenacity that makes a difference. If the change is that important to you, you have to be patient and persistent.*

We had a strategic alliance with the government. We both wanted to transform the community college system in Nova Scotia and we both wanted to build a world-class system. Then the government provided the funds for us to develop a master plan, which was the penultimate step. The province provided us with $900,000 to develop the master plan and it was a substantive piece of work.

So, it was not a matter of getting government onside, it was waiting for a set of conditions where the government could say "Yes." In March, 2003 our patience and perseverance paid off. Premier Hamm announced $123 million for capital infrastructure and an additional $29 million in operating budget to expand enrollment.

B.M.   *How did you keep the momentum up between 1999 when you became president and 2003 when the funding was announced?*

R.I.   *We had to make progress without losing the imperative to transform the community college system in Nova Scotia. I am a huge believer that resources track results. Between 1999 and 2003, we found funding from the federal government and used it to try several small-scale pilot projects, which confirmed some of the hypotheses that we had. For example we would do a small-scale pilot project with 15 people in one of our regions. When the pilot projects worked we knew that eventually we would be able to do the same for hundreds of Nova Scotians. We ran our internal budgets this way. We also had people who made things happen before they had the resources.*

B.M.   *Do you have any mantras or sayings that have influenced you as a leader?*

R.I.   *I have been aware of mantras since I was a teenager. I remember watching US Senator Sam Irving during the Watergate investigations and he* *had one of the most inspirational definitions about leadership that I had ever heard. Senator Irving said, "Leadership is about improving the lives of others and improving the systems they live under." Senator Sam's definition of leadership became my mantra when I became the President of the Nova Scotia Community College system some 25 years later; I worked every day to try to put Senator Sam's definition of leadership into effect.*

There is also a companion piece. When I was 16 or 17, I was reading Dante's Inferno and the sentence that has remained in my mind is that, "The hottest places in hell are reserved for those who claim neutrality in times of moral crisis." In a very real way, both of these quotations crystallized my thinking on leadership — although it took many years and a great deal of life experience for the lessons contained in these two quotations to become the basis of my philosophy of leadership.

B.M.   *Can you give me an example of how you use mantras at work?*

R.I.   *One mantra that I use has to do with helping others succeed. I frequently ask myself, "Who have I helped succeed today?" In fact, I would often start our staff meetings with the question, "Who have you helped succeed today?"*

A great way to bring your mantra to life is to measure it. In Ray's case, one of the ways he trained himself to operationalize and to bring his mantra to life is to start the day with half a dozen coins in his left pants pocket. Every time he helps someone else succeed that day, he moves one of the coins to his right pants pocket. The number of coins moved per day will tell Ray unequivocally how well he is doing in living up to his mantra. At the end of each day, Ray writes the number of times he used his mantra in his day-timer, which enables him to see how well he is living his mantra over time. I might add that I was so impressed with Ray's technique that I started to measure how well I was helping my staff and my children succeed.

Exercise 5-3: Please list the best mantras you have heard, seen and/or used.

Are there any mantras that have been used by the Master Leaders in this book that you would like to use?

Create a mantra that is personally meaningful for you that you would like to use more often – either at work, at home, or both?

The next step is to use the coin transfer technique for three to five days so you can hold yourself accountable to how well you are living your mantra. One way to do this is by keeping track of your progress in your daily diary, day-timer, or on a computer program such as Outlook™, etc.

Audit Your Decision-Making Process

> A journalist was interviewing a successful businessman. He asked what his success was based on. The reply was "decisions." Not being happy with the answer, the journalist asked, "What were those decisions based on?" The answer was "experience." Still not happy, the journalist asked "how did you get that experience?" The answer – "Bad decisions."
>
> — Anonymous

Every day we all make thousands of decisions. How often do we take the time to get feedback as to how well those decisions served us? The answer is not often. There is a great deal of psychological research to back the fact that we do not tend to be good observers of our own behaviour. One classic study asked a group of dieters to list, as carefully as possible, what they ate during the past week. The dieters were then put on the exact same diet that they recalled. What was the result? They lost weight because they forgot a significant number of items that they had consumed.

In order to monitor, and hence improve, your decision-making, the method that you can use has to be effective and at the same time relatively easy to use. Psychologist Gary Klein specializes in research on decision-making. Klein suggests that decision makers should become "reflective practitioners" by thinking about and articulating the elements that contribute to their decisions' success and failures. Klein recommends that one-third of all the time that US Marines spend in simulations that are designed to sharpen their decision-making process be spent debriefing those decisions and learning everything possible to improve their decision-making in the future. However, it is one thing to think that "reflective practice" or debriefing your decisions, is a good idea and it is another thing to actually do it. There are also those of us who ruminate and keep regretting our decisions but still don't formulate a plan for what we should do differently next time. A wise colleague of mine, Patricia Morgan suggests that we turn our resentments into commitments.[6]

Exercise 5-4: Turning resentments into commitments:

My first resentment is:

In the future I will:

My second resentment is:

In the future I will:

My third resentment is:

In the future I will:

In the final section of this chapter, we will examine three effective, yet relatively simple methods you can use to audit and improve your decision-making. In addition, excellent references on decision making can be found in Resources from the Masters: An Annotated Bibliography for the reader who wants to study this important area in more detail.

The first, and by far the easiest method to use is to write down your more important decisions in a small booklet that you can carry with you. Write down the probability that each decision will actually turn out the way you think it will. Track each decision to see if the percentage you chose was in fact correct, and if not, what did you learn or relearn. Then summarize what could help you make better decisions in the future.

For example, I decided to submit a proposal for this book to a publisher I worked with in the past and with whom I had a very positive, productive and professional working relationship. The major problem was that this is a book that was written almost exclusively for the Canadian market and this publisher was not publishing Canadian books at the time. I rated the probability that they would be interested in my book at less than 5%. However, when I spoke to the head of their marketing department, she told me that in one or two cases, they published a book that they were very interested in with their parent company in the US and then bought the book from the US division and sold it in Canada. She added that she was very interested in my book and would be pleased to see if they could make an exception. I asked her what she thought the chances were and she said 50%, which was much more favourable than I had dared hope for. What did I learn? I learned that there are always people who can make exceptions to any decision-making rule. I also realized on an even deeper level just how important relationships are when it comes to granting exceptions.

The second method to improve your decision-making is to debrief your decision-making with a peer mentor or a buddy. For example, my good friend Paul Wittes and I audit our major decisions at least once a month, in person, on the phone and through e-mail. To borrow a phrase from MasterCard – what is the value of being able to debrief my decision-making – priceless!

The third method of auditing your decisions is more complex, but the advantage is that you can collect more information and that information can help you make better decisions in the future. This method asks you to summarize the decision and the rationale behind the decision, then list the factors that were in your control and the factors that were outside of your control. Then you track the actual decision and write down what you learned and/or would do differently next time. I have had extensive experience with this form and one of the lessons I've learned is that we almost always have both more control than we thought and less control than we thought we had in making the decision. The important lesson is that this type of log or diary will help us learn how to make better decisions in the future.

This method is based on a form that was developed by Tom Stoyan, Director of the Coaching and Sales Institute.[7] Two examples, one positive and one negative, demonstrate how you can use the form to become a more effective decision-maker.

In the first example, a business leader I worked with did not do enough diagnostic information gathering to find out how trustworthy a person was before she decided to work with him. She put too much stock on her gut instincts. We also determined that she felt badly about her decisions for far too long, which was a waste of time that could and should have gone into something that would have a more positive outcome. In the second example, the person I coached used the information from the first decision – which did not turn out well – and used a much more thorough decision-making process in the second decision which turned out positively both for her and for her organization.

One of the best ways to learn from good and bad decisions is to use the decision-making self-critique form. An example of the benefits of debriefing both good and bad decisions appears in Figures 5-3 and 5-4, and a blank copy of the form that you can use appears in Figure 5-5.

Winston Churchill said, "Success is never final. Failure is never fatal. It is courage that counts." In this chapter we saw how the Master Leaders I profiled in this book had the courage to learn from both their decision-making successes and failures. However, there is a very important task that most leaders do not pay enough attention to – creating a culture that will help their organizations grow and succeed long after that particular leader has retired or moved on. How the Master Leaders I interviewed for this book built a sustainable culture that will last long after that particular leader retires is the subject of our next chapter.

Figure 5-3[8]
Decision Making Feedback Form: Example 1

Decision: <u>To hire Mr. 'X' to work in our firm.</u>

This Decision was:

☐ very successful   ☐ successful   ☐ weak   ☒ got me in trouble

	Question	Response
1	What happened that helped the decision making process? [external out of my control]	We were both ex-employees of the same organization and he seemed like a great potential partner, very bright, knowledgeable and personable
2	What happened that hindered the decision making process? [external out of my control]	I didn't know him very well
3	What did I do that helped the decision making? [within my control]	I didn't immediately say yes and we worked together and for the first four months it seemed like a very good fit
4	What did I do that hindered the decision making? [within my control]	I should have asked him for references and also check him out through my network. In other words I over relied on my own sense of being a good judge of character
5	What can I do better next time? [within my control]	Ask the questions about his past employment and contact people he worked with in the past and check out my inner and outer networks because it turned out he had a history of making a very good first impression and there were frequent moves because of an inability to maintain relationships over the medium and long term.
6	What results were achieved?	Very negative experience for both of us
7	What have I learned that I need to do better in the future?	Hiring is one of the most important decisions I have to make in my business. I need to collect more data and use behavioural based interviewing to make sure it is a good fit, and not overly rely on observation and intuition

Figure 5-4
Decision Making Feedback Form: Example 2

Decision: <u>To hire Ms. 'Y' to work in our organization.</u>

This Decision was:

☒ very successful   ☐ successful   ☐ weak   ☐ got me in trouble

	Question	Response
1	What happened that helped the decision making process? [external out of my control]	We both worked together in a voluntary organization. She stepped up to the plate and served as president for two years. I was able to observe her superb communication and organizational skills in addition to the initiative and creativity she brought to the organization
2	What happened that hindered the decision making process? [external out of my control]	I didn't know her very well at first
3	What did I do that helped the decision making? [within my control]	We worked together well. She had some very good ideas and she was very helpful when I asked for her help on an important project
4	What did I do that hindered the decision making? [within my control]	Not applicable
5	What can I do better next time? [within my control]	Not applicable
6	What results were achieved?	Very positive for both of us. I gained an excellent colleague and life-long friend
7	What have I learned that I need to do better in the future?	I need to be more vigilant in looking for talent in as many settings as possible as I expand my business

Figure 5-5
Decision Making Feedback Form

Decision: _____

This Decision was:
☐ very successful   ☐ successful   ☐ weak   ☐ got me in trouble

	Question	Response
1	What happened that helped the decision making process? [external out of my control]	
2	What happened that hindered the decision making process? [external out of my control]	
3	What did I do that helped the decision making? [within my control]	
4	What did I do that hindered the decision making? [within my control]	
5	What can I do better next time? [within my control]	
6	What results were achieved?	
7	What have I learned that I need to do better in the future?	

STRATEGY 6

Build a Culture of Excellence

Monkeys and Culture

Start with a cage containing five monkeys. Inside the cage, hang a banana on a string and place a set of stairs under it. Before long, a monkey will go to the stairs and start to climb towards the banana. As soon as he touches the stairs, spray all of the other monkeys with cold water. After a while, another monkey makes an attempt with the same result – all the other monkeys are sprayed with cold water. Pretty soon, when another monkey tries to climb the stairs, the other monkeys will try to prevent it.

Now, put away the cold water. Remove one monkey and replace it with a new one. The new monkey sees the banana and wants to climb the stairs. To his surprise and horror, all of the other monkeys attack him. After another attempt and attack, he knows that if he tries to climb the stairs, he will be assaulted.

Next, remove another of the original five monkeys and replace it with a new one. The newcomer goes to the stairs and is attacked. The previous newcomer takes part in the punishment with enthusiasm! Likewise, replace a third original monkey with a new one, then a fourth, then the fifth. Every time the newest monkey takes to the stairs, he is attacked. Most of the monkeys that are beating him have no idea why they were not permitted to climb the stairs or why they are participating in the beating of the newest monkey.

After replacing all the original monkeys, none of the remaining monkeys have ever been sprayed with cold water. Nevertheless, no monkey ever again approaches the stairs to try for the banana.

Why not? Because as far as they know that's the way it's always been done around here. And that, my friends, is how company policy [and organizational culture] begins.

Think out of the box ... (Source: unknown)

The above story aptly illustrates how corporate culture can be a negative force. However, if leaders are careful to build a positive, creative and empowering culture, it can be one of that leader's most important and long-lasting legacies. To better understand the critical importance of corporate culture, we will look at three definitions.

> 1) Corporate culture has been defined as "the collection of beliefs, expectations, and values shared by an organization's members and transmitted from one generation of employees to another."[1]

> 2) In their Harvard Business Review article, Measuring the Strategic Readiness of Intangible Assets, Robert Kaplan and David Norton state, Successful companies [have] a culture in which people [are] deeply aware of an internalized mission, vision, and core values [that they need] to execute the company's strategies. These companies [strive] for excellent leadership at all levels, leadership that could mobilize the organization toward its strategy."[2]

3) In their book on corporate culture, Deal and Kennedy state that, "Whether weak or strong, culture has a powerful influence throughout an organization; it affects practically everything – from who gets promoted and what decisions are made, to how employees dress and what sports they play. Because of this impact . . . culture also has a major effect on the success of the business".[3]

The most difficult and possibly the most important part of leadership is building a culture of excellence. In fact, changing your organization's culture can be one of the most significant, impactful and longest lasting things you can accomplish as a leader. However, if you do not succeed in changing your organization's culture – even when it should be changed – you are very often ostracized and/or scapegoated as the following example illustrates.

Sue was the president of a local chapter of a national volunteer association. Over the years, she couldn't help but notice that the organization was run very much like an old boys' and girls' club where neither diversity nor inclusiveness were valued. Sue was asked to chair a task force to increase both the level of diversity and inclusiveness among the leadership of the organization in question.

Sue was undecided about taking on this responsibility because she already had a lot of responsibility at work and she wasn't sure she wanted to add another task to her already very busy schedule. In the end, she told the national president that she would take on the task of working to increase the diversity and inclusiveness of the organization, but only if she had his full support. The president agreed and they shook hands to seal the deal.

After six months of hard work, Sue realized that the national president's word only applied to increasing the diversity and inclusiveness of the people whom the president and his supporters liked. After a great deal of inner struggle, Sue resigned from the organization. Although these events were traumatic for Sue, she learned the hard way just how difficult it can be to change an organization's culture.

I asked Sue what she learned from this experience and she said it was crucial in helping her learn when to take on a leadership role and when not to. The lessons became much clearer to her when I suggested that she read a remarkable book, *The Wisdom of Crowds* by James Surowiecki.[4]

The Wisdom of Crowds is like reading a great detective story, only the subject of the book is not who did it, but how they did it. And how they did it refers to one of the most important and least well understood topics we need to learn about – the influence of organizational culture. For example Surowiecki contrasts the culture of decision making that lead to the successful return of the Apollo 13 astronauts versus the Columbia Shuttle disaster. In the Apollo 13 case the decision-making was decentralized, independent and based on diverse points of view. Tragically, the decision-making regarding the foam that hit the wing on the Shuttle Columbia was centralized, dependent and diverse points of view were stifled. In Columbia's case, the team leader decided that the foam that hit the wing probably did not do any damage. She further decided that if it did damage the wing, they couldn't do anything about it. Lastly, she decided that spy satellites would not have good enough resolution to determine if there had been any damage. We will never know if the seven Columbia astronauts could have been saved. However, we do know, that based on the above decision-making model, they were condemned to death.

The Columbia tragedy illustrates the disastrous effects of dysfunctional leadership and organizational culture. On the other hand, developing the right type of culture can be a leader's greatest legacy. For example, in the fall of 2008, when the price of fuel skyrocketed, Air Canada and Air Canada Jazz, just like almost all of the world's airlines, were laying off pilots and flight crews and scaling back their routes. WestJet, however, was in the process of adding routes and hiring. Why? Because it had developed one of the highest performing organizational cultures in Canada as the following award attests:[5]

> WestJet is honoured to have been recently awarded the title of Canada's Most Admired Corporate Culture by Waterstone Human Capital for the third year in a row. This accolade is the result of our WestJetters' relentless commitment to our culture and values. The support from our guests over the past 12 years is appreciated and has helped us achieve tremendous growth and success. We believe that our unique, friendly and caring culture sets us apart in the airline industry. Our guests have embraced our vision for air travel and we truly appreciate your encouragement and loyalty.

WestJet has spent a great deal of time and effort developing its culture. However, it is one thing to build a corporate culture from the ground up in a new organization, and quite another to bring about change in an existing culture. This may be one of the things Kurt Lewin, one of the modern pioneers of social, organizational, and applied psychology, had in mind when he said, "If you want to know how something works, try changing it." And meaningful change in a unionized environment that has a history of very difficult union-management relationships is more difficult still. But that is exactly what Moya Greene decided to do when she was selected as the new President and CEO of Canada Post Corporation.

Two of the biggest mistakes leaders make are trying to change an organization's culture too quickly — especially when the new leader hasn't taken the time to get to know and understand the present culture — or *not* changing those aspects of an organizational culture that should be changed because the task is so daunting. An illuminating example of getting it just right is reflected in the following excerpts from my interview with Moya.

B.M.   *I understand that your first six months on the job were a bit unusual in that you actually did many of the jobs that Canada Post workers do. How was that received, how helpful was it and where did this idea come from?*

M.G.   *I didn't come from a postal or logistics industry background and Canada Post has a strong history in terms of its operating culture and I wanted to learn it firsthand and from the ground up. I wanted to have my own experience, short though it may be, in some of our key jobs. It was a way for me to take my own measure at how well we were doing. I got a firsthand sense of how complicated, complex and difficult it is to move 40 million pieces of mail a day to 14 million mailboxes. Our mission is to deliver the mail to all Canadians at a reasonable rate and to be financially self-sustaining. There is only one way to see it and that is to observe it and talk to the people who put their heart and soul into it.*

B.M.   *How much time did you spend in the field during your first six months?*

M.G.   *I was on the road 50% of the time. I got to see our postal workers trying to deliver the mail while having to contend with everything from untethered Rottweilers to having to contend with criminals who wanted to steal your mail. I sorted mail in rural and urban areas across Canada and I worked on the loading docks. I got to work with some of our supervisors and staff who have hero jobs, trying to deliver the mail with inadequate technology, which just increases their logistical challenges. To have the actual experience, even for a short period of time, certainly gave me a real perspective of the challenge we face.*

B.M.   *Do other people on your executive team have the same type of experience?*

M.G.   *Each of our executives has to do a specific number of front line operations quarterly. People all across the country get to see and hear the executives. Because of this experience, as a team, we have a much richer perspective and we have much richer discussions than we had four years ago. How well the executive engages our employees is tied into their compensation. In fact, employee engagement is 25% of our balanced scorecard. The result is that our employees, in the vast majority of cases, feel that they now have a voice and that they are listened to at all levels of the organization. We also have many channels and everyone knows that they can get to the top of the organization.*

I didn't have to go very far to learn that Moya's openness in communicating with Canada Post's employees was real. Moya has a blog and anyone at Canada Post can e-mail her. I had a student, Todd Kennedy, who works for Canada Post in my leadership class. I asked him whom I should speak with to get an interview with Moya. Two days later, I was surprised and delighted when I found out that Todd had e-mailed Moya and all I had to do was contact Moya's assistant to set up a time for the interview. This is an outstanding example of how responsive Moya is to her employees and how comfortable her employees are in approaching her.

Culture is so pervasive that, like a fish in water, leaders often don't see it and worse yet, take it for granted. Often organizational culture can be best seen indirectly rather than directly and is expressed symbolically or metaphorically through stories. I've found that one of the best ways to find out about an organization's culture is to listen to the stories that people tell when they talk about the organization at its best and at its worst. These stories contain the organization's DNA, and tell us a great deal about that organization's culture and the way that the culture impacts the organization.

In this chapter we are going to explore seven types of organizational cultures that the Master Leaders profiled in this book grew and nurtured. Please note that even though these seven types of cultures are listed separately, there is often a high degree of overlap and synergy among these different types of cultures:

1. Trust

2. Continuous Learning

3. Innovation

4. Operational Excellence

5. Customer Service Excellence

6. Inclusion

7. Social Responsibility and Environmental Sustainability

Trust

> Trust is the foundation of leadership.
>
> — John C. Maxwell

In the past, the relations between management and union at Canada Post have been very contentious. For the first time ever CUPW or unionized employees at Canada Post were paid a bonus. I asked Moya Greene how that came about and what were the results.

M.G.   *It was tough, but I believe in incentive and performance-based compensation with clear set targets in advance. I believe that if people understand that, they buy in and they buy in even more so if there is money attached to it. Everyone is attached to the same scorecard which gives them an ownership mentality. All we need to do to stay competitive is to change the culture so that driving for success becomes more and* *more ingrained. For example, under our union contracts, every aspect of compensation has to be negotiated. Our cost structure is very high. The bonus helped us change the culture at Canada Post — from a culture of grievance to a culture of ownership.*

One way Kevin Hamm, President and CEO of DownEast Communications, increased the trust and loyalty of his employees was to acknowledge and reward them for their outstanding efforts by offering each employee Friday afternoons off once every other week during our short Canadian summers. There was only one caveat. The employees had to write, and Kevin had to approve, "The Rules of Engagement." The Rules of Engagement that the employees developed for this program follow.

The Rules of Engagement

1. This opportunity is valid only from May 1 to August 31. An employee wishing to leave at noon on a given Friday must be up to date in their workload.

2. An employee must not have taken any paid sick/personal time in the previous two weeks.

3. All employees wishing to take part in this rotation must have their Friday afternoon schedules confirmed with their direct Supervisor/Manager. All employees will not have the same Friday afternoon off, as we must ensure that our sales and service departments continue to be supported.

4. Employees must be present (at work) on their scheduled Friday in order to take advantage of this offer. If an employee is out sick or on vacation, they will be deducted for the full day of vacation or sick/personal time.

5. Employees must be in good standing as far as performance to take advantage of this offer. Employees recently on performance counseling may not qualify.

The outcome of Kevin's experiment is that his employees feel more happy and satisfied with their work/life balance. These employees are more productive at work and the number of sick days has decreased. Kevin summarized the program's impact when he said, "the bottom line is that it was a great shot to our M & M. I am a big fan of reading a company's M & M Meter. M & M stands for Morale and Momentum, which is just as important as any financial metric in how a company is doing ... especially with today's workforce."

A third example demonstrates how an organization used job sharing with a twist to increase the trust and loyalty of its employees. Two women, each named Kelley, were young mothers who had similar qualifications and positions. They approached their manager with a proposal for job sharing. The twist was that neither could afford to work half time, so they proposed that they each work three out of the five days a week with both being in the office on Wednesdays, which would also lead to a much more seamless and cohesive running of the unit.

The outcome from this proposal was a win, win, win. Both Kelleys could spend more time with their young families, the organization gained increased productivity and increased loyalty and they developed a model that could work equally well for others in the future.

One of the best ways to engender loyalty is to reward people with something that is meaningful to that person. This is not the case of The Golden Rule; it is the case of applying The Platinum Rule. The Golden Rule states that we should treat others the way we would like to be treated. The Platinum Rule states that we should treat people the way *those* people want to be treated. In point of fact, Master Leaders often walk a fine line by knowing when to apply The Golden Rule and when to apply The Platinum Rule.

As the above three examples illustrate, trust, fairness and loyalty are three of the primary characteristics that form the foundation of an organization's culture; however, trust, fairness and loyalty, although necessary, are not by themselves enough to ensure success. To these three important parts of an organizational culture, we must add learning, growth and personal development.

Continuous Learning

> Continuous learning drives everyone to find a better way,
> every day. It's not an expense; it's an investment in continuous
> renewal.
>
> – Jack Welch

In most organizations, when the economy takes a downturn and demand for those organizations' products and/or services decreases, staff training is one of the first departments to have its funding decreased. Not so at Michelin. Michelin sees this as an opportunity to do even more staff training and development.

I have been working with Michelin, which is one of the world's premier manufacturers of tires, for the past 16 years. Michelin has a very strong corporate culture and that culture[6] is responsible for a great deal of Michelin's continuing success. One of the first things I noticed when I began working with Michelin was the length of the training day. In most organizations, training goes from 9:00 a.m. to 4:30 p.m. with an hour for lunch and two 15 minute breaks – which leaves six hours a day for training. However, the typical training day at Michelin is 8:00 a.m. to 4:30 p.m. with 45 minutes for lunch and two 15 minute breaks. This is equal to an additional one and a quarter hours per day, or two and a half hours in a two-day training course. Compared to most organizations, that is a 20% increase in time per course. Michelin Canada has approximately 3,500 employees. These employees received approximately 368,000 hours of training per year – 368,000 times 20% equals 73,600 extra hours of training for all of its employees in the past year.

Michelin is known for its passion for research and development (R&D). Michelin spends a higher percentage of its profit on R&D than any other tire manufacturer in the world. The emphasis on R&D has paid off for Michelin, which has "over the decades, invented everything from steel-belted radials to 'regenerating' tires (as the tread wears, new water-planing grooves emerge, extending tire life by 25%)."[7] Michelin's newest tires have rolling resistance that "accounts for 20% of a car's fuel consumption" (and 3% for a truck's). At current gas prices Michelin figures European car drivers on Energy Savers will cut their fuel costs by an average $2.90 every time they fill the tank, while also reducing by 6.5 grams per mile the amount of CO_2 emissions."[8] What most people don't know is that Michelin is equally passionate about coaching and development (C&D). Let me give several examples.

In the fall of 2000, I was teaching for Michelin right in the middle of the massive Firestone tire recall, which was associated with the instability of Firestone tires on the Ford Explorer. As you may remember, there was a problem with rollover accidents in the Ford Explorer. Michelin and other tire manufacturers could not produce tires fast enough. I was scheduled to teach the "Become a Master Negotiator" course for participants from the credit department at Michelin. The credit department was inundated with extra work. They had new clients lined up wanting credit so they could sell Michelin replacement tires for the Ford Explorer. At the same time, Michelin's traditional customers were asked to radically increase their credit level so they could meet the increased demand. Michelin had to please both its new and existing customer base. The credit department uses a complex computerized program to help determine the right level of credit for its on-going and its new customers. To say that the credit department was horrendously busy would have been an understatement. Ninety-nine percent of companies would have cancelled the negotiation course – not Michelin. This story has a strong message for the employees of this department, but also for every employee – C&D is of paramount importance at Michelin – not just in words, but in actions.

Innovation

> The goods-based economy is being replaced by the innovation-based economy.
>
> – Rebecca Ryan

An excellent example that illustrates the above quote appeared in Canada Post's internal magazine, Performance Special Report. In the interview, Moya Greene stated that her 16-year-old daughter had never been to a post office. I asked her what this says about the future of Canada Post. Moya replied:

M.G.   *Today, she is 20 and still hasn't been to a post office. It will force us to be a real multi-channel intermediary. Today, there is still a lot of paper in the postal system. In the future things are going to be quite different. For my daughter's generation for example – when she has her own household, she will be getting her bills exclusively electronically. I am more comfortable with paper. She may want it on her smart phone because she uses these tools in a different way. She and her friends are more adept and comfortable with the new technology. They communicate through text-messaging even when they are talking to the same person on the phone. In other words, we will need to go where our customers are going. Increasingly, that means using information electronically and we will have to make sure that it is secure in whatever device the end-recipient wants to see it. And just like radio did not come to an end when television was introduced, I think we will always have things come in the mail.*

David Foote, best selling author of *Boom, Bust and Echo*,[9] states that two-thirds to three-quarters of any trend can be explained by demographics. In relation to Canada's lack of population growth, author and consultant Rebecca Ryan states:

> If all adults aged 15 to 99 were working [full employment], there would still be a shortage of 3.9 million workers in 2022 … The demographic issue simply is "We don't have enough young people to backfill for all those baby boomers who have been populating developed countries."[10]

Further evidence of this trend comes from the Conference Board of Canada, which predicts that by the year 2031, we will only have 23 people available to do the work that 50 people do today. I asked Moya Greene how Canada Post is preparing for the workplace of the future.

M.G.   *One-third of our workers will retire in the near future. We also have started a $1.9 billion modernization over the next five years. Much of our equipment and infrastructure is very outdated. The investment will entail $1.9 billion in capital expenditures over a five-year period, and* *it will place Canada Post, once again at the forefront of the business that it does. Right now some of our equipment is five generations old. Some of the equipment we use is in the U.S. postal museum and other pieces of equipment are so old that the manufacturer no longer stocks replacement parts so we have had to go to advertise on eBay and see if anyone has the parts we need.*

The change will also support renewal of Canada's largest corporate fleet. We operate almost 7,000 vans and trucks, and during this modernization we will have the opportunity to capitalize on other modes and technologies that are far more fuel efficient, environmentally friendly and more ergonomically appropriate than what we use today.

In other words, we have a unique opportunity to modernize now because we are facing some of the same problems other organizations are and will be facing. We definitely need to synchronize our plan for modernization of our facilities with the pace of these retirements and improve our operations and level of service so Canada Post will be the most effective and efficient postal system in the world.

Try to imagine what would happen today if almost half of the workforce was gone tomorrow. The only way to circumvent the problems that this shortage of workers would create is through innovation, innovation and even more innovation. Fortunately, the Conference Board of Canada report also predicts that the answer to the upcoming labour shortage will be the increasing use of technology and self-service.

For example, 20 years ago, who would have thought that we would become our own gas station attendants? Or that we would arrive at an airport and be our own check-in agents by inserting our credit card or frequent flyer card in a machine that would ask us how many pieces of luggage we had and then print out our boarding passes? The most recent innovation is that we can even bypass the kiosk machines by printing out our own boarding passes which are e-mailed to us, or storing the boarding pass on our PDA or smart phone. To encourage passengers to use their own computers to print out their boarding passes or store them on their PDAs, Air Canada has separate – shorter – lines and check-in areas for Web-Based Boarding Passes only. This example is just a small indication of what will come because of the impending labour shortage.

Nowhere else will the problem be more critical than in health care. Innovation, in the form of Star Trek medicine will come to the rescue. For example, in the future we will have smart bandages. With smart bandages, when a person injures one of their fingers, they will put on a smart bandage and that bandage will be able to tell if the wound on the patient's finger is getting better, in which case the patient will carry on. If the wound is beginning to get infected, the bandage will change colour to alert the patient that all is not well and they should book an appointment to see a doctor. Another type of smart bandage, "may completely do away with the need to use needles for testing cholesterol, insulin and blood chemistry ... the bandage could determine internal chemistry and other essential ... information without breaking the skin."[11]

In today's competitive world, all organizations must innovate or die. Let me give some specific examples. The original disposable diaper, Pampers, officially came onto the market in 1964. They did not have any tape so customers had to use safety pins just like cloth diapers. If Pampers still used safely pins today, they would have gone the way of the Osborne luggable laptop or the Wang Personal Word Processor – two products that were very innovative when they first appeared but now can only be found in technology museums because they stopped being innovative. Let's look at a few more contemporary examples that illustrate the need to innovate.

Now more than ever, organizations of all types are using digital technology in ways that we never would have dreamed of. Now Apple wants to develop on-demand television programs and on-demand movies the same way it developed downloading music through iPod and iTunes.[12] However, Apple is not alone as several other companies are developing 5,000 channel television and download-able movies right to your computer or computer-aided entertainment system.

Another contest to watch is Airbus versus Boeing. I fly extensively and have a keen interest in the aviation industry; after all, I trust my life to airplanes many times a year. Ten to 15 years ago, 80% of the planes I flew on were made by Boeing. Today, 80% of the planes I fly on are made by Airbus. Airbus has bet its future on the A380, the largest jumbo jet in the world. It can hold up to 825 people. New boarding ramps are being built to load and unload the giant double-decker. And for the first time ever, Airbus will have a plane larger than the Boeing 747. The A380's wingspan is so wide that at some airports they will have to close the adjacent runways when it lands or takes off. But the contest isn't over. In the mean time, Boeing developed the 787 Dreamliner. These planes are being made of light alloy materials and will be 30% more fuel efficient than anything else on the market, it just could be that the bet will be won by Boeing.

However, the advantage that Airbus has is that as our airports are getting more and more crowded, one way to increase efficiency is to use larger capacity planes so fewer planes would have to land and take off. So stay tuned, the rivalry between these two companies is intense. Their leaders' ability to innovate and to keep innovating will be the winning edge.

The next great competition between Boeing and Airbus will be to see who most successfully develops the next generation of some of the most widely used jetliners to replace the Boeing 737 and the Airbus A320. However, both Boeing and Airbus are having significant problems in getting the Dreamliner and the A380 into production. In the meantime, Pierre Beaudoin and Bombardier are going ahead with the C series. For the first time Bombardier will have a plane large enough to compete with Boeing's 737-600 and Airbus' 318. The C series is scheduled to be available by 2013 with new Pratt and Whitney engines that will be 20% more fuel efficient. Other countries such as Russia and China are also eyeing this market – so this will be an especially interesting contest to watch with potential sales in the tens of billions of dollars.

It is clear that leaders have to know when and how to innovate. For example, at General Electric (GE) every product and brand manager is responsible for developing three breakthrough ideas per year: GE does not leave innovation to chance. Now, let's look at three Canadian innovative examples in three very different industries: telecommunications, food services and post-secondary education.

Innovation in Telecommunications. There are few businesses that are as competitive as the mobile phone industry. Cell phones come in all shapes and sizes, and there is a plethora of tasks they can handle, from being a phone, to working hands-free in your car, to being a digital recorder, camera, MP3 player, Web browser, game device, to a PDA/phone combination that serves as a hand-held computer. I am sure that there are other functions I haven't mentioned, such as GPS and other features that are being added on a daily basis. It seems as though you need a chief financial officer to help you figure out which payment or leasing plan would work best for you, keeping in mind how soon you may want to upgrade.

In their remarkable book, *The Experience Economy: Work Is Theater & Every Business a Stage*,[13] Joseph Pine and James Gilmore state that we live in an experience economy — which is to say that customers rate the organizations that they support and/or buy from based on the sum total of their experience with that organization. For example, Kevin Hamm, President and COO of DownEast Mobility, and his team came up with a strategy to design a new experience-based environment that was both congruent with their products and would resonate with their customers. The first new store was opened in Saint John's, Newfoundland, and the second in Halifax, Nova Scotia, and were designed to be as interactive as possible. Work stations are available where you can check your e-mail and there are games galore for kids to play. These stores also became the first mobile phone stores in Canada where you could both look at the latest technological innovation *and* try it out.

What was the result of opening up these new stores with up-to-date marketing features hard-wired into the store? The Retail Council of Canada awarded DownEast Communications the prestigious Retail Store Design Concept Award for 2006 and now similar stores are being rolled out across the Bell Network of companies throughout Canada (see Figures 6-1 and 6-2 for the award-winning stores). However, as interesting as all of this is, what I found most interesting was that Kevin was in no way going to rest, nor let his employees rest, on their laurels. Kevin has already said that they have to look for improvements and/or come up with better and maybe even completely different, innovative environments in order to stay competitive in the future. Excerpts from my interview with Kevin follow.

K.H.   *When I became President and COO of DownEast Communications, I didn't have any experience in the cell phone and telecommunications industry. However, I did have a lot of experience in selling, merchandizing, and marketing. The cell phone and telecommunications industry is hyper-competitive and I knew we had to be the best from the first point of contact with the customer and I also know that our* *reputation was only as good as our last point of contact with the customer. I also knew that we had a very diverse customer base. In other words, the products and displays that would appeal to now retiring baby boomers would not necessarily appeal to the younger primary, junior and/or senior high school students who were getting their first cell phone. Therefore store design – that first point of contact was critical to our success. So we worked hard to come up with a new store design and won the National Retail Award for Retail Store Design.*

B.M.   *Why do you think you won the award?*

K.H.   *We have been and are very careful when we design a new store because that store and its design are part of our brand. We wanted our new store design to be warm, inviting, interactive, engaging and enticing. Look at the signs that say, "Please handle the merchandise." That is a statement that we have in mind when we design a store. That statement is built right into the fixtures. I believe that we were the first communications store in Canada and maybe North America to have live products in our stores. We now have over 75% of the products live in our new stores and we are working towards 100%.*

Our objectives in redesigning our stores were to appeal to the youth market, increase traffic to the store, increase sales, build our brand and showcase our passion for customers. The store's redesign is a hit with youth who especially enjoy the Internet and gaming areas. A traffic study indicated a substantial increase in traffic and we experienced significant sales increases across all lines of business.

Figure 6-1
Award Winning Store in the Avalon Mall,
St. John's, Newfoundland

Figure 6-2
"New Look" stores – featuring live product displays,
digital screens, etc.

Store design is not the only area where Kevin is innovating. DownEast is booming as a company. Revenues are soaring in one of the most competitive industries and DownEast's competitors are also relentless innovators. Roger's has the exclusive right to sell Apple's new iPhone in Canada. Given the extreme loyalty that people have to their iPods, this is going to be an innovation match to watch and it will be just as interesting and just as intense as the Stanley Cup playoffs or the Wimbledon Tennis Tournaments.

Innovation in Food Services. In March, 2007 I was asked to present at the Newfoundland and Labrador Organization for Women Entrepreneurs national conference in St. John's, Newfoundland. The first morning's keynote presenter was Cora Mussely Tsouflidou, the founder and owner of Cora's Restaurants. When Cora took the stage she looked like everyone's favourite grandmother. However, when she told her story, it was absolutely clear to all of us that Cora was an exceptional leader, entrepreneur, negotiator and presenter.

In 2005, the Harvard Business School Press published *In Their Time: The Greatest Business Leaders of the 20th Century* by Anthony Mayo and Nitin Nohria. The authors identified three prototypical leadership types – the entrepreneurial leader, the leader as manager and the charismatic leader. It turns out that Cora Mussely Tsouflidou is all three.

Cora was born into a modest family in a little village in the Gaspé Peninsula. From an early age Cora felt a passion for fine art, but her father wanted her to study stenography so she could become a "good secretary." However, Cora had her own vision for her future. She enrolled at Montreal's Cardinal Léger Institute, promising to pay for her education to prepare herself for a professional career. However, when she found out that she was expecting her first child, she quit college during her final year to devote herself to her family, and to the two other children who would soon follow.

> Great companies need both a visionary leader and a skilled executive: one for the top line, the other for the bottom line.
> **Howard Schultz**

When her husband left her and abandoned their children, Cora was suddenly a single mother with three teenage children to support. With her characteristic aplomb, Cora bought a small neighbourhood canteen, worked hard, tripled its value and sold it. She then became a hostess in a well-known Montreal restaurant, where she worked her way up the ladder as a day manager, general manager and junior partner. For the next five years, Cora perfected her knowledge of the food service industry until she mastered all aspects of the hospitality trade.

In 1987, Cora decided that she wanted to be her own boss again and bought a small snack bar in Montreal. After a few months, Cora transformed the snack bar into a whole new breakfast concept, one that blended the best of traditional breakfasts with new health food trends.

Now that you understand a little bit about Cora's background, you will be able to learn more about how she created and nurtured her organization's culture through my interview with this Master Leader and Entrepreneur.

B.M.   *Where did you get the nerve to start your own restaurant?*

C.T.   *When my husband left me with three children and absolutely no support, I decided that I would have to be in the driver's seat. Going on welfare never crossed my mind. I could have become a waitress, but I decided to sell our house and buy a restaurant.*

B.M.   *How did you decide to open multiple restaurants?*

C.T.   *We couldn't serve all of the people who were lined up for lunch and breakfast. It was a small 32-seat restaurant and I was barely making enough money to survive. So we decided to open up a second, larger restaurant. We then opened two more restaurants, which were all run by my children. At this point, I ran out of children and a friend of mine approached me and wanted to run a Cora's so we went into business together with me being the majority shareholder.*

B.M.   *How did you decide to franchise?*

C.T.   *Eventually, we had nine restaurants and another friend of mine said that she wanted to buy a franchise. I didn't know what a franchise was, but I had always been a very good student so I went to the library and read everything I could find on franchises. I had several customers who ran franchises and they let me see some of their contracts. A year later, I felt that I knew enough and I started my first franchise.*

I then had a vision of having franchises throughout Quebec. I really did not know if the Cora's concept would work outside of Quebec, but I decided to give it a try. It seemed that wherever we opened a Cora's, people would line up to get in, so we had no problem selling franchises throughout Canada — at last count we had 103 restaurants.

B.M.   *How do you, as a leader, ensure that each restaurant provides the same quality of food and service that you yourself would provide?*

C.T.   *We are incredibly systematic in everything that we do, from the meal preparation manuals to marketing and public relations, to the layout and design of our restaurants. We are very close to our franchisees. Every five years they come to Montreal and the head office staff celebrates our accomplishments and we serve them a fantastic meal. We visit their restaurants and if something is not right, we help them as much as possible. In the end if it is not working out, we part ways because it is not good for any of us if the brand becomes diluted.*

B.M.   *How would you describe your leadership style?*

C.T.   *My style is like a mother hen. I believe in being outrageously supportive of the people I work with and that has carried over to everyone who works with me. For example, we had an employee who lost a child. She was entitled to one month's bereavement leave. We gave her four months because it was the right thing to do.*

B.M.   *How did you develop your style?*

C.T.   *I am not sure. I think it just came naturally. We learned that giving does not make you poorer; it makes you richer. So early on, we started taking some of our profits and used them to support a program in Quebec that works to make sure that children go to school having had a good breakfast. Now we are doing that across Canada and it is the purpose of the Cora Foundation.*

B.M.   *At this point, you have left the day-to-day operations of the company in the hands of your son Nicolas. Was that hard to do?*

C.T.   *Yes and no. I still work on special projects. For example, we are currently in the process of implementing a new extranet to automatically receive and transmit information between the franchiser and its franchisees. More than just transmitting data, producing automated reports and managing e-mails, this system will also offer on-line multimedia training sessions. With the simple touch of a computer screen, employees can access numerous job-specific training programs. Timely, fast and efficient, this new training tool will give Cora's the two most important ingredients in the restaurant business: premium products and superior service.*

B.M.   *What are your plans for the future?*

C.T.   *For me, the future means the development of the Cora's brand all over Canada and North America. I now work mostly in the area of PR and as a trusted advisor to my son. I would also like to give more speeches like the one you heard in St. John's to inspire others to live their dreams – especially woman. Lastly, I want to continue growing our foundation in order to insure that every child in Canada starts the day with a wholesome and nutritious breakfast.*

The growth of Cora's brand is a result of Cora's dedication to building a culture of excellence. In the next example, you will see how Ray Ivany also built a culture of excellence that continues to flourish even after his departure.

Innovation in Post-Secondary Education. Master Leader Ray Ivany is credited with transforming the Nova Scotia Community College system (NSCC) from the worst community college system in Canada to one of the best.[14] He accomplished this by developing a culture of excellence through learning and innovation.

R.I.   *We are the first and only community college in Canada where developing a portfolio is a requirement of graduation. Our students are producing a document and that document can take many forms. It could be a document, a CD or even a Website that provides an actual demonstration of what students can do. It goes beyond a diploma or a CV to both demonstrate and celebrate what our students can do and* *what they bring to prospective employers. But it is more than that. It is a process that we take students through that requires them to take stock of where they are in their lives, how they got there, where it is they want to move to and what is it they need to do, both in their learning and otherwise in order to get there. And that provokes some very powerful self-reflection.*

Portfolio education challenges some of the assumptions about technical education and its narrowness because people have to develop some very sophisticated skills and abilities in addition to the technical skills that they learn at the college. It is also about developing the whole person and that can be demonstrated much more effectively with a portfolio than with a piece of parchment and a CV.

B.M. *So you are saying a person can talk about the fact that they have initiative until the cows come home, but it is so much more powerful to be able to demonstrate that they have initiative and that can be shown very effectively through the portfolio that they have developed.*

R.I. *The best way to illustrate how our students feel about the portfolio program is to quote one of our students. Michael Richards, who is a graduate from our Business Administration – Marketing program ... said, "I knew the College experience was going to be different. One reason for that was portfolio learning. A portfolio education empowers the student to demonstrate immediately to employers the value they can bring to their business." Another example is a student in our entrepreneurship program where our students actually have to go out and start a business. This same student then went to a bank and actually got a loan based on his business ideas that were documented in his portfolio. The portfolio gave the bank manager deeper insight into the student and from this insight the manager made a better decision about taking the risk to make that loan.*

The portfolio documents what our students can do, not just what they say they can do, and this gives our students and their prospective employers more confidence in our students' knowledge, skills and talents. And it is not just based on what they learn at the college. We also have a Prior

Learning Assessment Centre where we help our students document that important learning that they acquired before they came to the college.

Additional comments by students, faculty and staff about their experience with the portfolio program follow:

> ➢ As a student, it helped me gain a lot of self-confidence.

> ➢ Some of my class did their portfolios on a CD. What a learning experience! It made our program that much more meaningful!

> ➢ When I went for a job interview, I was able to present myself more effectively, not only because I had a portfolio binder in my hand but because the process made me more prepared for the questions... and I got the job!

> ➢ As an instructor, portfolio development is the best thing that happened to my teaching in twenty years.

The portfolio program at the NSCC is designed to help the students secure gainful employment because they can express themselves more effectively when they can show samples of their actual accomplishments. This also helps the students increase their self-confidence because they can see, in real terms, what they have learned and what they bring to their prospective employers. Once a student sees the value he or she has created in his or her portfolio, they are more likely to add to it as their learnings and their experience grows. Faculty and staff are also encouraged to have their own portfolios. You know it is part of their organizational culture because NSCC is now known as the portfolio college.

Master Leaders like Kevin Hamm, Cora Tsouflidou and Ray Ivany didn't leave innovation to chance. They lived and promoted a culture of innovation. Some even had an innovation to-do list where they listed the innovations they wanted to accomplish month-by-month, and the innovations they wanted to accomplish year-by-year and even for longer time periods. They used that list to hold themselves accountable to create innovative ideas, to implement those ideas and to measure the success or failure of those initiatives, and then to reflect on what they learned, and start the innovation process all over again. The following exercises have been designed to help you become more innovative.

Exercise 6-1: Describe one or two innovations – either at work or in your personal life – that you have implemented in the last six months.

Do you have an Innovation To-Do List? If not, this is the perfect opportunity to start one in the space below.

1.

2.

3.

4.

5.

6.

7.

8.

Operational Excellence

There is a cartoon that shows a group of mothers trying to one-up each other. The first mother says that she wants her son to become a doctor, the second a lawyer, and the third said she wants her son to start an Internet company that would be bought by Google. Mothers and fathers have traditionally encouraged their sons and daughters to become doctors, lawyers and other professionals. It is rare that a parent suggests that their son or daughter go into operations or manufacturing. To make matters worse, there has been a steady trend of manufacturing jobs leaving Canada because it is less expensive, at least in the short term, to ship jobs overseas. Fortunately, there are two major exceptions. One is Michelin and the other is Bombardier. Both of these well-known companies have taken similar approaches in developing cultures of operational and manufacturing excellence.

> *Sustained great results depend upon building a culture full of self disciplined people who take disciplined action.*
> **Jim Collins**

Michelin Manufacturing Way: Towards Operational Excellence. Michelin has set a goal to increase productivity through the systematic implementation of best practices, called the Michelin Manufacturing Way (MMW), by 20% by 2010.[15] The goal is "to align all of its plants on the best practices of its higher-performing factories by 2010." Best Practices are based on demonstrated performance in the field. There are 12 leading MMW sites that actively train all the other plants and results are measured by four progress tools and key performance indicators including: work accident frequency and severity rate, order fill rate, raw material waste and product quality.

There are several things to notice here. Safety was listed first – and that is no "accident". The Centers of Disease Control in Atlanta stipulate that 90% of accidents are predictable and preventable. I had the good fortune to be able to tour several Michelin plants. These plants represent massive amounts of investment and run 24/7. Everything is measured and I mean everything. Large flat screen television monitors are located strategically throughout the plant, so that employees know instantly how well the plant is doing in terms of number of days without accidents, productivity, quality and waste. At the eight a.m.

shift change, vital information, which is displayed on these flat screen television monitors, is transferred from the night team to the day team, daily goals are set, and everything that needs to be addressed is discussed in the standing meetings (where people actually stand).

In addition to manufacturing excellence, Michelin is committed to helping to cut fuel consumption in automobiles as the following statement in Michelin's annual report attests.

> On average, 20% of a car's fuel consumption – 30% for a truck – are used just to overcome tire rolling resistance. Therefore, tire performance plays a key role in reducing both consumer fuel spending, fossil fuel consumption and greenhouse gas emissions. Michelin's radial technology first reduced rolling resistance by 30% and its green tire technology by a further 20%. In Europe alone, if all passenger cars were fitted with green tires, some 6 billion litres of fuel would be saved every year and 15 million metric tons of CO_2 would not be released. And the Group is preparing the way for a further technological breakthrough which will have rolling resistance yet again.[16]

Just as the Michelin Manufacturing Way has contributed to Michelin being a world class tire manufacturing company, the Bombardier Manufacturing System[17] (BMS) has contributed to Bombardier being a world class recreational vehicle, train and plane manufacturing organization.

Bombardier Manufacturing System. Like the Michelin Manufacturing Way, the Bombardier Manufacturing System is not just a way to doing things; it is a way of thinking that has become part of Bombardier's culture. BMS is based on Kaizen or continuous quality improvement, total quality management, and just-in-time-delivery. At Bombardier, these things are not fads – they are a fact of everyday life. Another part of the BMS is that different departments don't engage in tribal warfare because they are jointly accountable for the success of their product lines. An example of tribal warfare in another organization is the sales department calling the credit department – "the non sales department".

However, if the credit department ceased to exist – the company would cease to exist because there would not be a department to process and collect outstanding bills. Without proper funding, sales would have nothing to sell. Therefore, when Bombardier decided to develop a new product – like the C Series jetliner – they made sure that design, manufacturing, marketing and procurement work closely together from the initial starting phases of design in order to ensure that Bombardier can produce the right plane at the right cost and at the right time.

One of the best practices that Bombardier uses is Six Sigma. Six Sigma was developed by Motorola in 1986. The goal of Six Sigma is to improve both customer satisfaction and profitability by using advanced measuring and statistical analyses to reduce and eliminate defects. Every aspect of the product cycle from design, procurement, manufacturing costs, product quality, defect rates and scheduling are measured and benchmarked. Six Sigma stands for six standard deviations from the mean. Therefore reducing defects by six standard deviations mean 3.4 or fewer defective parts per million. As of 2006, it is estimated, that since its inception, Six Sigma has saved Motorola $17 billion.

Using Six Sigma also resulted in large savings at Bombardier[18].

> Six Sigma shaved $242 million off costs in fiscal 2001. One example of the successful application of Six Sigma techniques involved the paint shop in the aerospace group. After five years of trying to solve a problem with paint peeling off freshly minted regional jets, a Six Sigma team was asked to take a look. It was a knotty conundrum because there were at least 10 possible causes, all interacting with each other. Within five months, however, the group discovered that the solution laid in changing the thickness of the undercoat.

More recently Bombardier has married Six Sigma and Lean Manufacturing to eliminate even more defects and reduce waste through continuous data gathering.

Exercise 6-2: What is the best example you are aware of that demonstrates operational excellence?

What are three steps you could recommend to improve operational excellence where you work or in an organization that you volunteer for?

Customer Service

When terrorists tragically turned commercial airliners into incendiary bombs on September 11, 2001, 41 planes, the most planes at any Canadian airport, were diverted to Halifax International Airport. Many of the passengers were taken to Exhibition Park,[19] where mattresses, food and televisions were provided. Since the event was totally unexpected, dinner consisted of hot dogs and hamburgers. However, on the second day of the passengers' unanticipated stay, something totally unexpected happened. Under the direction of Fred MacGillivray, President and CEO of Trade Centre Limited, all the people who were stranded at Exhibition Park were given hotel quality food as if they were attending a convention. The wait staff was even dressed for the occasion wearing black and white serving attire. In addition, the men and women were also wearing their traditional Nova Scotian tartan bow ties and cummerbunds. Fred MacGillivray could have sent out 50 million memos telling the employees at Exhibition Park that they were in the hospitality business. However, it would not have had nearly the effect that this one story had in exemplifying Fred McGillivray's and his staff's commitment to "Down East Hospitality."

Another good example of enhanced customer service at Canada Post is the Canada Post Flat Rate Box for eBay.[20] There was a problem for both buyers and sellers on eBay. As part of the transaction, both the buyer and seller had to know what the price for shipping would be and that meant that the seller would have to box the item they wanted to sell, take it down to the post office, get it weighed and measured and then go home and confirm the shipping price by e-mail. So Canada Post developed the Canada Post Flat Rate Box. The Canada Post Flat Rate Box is a standard box that will hold 90% of the items that Canada Post ships. Canada Post also developed a standard rate for shipping anything in the Canada Post Flat Rate Box. Therefore, both the buyer and the seller can more easily complete their transactions. In the future, Canada Post will offer even better customer service. For example, if you are going to be away from your house when your shipment is scheduled to arrive, you will be able to let Canada Post know via the Internet and your shipment will be delivered to the alternative address specified. All this will provide services well beyond what is offered today.

Examples of cultural excellence can be found in unexpected situations. My son and I went on a cycling vacation in Quebec City, which has 150 kilometers of some of the best and most well maintained cycling paths in the world. We cycled 20 kilometers out to Montmorency Waterfalls, hiked up to the falls, crossed the suspension bridge, had a wonderful lunch on the balcony of the manor house overlooking the falls, climbed back down and cycled back to the small pensione where we were staying.

All in all, it was a perfect day. The only thing that would have made it more perfect for me was a cool refreshing swim. Our pensione was a stone's throw from the world famous castle-like Chateau Frontenac which is a Fairmont Hotel. So I walked over to the hotel, told the receptionist that I was a President's Club member, which is their frequent guest program, and asked if it were possible to use the pool as a non-registered guest. She asked me if I had my President's club card with me and I said no, it was at home. She said that that was not a problem because she would look me up on the computer and issue a temporary card, which she did.

> *For every 1 percent improvement in the service climate, there's a 2 percent increase in revenue.*
> **Daniel Goldman**

I asked what the cost would be to use the pool and she said it was complimentary as I was a President's Club Member. To this day, I can still remember how pleasantly shocked I was and how refreshing my swim was in that wonderful open-air art deco pool. This is more than an example of stellar customer service — this is an example of a living brand – as a member of the President's Club at the Fairmont Hotel you are treated as a first class guest even when you are not an official guest. At the Fairmont Hotels – there are no little things. But excellence in customer service doesn't happen by chance. It must be carefully developed from the ground up as Annette Verschuren stated.

I talk to consumers about how they buy. In fact, I spend as much time with customers as I do with my staff. Yes we use consultants; yes we do assessments as to what the customer service level is. However, I think it is very important to get close to where the action is and really understand it.

To really understand what is happening I go to where I am uncomfortable and I have always done that. In the same way it is easy for me, or for executives to lock themselves in an office, it is also easy to look good by asking questions that you know the answer to. We often learn much more by asking questions that we don't know the answer to. The more leaders stretch themselves into areas outside their comfort zone, the better they become.

The first day I joined Home Depot I met the people at the head office and that afternoon I worked with the cashiers and bagged the product. Now I spend at least one or two days a week in the stores, walking, talking, and working with people. Also one day a quarter, all the people in the Home Support Center – we don't call it a head office – goes out and works for a day in different departments so that we don't lose sight of who we really are. Personally, I love working the lot and helping to put [the customers'] merchandise in their cars, that's when they tell you everything about their experience at Home Depot.

B.M.   *Do you tell them that you are the president of the store?*

A.V.   *Only when I bloody well have to. If one of the associates tells them that the person who just helped them put their purchases in the car was the president of Home Depot Canada, they usually just plain don't believe it. It's much better to get information without people knowing my status; otherwise they filter what they say. And I do that regularly. The great ideas in this company – that's 95% of them – come from the floor. We are 16,000 people who work in the Canadian operations. We will be one of the biggest retailers in Canada very soon, both sales-wise and people-wise. We get very excited about developing ways in which to improve customer service. And I will tell you that the great ideas come from the field.*

Unlike the examples listed above, many organizations only pay lip service to the importance of customer service and underestimate its importance. There is actually a logarithm that predicts: "For every 1 percent improvement in the service climate, there's a 2 percent increase in revenue."[21] To help you get a better sense of the culture of customer service at your organization, try the following exercise.

Exercise 6-3: If you had to tell one story that best illustrated the exemplary positive culture of customer service at your organization, what story would you choose? Briefly describe the story below.

If you had to tell one story that exemplified the worst aspect of customer service at your organization, what story would you choose? Briefly describe the story below.

Just like Exhibition Park or Fairmont Hotels how could you improve the culture of customer service at your organization?

Has your organization's culture affected you for the better?

Has your organization's culture affected you for the worse?

Inclusion

Cultures of excellence have to be inclusive both in regard to utilizing their own resources to the fullest and in appealing to their ever increasingly diversified customer base both domestically and internationally.

Most people think that ROI stands for Return on Investment. However, Brian Warren, President and CEO of Kidsfest, an organization that is dedicated to helping underprivileged children, has a very different definition of ROI. For Brian, ROI stands for Return on Inclusiveness. Brian Warren is not alone. For the first time in its history, when IBM was in serious difficulty, it hired Lou Gerstner, an outsider, to become President and CEO. Gerstner knew that the direction and culture of IBM had to change if it were to survive in the new technological age. The direction of the company changed from silos where divisions competed against each other, both internally and externally, to starting to act as one company with an integrated mandate. There were other significant changes to IBM's culture as the following quotation points out.

[Gerstner] introduced many seemingly small changes to IBM's corporate culture that in the end had a huge impact. He insisted, for example, that all employees at every level of the company be referred to as "colleagues." This policy of "inclusion" was new for a company with such an extensive and rigid hierarchy.[22]

A much more contemporary example of inclusiveness can be found at www. monster.ca, an employment website and click the Diversity and Inclusion message board and then look for the heading Diversity 101. Among the issues listed under diversity on their website are:

Sexism

Homophobia

Ageism

Discrimination against people with disabilities

Sexism. An example that illustrates a cultural change from that of an old boy's network to that of inclusion is illustrated in the following story about Nelson Mandela in Rosabeth Moss Kanter's seminal book *Confidence*:

The message that all races should work together for the good of the whole nation started at the top and was embodied in Mandela's choice of colleagues. Indeed, Mandela demonstrated this belief soon after his release from prison. On May 2, 1990, Mandela met President de Klerk at de Klerk's residence near Cape Town, each accompanied by an eleven-person delegation. While de Klerk brought an all-male, all-Afrikaner team, Mandela's group included two whites, one Indian, one colored, and seven [black South] Africans, with two women among them[23].

Mandela's enlightened approach aside; there is still a great deal of work that needs to be done. Only two-percent of CEOs of corporations in Canada are women, only about 20 percent of the seats in Canada's legislatures are women. The following statistics shed even more light of the lack of inclusiveness when it comes to gender. The percentage of fulltime female faculty is 29% and their average earnings in 2003 equaled 85.5% of their male colleagues. The percentage of women university presidents was 13.7% and female university presidents' average compensation as a percentage of their male counterparts was 91.6%.

There is no question that with the upcoming war for talent and the fact that women now equal 66% of university graduates, that these statistics should start changing. The only question is how long will it take.[24]

Homophobia. A recent example of inclusiveness is the Canadian Armed Forces. For the first time ever, gay, lesbian and transgender members of the Canadian Armed Forces marched in uniform in the 2008 Gay Pride Parade in Toronto. Even more interesting is the fact that the Canadian Armed Forces set up a recruiting station at the parade. The message was loud and clear. The Canadian Armed Forces is inclusive and is open to recruiting the best talent possible regardless of race, colour or sexual orientation. You can contrast this with the American military's policy of "Don't ask, don't tell." The Canadian Armed Forces has reached a new level on inclusiveness and will be better prepared for the upcoming war on talent because of it. And the Canadian Armed Forces are not alone. Canadian businesses are also being ranked, both formally and informally, as to how inclusive they are.[25]

Ageism. Ageism is a factor in today's workplace now that forcing people to retire at age 65 has been legislated to be discriminatory for many occupations. Among the issues that are and need to be addressed are the impact of older workers choosing to work long past traditional retirement, and how to help aging baby boomers and Generation "X" and "Y," also known as the Millennials, better understand and work with each other.

Increased awareness of what older workers have contributed and can contribute is also critical. Alex Comfort wrote *A Good Age*; what is most remarkable about his book is that it is illustrated with older workers – each of whom made their greatest contribution in their careers – after age 65. Among the people who made their greatest accomplishments later in life are Margaret Mead, Albert Switzer, and Nelson Mandela. Even more telling is the fact that Grandma Moses didn't start painting until she was in her mid-seventies and painted 25 pictures in the last year of her life – at 101.

Discrimination against people with disabilities. Another area where there is more work to do is in including workers with visible and invisible disabilities. A visible disability that is easy to recognize is a person in a wheelchair. An example of an invisible disability could be a person with a learning disability, such as dyslexia or a progressive degenerative disease such as MS. Both sides of the question of how to best help workers who have disabilities and learn how to profit from their talents will benefit from the articles on monster.ca and the references that are provided to break down barriers vis-à-vis inclusiveness in each of these four areas.

A unique idea to increase inclusiveness is National Chief Phil Fontaine, suggestion that:

> *Every university student who is pursing a degree must take a native studies course as a mandatory requirement before a university degree is awarded. That would be so incredibly helpful in transforming this country because right now you have to take a science course, what should be mandatory is a native studies course.*

In fact, his suggestion might be even more effective if native studies were part of the elementary school curriculum to influence children before stereotypes are formed with more in-dept coverage of native culture and issues as these students progress in their education. This is important for many reasons, not the least is that the native population is growing six times faster than the non-native population and this is happening as the number of people retiring from the workforce will be greater than the number of people entering the workforce. [26]

So it looks like Brian Warren is correct – ROI does stand for Return on Inclusiveness – and it is not so different from Return on Investment after all, as the following example points out. A study was done on the number of suggestions employees made per worker and the percent of those suggestions that were adopted. The study attests, the employees whose ideas were welcomed and implemented had a higher ROI in both inclusion and investment.

Company	Number of Adopted Suggestions	Per Worker	Percent
Toyota	27	1	80
Canon	50	1	80
Fugi	80	1	80
GM	1	40	20

Exercise 6-4: Is the culture in your organization inclusive enough?

Are there ways that you could help make the culture in your team or organization more inclusive? If yes, what would you do? What resources do you need? Who else needs to be involved?

Social Responsibility and Environmental Sustainability

[C]customers will make a purchase decision based not just on what you sell, but on what you stand for.[27]

— Roy Spence

With talent in short supply, employers' CSR [corporate social responsibility] reputations are an important tool to attract and retain employees. Companies are also recognizing that they are being held mutually accountable, along with the public sector, for the socioenomic well-being of the regions in which they operate.[28]

— The Enterprise of the Future

Social responsibility, environmental protection and economic growth do not have to be at odds. In fact two Canadian institutions that are leading the way in being both environmentally and organizationally sustainable are VanCity Savings and Loans and Mountain Equipment Co-op because corporate social responsibility is an integral part of their cultures.

I remember walking down Robinson Street in Vancouver in May, 2007 when a sign in the window of one of VanCity's branch offices caught my eye. The sign said that VanCity would be carbon neutral by 2010. VanCity also offers "Clean Air Auto Loans." Clean Air Auto Loans are car loans at lower rates if the borrower is purchasing a low CO_2 low emission vehicle. Currently VanCity lets you borrow at prime if you are buying Tier 1 vehicles such as the Toyota Prius, the Honda Civic Hybrid and the Smartcar. If you are buying a Tier 2 vehicle, such as the Hyundai Accent, Kia Rio, Toyota's Corolla and Yaris, the Ford Escape hybrid and Volkswagen diesel-equipped models – those that emit significantly less CO_2 but are not as fuel efficient as the Tier 1 cars – the loan is pegged at prime plus one.

Another Canadian organization at the forefront of social and environmental sustainability is Mountain Equipment Co-op, more affectionately known as MEC. I was very fortunate to be able to hear Peter Robinson speak in his last public appearance as President and CEO of MEC just before he became the President and CEO of the David Suzuki Foundation. Peter concluded his presentation by saying:

> *The bottom line is that MEC believes strongly that being concerned about the environment and being in business do not have to be at odds. For example, we have a vice-president of sustainability, but we don't want the responsibility for sustainability to reside with one person. Therefore, sustainability is part of everyone's job description. And not only is it a part of their job description, each manager has sustainability targets written into his or her yearly objective and merit increases are also based on hitting those sustainability targets. For example, in Calgary, we buy a part of our electricity from wind power, which is sustainable, not from fossil fuels, which is not unsustainable, even though it is more expensive in the short-term, it is a better investment in the long-term. I should point out however; in most cases we save money by going green.*
>
> *Sustainability is part of the fabric of who we are. It is embedded in our culture, our DNA and it is good business as well as good environmental practice. In Calgary where the labour market is extremely tight, MEC has a long list of job applicants.*

B.M.   *In the Scandinavian countries, business and government are working together to help prevent climate change. Unfortunately the current government in Canada is dragging its feet on climate change.*

P.R.   *That may be true at the federal level, but we are making some significant progress at the municipal level. Cities and states in the US have signed onto the Kyoto accord. Also three of our biggest provinces, British Columbia, Ontario and Quebec have signed onto Kyoto. At this point we need to apply more pressure at the federal level and that pressure has to start from the ground up.*

We just completed a project where we were looking ten years into the future. The project started in 2006 and it was called The Futures Project 2016. We looked at how [MEC] . . . should evolve in 2016 and then developed three long-term goals that were congruent with that vision:

1) *Increase participation in outdoor recreation in Canada*
2) *Create and protect wilderness areas, parks and outdoor recreation areas*
3) *Change the market place to increase economic and environmental sustainability*

In other words, we will be a leader in the emerging green market. Making a profit is like breathing, you have to do it to stay alive, but it is not a reason for living. We are the healthiest and wealthiest generation of Canadians ever, and this has led to short-term thinking, but short-term thinking is the riskiest risk of all.

Going green is a competitive advantage when it comes to recruitment and employee retention. A recent survey by monster.ca found that 80% of the people it surveyed stated that they would, "leave their current employer for greener pastures." Developing and/or enhancing your company's culture of being green and environmentally friendly is smart as it "will pay off in terms of recruiting and retaining employees." Likewise, Tim Sanders, who is Yahoo! chief solutions officer and author of the book *How to Save the World at Work* states:

> Businesses will be forced to embrace corporate social responsibility (CSR) by their younger employees who have been raised to understand that their survival relies on the kindness of strangers.

Sanders says companies that do not fully participate in the Responsibility Revolution risk significant disruption in ways not seen since the U.S. Quality Revolution of the 1970s and 1980s. By 2010, there will be a war for talent, and only the cleanest companies will attract the employees necessary to succeed.[29]

It is not just businesses and organizations that are going green — so are associations and conferences. The following results are from a Meeting Professionals International (MPI) survey entitled "Corporate Social Responsibility: Where We Stand." [30]

> ➤ Eighty percent of respondents agreed or strongly agreed that the industry has a moral obligation to practice CSR

> ➢ Seventy-one percent of respondents agreed or strongly agreed that CSR is important to the meetings industry because the industry is very dependent on environment and society

> ➢ Eighty-six percent of respondents agreed or strongly agreed that more organizations will practice CSR in the future

> ➢ Seventy-four percent of respondents indicated that the biggest driver for CSR in their organization is their leadership

> ➢ Only twenty percent of respondents indicated they were participating in transformational CSR activities

> ➢ Respondents identified that the development of a CSR trends and best practices library was most vital to their success with CSR initiatives; a close second was the creation of online tool boxes and CSR measurement tools

There is clear evidence that our current environmental practices are not sustainable and the First Nations proverb had it right, "We do not inherit the Earth from our Ancestors; we borrow it from our Children." Europe has a similar standard of living and population size to North America, yet through conservation, their oil consumption is half the amount of North America. Master Leaders also see this as an opportunity while their less masterful counterparts deny that there is a problem or that we should do anything about it. Canada is a world leader in many areas, however in the area of environmental sustainability we have yet to fully "step up the plate." One person who is working tirelessly to help North America become more environmentally sustainable is Jim Reid.

Jim Reid was a prominent businessman in the UK. As faith would have it, he was flying to North America from the UK on September 11, 2001 and his plane was diverted to Halifax. He ended up staying with friends in Bridgewater, Nova Scotia and in the process fell in love with that part of the world. Three years later he started Green Solutions North America Inc. (GSNAI). Jim says that 98% of the materials that goes into landfills was never designed for that purpose. Also, a great deal of the material that goes into landfills can be re-purposed. Two of his programs are "Schools in a Box" and "Doctors in a Box" which supply school and medical furniture and ancillary supplies where they are most needed in the third world. One of the best examples is a school in the Atlas Mountains of Morocco. That school now has a full set of furniture and computers for its students. However, the students have to pay one cent to use the computers for an hour. Of course, the students have no money. And here is the great part. The students get to use a computer for an hour if they bring in one kilo of garbage from the village. The net result is that it raises the students' self-esteem and they now live in a much cleaner village.

Green Solutions currently has offices in Nova Scotia, Toronto and Calgary in Canada, and Minneapolis in the US. GSNAI plans to open offices in Montreal and Vancouver. Recently, Jim met with an official in Veterans' Affairs and they have 38 warehouses full of old furniture that would go into landfills and Jim is going to work with them to divert it to where it can be used for good. An added bonus is that when the furniture and equipment are transported in shipping containers they can be reused/repurposed to permanently alter the lives of people in the communities they are sent to. At the same time, many organizations would like to balance their environmental and social strategies within a corporate social responsibility (CSR) framework; however they do not have a processes in place to easily carry this out. Jim founded GSNAI to do just that – help companies do the right thing by providing an environmentally sensitive and socially responsible solution to dispose of corporate assets, thereby "turning policy into process."

Exercise 6-5: Where do you and your organization stand on Corporate Social Responsibility?

What could you and your organization do to increase CSR?

Does your organization have any policies or programs in place on "Going Green?"

What could you and your organization do to establish or increase an existing green initiative?

Harvard's Rosabeth Moss Kanter is one of the most respected experts on leadership and organizations. In her book, *Confidence: How Winning Streaks & Losing Streaks Begin & End*, she states, "getting good habits in place takes a lot longer than eliminating bad practices; it takes the long march of culture change in which many individuals change their behavior in order to head in the same direction."[31]

Most leaders do not pay enough attention to developing a culture that will help their organizations grow and succeed long after that particular leader has retired or moved on. In this strategy we looked at how the Master Leaders I interviewed developed seven different types of cultures and/or combinations thereof. I also challenged you to look at the type of culture you are building as a leader. By doing so you will gain in-depth insight into what is working in your organization's culture and will be able to make recommendations to improve it. In the next strategy we will look at how Master Leaders transform their competencies into mastery.

STRATEGY 7

Transform Competence to Mastery

Three samurai warriors seated in an inn noticed a lone swordsman as he entered. They immediately determined that they were going to take away his magnificent swords. They felt that this would not be a problem, knowing that they could overcome him by sheer numbers. They conspired to goad him into a fight. He sat at a table and ordered food. As the lone swordsman started to eat with his chopsticks, several flies flew around him. He took the chopsticks and caught the four flies on the wing with four quick movements. He then laid down the chopsticks. On seeing this, the three other samurai left the room. Object lesson: People who have attained mastery of an art reveal it in their every action.[1]

—Robert Frager

The Master Leaders I interviewed for this book developed themselves, but this was not development as we normally think about it. The type of development I observed was transformational: from competence to mastery. Competence is defined as having skills that are very well developed. Mastery means having skills that are developed to the highest level possible and being able to use the right skill or right combination of skills in the right place and at the right time.

Master Leaders move from competency to mastery by:

> ➤ setting tipping point goals

> ➤ translating their tipping point goals into doable activities

> ➤ making higher-order commitments

> ➤ taking advantage of compound learning

> ➤ committing to life-long organizational growth

Tipping Point Goals

Malcolm Gladwell's best-selling book, *The Tipping Point*,[2] demonstrated in case after case how one goal, which I call a tipping point goal, can make an even larger difference by starting a positive domino effect. Let me give an example of the power of tipping point goals.

Heather Reisman is the President and CEO of Indigo/Chapters. Indigo and Chapters were bitter rivals, each of which was working to have the biggest presence in the big box bookstores in Canada — that is until Indigo took over Chapters in 2001. At the time of this writing Indigo/Chapters has 200 bookstores in Canada and accounts for an astounding 65% of book sales in Canada.

Heather strongly believes that leaders have a moral responsibility to help make their communities, countries and the world a better place. And like all of the other Master Leaders you have met in this book, she has a detailed and specific plan to do so. Her plan is to infuse 17 billion dollars into the Canadian economy. How does she plan to do it? By decreasing the level of illiteracy among adults. Statistics Canada estimates that 42% of Canada's adult population is functionally illiterate. Decreasing that number by just 1% would add $17 billion to Canada's economy.

Twenty years from now you will be more disappointed by the things you didn't do than by the ones you did do.
Mark Twain

For example, 80% of the adults in Canada's prisons are functionally illiterate. This represents a group that is one of the biggest drains on our country's resources. On the other hand, any prisoner in Japan who is in prison for a year or more, has to learn to read before they are released. This very well could be why Japan has one of the lowest recidivism rates in the world. The recidivism rate is the number of people who leave prison and subsequently return.

For many of us, literacy starts at kindergarten and what we have done is robbed our schools of books. In the 1970's, the typical public school got three new books per child per year. Therefore if a school had 200 children, 600 books would be added each year. The current rate is less than one-third of a book per child. Therefore if there are 200 children in a school, only 67 books are added per year which translates into an 89% decrease. In many cases our school libraries are dying.

In middle and upper income areas, parents are raising money to put books back into libraries, sadly this is not and can not be the same in lower-class areas. To help rectify the imbalance, Heather has established the Indigo Love of Reading Foundation and has visited over 700 school libraries. She is currently fundraising from both the public and private sectors to put more books in our libraries. Every year the Indigo Love of Reading Foundation gives $150,000 to 10 schools across Canada for their school libraries.

The bottom line for Heather, is that by increasing adult literacy, we will start to achieve multiple goals simultaneously. We will have a better educated and therefore more competitive workforce, we will have fewer people in prisons and a larger number of those coming out of prison will be able to find jobs and thus be less likely to return to prison. In addition, a well informed population is a healthier population and our school libraries will be able to serve their schools better. If this is not a stellar example of bold and innovative thinking that is also a tipping point goal, then I don't know what is. You can learn more about these efforts by looking at a documentary entitled, "Writing on the Wall" at www.loveofreading.org.

Once I understood the concept of tipping point goals, I began to think about how they applied to the other Master Leaders in this book. For example:

> When Hazel McCallion first became mayor of Mississauga,
> it was a bedroom community of Toronto. Mayor McCallion
> wanted Mississauga to have its own economic engines and

she wanted the city to be run like a business, so it could be the master of its own destiny. Today Mississauga is home to 79 Fortune 500 head offices in Canada, has no debt and $700 million in reserves.

Peter Robinson wanted MEC to be both economically and environmentally sustainable, while promoting the enjoyment of outdoor recreation at the same time.

Craig and Marc Kielburger wanted to develop a world-wide network of children helping children and at the same time help to develop the leadership capacity of youth.

I also began to think about how I could develop my own tipping point goals. In 2007, I had the pleasure of hearing Pat Voss speak at the national CAMX conference[3] in St. John's, Newfoundland and Pat changed the way I see the world and my role in it. Pat quoted a study by the Conference Board of Canada that said that by the year 2031, we will have 23 people available to do the work that 50 people do today. Pat further commented that we will only be able to accomplish this with the increased use of technology and self-service. I thought about these observations for a long time. I began to realize that the transfer of learning from my teaching wasn't as good as I had thought or had hoped it would be. Students in my advanced negotiation courses did not retain as much from the basic negotiation course as I had hoped in spite of everyone's best intentions. Therefore, my goal was to use technology and self-service to increase transfer of learning from the courses I taught.

> **Great things are not done by impulse, but by a series of small things brought together.**
> **Vincent Van Gogh**

I discussed my dilemma with my friend and colleague Tim Paulsen. We subsequently developed the Master Negotiator's Digital Coach, which can be installed on our participants' computers. The Digital Coach makes it much easier and more convenient for the user to fill in the Master Negotiator's Preparation Form, get salient feedback from friends and colleagues, archive records of their negotiations, and keep track of their progress. The Digital Coach became a tipping point goal when we realized that it changed multiple aspects of our training. The Digital Coach takes advantage of the multiple ways in which people learn, how they remember and retain what they learned. It also provides us with another way to measure what has been learned.

This example may help to clarify the difference between a goal and a tipping point goal. Sometimes, we are able to realize right away that we have set a tipping point goal. However, more commonly, we set a goal and only realize afterwards, when we see the deeper implications from achieving that goal, that we have actually set and/or the original goal transforms itself into a tipping point goal. When we first developed the Digital Coach we had only one goal in mind — to increase transfer of learning. Now we realize that we can take advantage of different learning styles and better measure the results from the negotiation training, but also in other courses that we give and our colleagues provide.

What these stories point out is that sometimes we can set tipping point goals consciously. At other times, we only realize in retrospect that we set a tipping point goal. However, much like the Master Leaders I profiled in this book, once you understand the concept of tipping point goals, you will be much more likely to set them deliberately.

Exercise 7-1: Your Tipping Point Goals

In the space below, please list up to three tipping point goals you want to set for yourself and/or for your organization. You may want to list your goals on a separate sheet and then see if any of them are or could be turned into tipping point goals. In addition, you may want to discuss setting tipping point goals with a trusted friend or advisor. You might also want to think back on some of the goals you have accomplished and see if any of those goals were in fact tipping point goals. It might help to remember that tipping point goals results in multiple accomplishments.

1. Tipping Point Goal Number One:

2. Tipping Point Goal Number Two:

3. Tipping Point Goal Number Three:

Translating Tipping Point Goals into Doable Activities

Identifying your tipping point goals, no matter how clear and desirable they are, is not enough. To transform your "tipping point goals" into "tipping point actions", you need to list the benefits that would accrue to you from achieving these goals. Next, break your goals into doable activities. For an activity to be doable, it must pass the "Yes-No test". The Yes-No test states that the activity must be defined so specifically that you can easily say "Yes I did it" or "No I did not". For example, working on a funding proposal does not pass the Yes-No test. Working on the funding proposal Saturday and Sunday mornings between 8:00 a.m. and 11:30 a.m. does pass the Yes-No test.

> *It is a paradoxical but profoundly true and important principle of life that the most likely way to reach a goal is to be aiming not at that goal itself but at some more ambitious goal beyond it.*
> **Russell Baker**

Exercise 7-2:

Activities List for Tipping Point Goal 1

Goal: _____

_____

_____

Benefit: _____

_____

_____

Activities: _____

_____

_____

_____

_____

_____

_____

_____

_____

_____

_____

_____

_____

_____

_____

_____

Activities List for Tipping Point Goal 2

Goal: _____

_____

_____

Benefit: _____

_____

_____

Activities: _____

_____

_____

_____

_____

_____

_____

_____

_____

_____

_____

_____

_____

_____

Activities List for Tipping Point Goal 3

Goal: _____

_____

_____

_____

Benefit: _____

_____

_____

_____

Activities: _____

_____

_____

_____

_____

_____

_____

_____

_____

_____

_____

_____

_____

_____

Now that you have identified your tipping point goals, realized the benefits of accomplishing them and developed your list of activities to accomplish them, you will need to ask yourself how committed you are to performing the necessary tasks.

Making Higher-Order Commitments

McClelland's research on the psychology of high achievers demonstrated that high achievers:

➢ want more

➢ expect more

➢ do more

➢ get more

The following story illustrates the value of effort and commitment.

THE 212ᵗʰ DEGREE

At 211 degrees [Fahrenheit], water is just hot water — inert — powerless.

At 212 degrees, water is live steam, with more power inherent within it than man has ever been able to harness with true and full efficiency, even with all his knowledge and skill.

At 211 degrees, the water in a locomotive boiler exerts not one ounce of pressure.

At 212 degrees, the water in a locomotive boiler gives it the power to haul a mile-long train of cars across a mountain pass.

At 211 degrees, the locomotive is as powerless as if the firebox were empty and cold; at 212 degrees; it has the power to pull a mile-long train of cars rattling along the right of way at 70 miles per hour.

Most people today are walking around at 211 degrees who, for the want of one more degree of temperature, are relatively powerless, and far less effective than they should be. Many people are walking around at 211 degrees who, if they would but throw another log on the fire, another lump of coal could raise their temperature to 212 degrees, and increase their power to infinity.

That one last degree out of 212 degrees seems insignificant by itself, yet it is one of incomparable importance. The person who will never lift his temperature to the boiling point may never achieve anything worthwhile in this world. He who can and will keep his temperature above 212 degrees and who can and will keep his boiler at full steam by using the fire of enthusiasm and with a desire can achieve anything in this world to which he may reasonably aspire.

– Author Unknown

The story of the 212th degree can be applied to your tipping point goals, in that one extra degree of effort and/or commitment could make the difference between you achieving them or not. A very good way to look at your level of commitment is through the three levels of commitment:

> ➢ Intellectual,

> ➢ Irregular, or

> ➢ True Commitment.

At the intellectual level, a positive attitude exists towards doing a certain activity, but the intention is not translated into behaviour. For example, you want to exercise to get into better shape, but you just have too much to do right now to start. At the irregular level, people work on their goals sporadically. At this level of commitment, you go to the gym every other week, which is not enough to get much of the benefit from exercising, and you might actually be doing more harm than good. At the level of true commitment, you overcome all obstacles in order to accomplish your goals. In fact, you transform obstacles into opportunities to problem-solve and use your creativity. In the exercise example, you exercise with a "buddy" or you get up a half an hour early three days a week and work out on your exercise bike for 20 minutes to half an hour before you allow yourself to have that first cup of morning coffee.

An example of true commitment is Bombardier's July, 2008 decision to produce the new C Series regional jet. At the time this decision was made, almost all of the world's airlines were losing massive amounts of money because the price of jet fuel had doubled. On the surface this would seem to be the worst time to invest in building a new multi-million dollar plane. Bombardier, on the contrary, thought it was the best time because they would build the new C Series with lighter composite materials and with a newly designed more fuel efficient jet engine that will lower fuel consumption by 20%.

Not only is this a very difficult time for the airlines, there is intense competition from Bombardier's fierce rival Embraer of Brazil, and the Chinese and Japanese also have their eyes on this market as well. In fact, this could be a make or break the company decision according to Bombardier's president, Pierre Beaudoin.

Which level of commitment best reflects your own behaviour in relation to the Tipping Point Goals you set?

Intellectual

Irregular

True Commitment

Next to each activity you listed above for Tipping Point Goal Numbers 1, 2 and 3, go back and write in the margin, the estimated percentage likelihood from 0 to 99%, that you will actually complete each activity. Because half-hearted commitments are always counterproductive, if your commitment level is under 80% you are at risk of not completing that activity. If you do not honour your commitments your self-esteem diminishes and when your self-esteem diminishes you don't manage your time as well as you could or should. When our self-esteem is higher we tend to manage time more effectively.

I am not saying that we have to do *everything* we commit to, that would be as foolish as not keeping our commitments. What we need to do is be more careful about managing our commitments because our commitments determine what we get done. And what we get done in turn affects our self-esteem which in turn influences what we chose to do, how committed we are, and if we ultimately accomplish our goals which in turn help to raise our self-esteem – thereby creating a virtuous circle which keeps spiraling up.

If your level of commitment for any particular activity is below 80% you should consider not doing it, doing it at a later time, or breaking that activity into smaller doable steps to the point where your level of commitment increases to 80% or more. If you still are having difficulty or find yourself resisting, talk your tipping point goal(s) over with a trusted friend and/or advisor. It may not be the right tipping point goal or it might be the right goal but the wrong time.

Compound Learning

A stellar example of a Master Leader who applied compound learning to achieve her tipping point goals is Mayor Hazel McCallion who is the oldest person I interviewed for this book. At the time of the interview, Mayor McCallion was 87 years old, had been the mayor of Mississauga for 30 years and was in the middle of her 10th term as Mayor. When her current term as Mayor expires in 2010, she will be 89. She hasn't made up her mind if she will re-offer or not. Mayor McCallion's moniker is Hurricane Hazel because she is always on the move. As a role-model, I don't think I could have found a better example of a life-long learner. She is an inspiration to all of us to keep learning, living and contributing for as long as we choose to.

An example of how Mayor McCallion used compound learning was in setting the tipping point goal of developing bio-technology as an economic engine for the City of Mississauga. First she recruited one, then two, then a third biotechnology firm to locate in Mississauga. Over time she learned how to become a better and better salesperson for the City of Mississauga.

Once the infrastructure was in place so that developers could get their applications approved and build the buildings with the help, not the hindrance, of city hall, she then approached the University of Toronto to offer the only master's degree in Bio-Technology in Mississauga. Of course, all of the bio-technology firms need vendors and supplies close by, and as Mississauga's chief salesperson, Mayor McCallion helped to recruit them to Mississauga as well — and she not only recruited companies in North America to locate in Mississauga — she recruited internationally.

One of the secrets to Mayor McCallion's success and to the success of all of the Master Leaders I interviewed for this book is the power of compound growth through compound learning as the following example by Harvard's John Kotter points out.[4]

> Between age thirty and fifty, Fran "grows" at the rate of 6 percent — that is, every year she expands her career-relevant skills and knowledge by 6 percent. Her twin sister, Janice, has exactly the same intelligence, skills, and information at age thirty, but during the next twenty years she grows at only 1 percent per year. Perhaps Janice becomes smug and complacent after early successes. Or maybe Fran has some experience that sets a fire underneath her. The question here is, how much difference will this relatively small learning differential make by age fifty?

> Given the facts about Fran and Janice, it's clear that the former will be able to do more at age fifty than the latter. But most of us underestimate how much more capable Fran will become. The confusion surrounds the effect of compounding. Just as we often don't realize the difference over twenty years between a bank account earning 7 percent versus 4 percent, we regularly underestimate the effects of learning differentials.

> For Fran and Janice, the difference between a 6 percent and a 1
> percent growth rate over twenty years is huge. If they each have
> 100 units of career-related capability at age thirty, twenty years
> later, Janice will have 122 units, while Fran will have 321. Peers
> at age 30, the two will be in totally different leagues at age 50.

What accounts for the amazing difference between Fran and Janice? Was Fran just more lucky in finding a career that was a better fit than Janice? Did Fran find her true passion while Janice didn't? The difference can be better accounted for by examining the research McClelland completed on high achievers. McClelland found that high achievers most differed from their less successful counterparts in four important areas: high achievers wanted more, but wanting more was not enough, they expected more, but expecting more wasn't enough either, they did more; and because they wanted more, expected more, and did more – they got more. They used their vision and passion to inspire others to want, expect, do and get more. And, as we've seen from the Master Leaders profiled in this book, it didn't matter if that goal was in the private sector such as Kevin Hamm or the public sector such as Mayor Hazel McCallion or the volunteer sector such as Rick Hansen.

The Master Leaders we met in this book believed deeply that their opportunities and methods for learning have never been greater – in fact, we can easily say that they believed that, "The World is their Classroom." Often the addition of one piece of critical information, critical learning or the application of that information/learning made the difference between their achieving and not achieving their tipping point goals. Seven sources of knowledge that you can leverage to help you achieve your tipping point goals are:

- Mentors and Coaches
- Mastermind Groups
- Interviews
- Conferences and Courses
- Print Media, Audio/Video Resources, and the Internet
- 360 Degree Feedback
- Developmental or Special Assignments

Mentors and Coaches

To help them move from competence to mastery, most of the Master Leaders I interviewed use of outside resources such as mentors and coaches. Both mentoring and coaching involve a one-on-one relationship. However, mentors are usually in more senior positions in an organization who help the people they mentor. They assist in skill and strategy development and can help in analyzing the way things get accomplished in an organization. The other major difference is that there is no fee for the services of a mentor and the mentoring process is more informal than the coaching process. Sometimes organizations set up formal mentoring programs; however, most often the mentoring relationship is initiated by one party or the other. Often finding the right mentor rests on both parties finding the mentoring relationship mutually advantageous.

Coaching, on the other hand, is a more formal process, which typically has more clearly defined goals. The coach may be paid either by the individual or by the organization. Coaching may focus more on a specific skill such as a presentations coach, or on integrating several skills. In her incisive book entitled *Coached to Lead,*[5] Susan Battley states:

[C]oaching helps the best get better. At championship levels, even small incremental gains in performance can have a profound effect on the result, often being the difference between winner and runner-up, between capturing the gold medal or the bronze.

Research from the Centre of Creative Leadership in Greensboro, North Carolina reveals that 35% of leaders "derail." This means that at some point their career comes off the "tracks". This can result in a person being fired, demoted, or put into a position where his or her career stagnates with little or no opportunity for future advancement. There are many causes of derailment. As one moves up the hierarchy, different skills are required and sometimes what was once considered a strength, becomes a liability. The person lacks tact/diplomacy, micro-manages, over relies on a mentor, is not politically astute, or lacks specific skills, interpersonal or otherwise, to be successful when they move up a level in the organization.

An excellent way to help prevent career derailment is coaching. It has proven to be very effective in helping leaders at all levels learn from their experiences – both good and bad. In addition, research shows that when participants receive coaching after a training session, the training session is 80% more effective[6].

Therefore, the decision to hire a coach and to make sure that the fit between the coach and the person being coached has never been more important.

Another potential problem is that the further you move up the professional hierarchy, the less likely you are to get feedback — this phenomenon of being isolated from the feedback even has a name — the CEO Disease. Often by the time the person receives feedback, the damage is done and it is too late. This is an expensive way to learn — expensive both for the individual who is let go and for the organization that has invested so much time and resources hiring and training the person in question. [7]

An example of how coaching helped to lead to stellar results in the sports world is Elvis Stojko. Elvis won silver medals in men's figure skating at the 1988 and 1994 Winter Olympics. He also won three World Figure Skating Championships and seven Canadian Championships. At the 1991 World Championships, Elvis became the first person to land a quadruple-double jump combination (a jump with four revolutions followed by a jump with two revolutions). In the 1997 Grand Prix finals, Elvis again made history by being the first skater ever to land a quadruple-triple combination. [8]

I interviewed Doug Leigh, [9] Elvis Stojko's coach throughout his stellar career, and asked him how long it took Elvis to learn how to do the quadruple triple jump combination. His answer was:

> Basically a lifetime. Part of the process is training the muscles and memory system until you get the blue print in your mind so you can do it on automatic pilot. At the same time you had to have developed amazing edges and astounding strength to do the jump. Another critical part of the process is developing incredible patience and determination. It takes a very special mind set. In other words, he had to develop emotionally, physically and mentally. Elvis then started to knock off his goals, one at a time.

Clearly, doing a quadruple jump was a tipping point goal for Elvis. I interviewed Elvis and asked him how coaching was helpful to him. [10]

E.S.   *Basically I started skating when I was 4. I made my first attempt at the quad when I was 14 or 15. The quad was difficult because it takes a lot of power; in fact your power, technique and timing have to be near perfect. There are days when the quad just doesn't work and it is very hard on the body I landed my first quad two years later when I was 17 at the national championship exhibition practice in Sudbury, Ontario.*

B.M.   *How helpful was Doug Leigh's coaching in helping you learn to land the Quad?*

E.S.   *Doug Leigh was great. He is very straightforward. He knows how to train you in being consistent. I had to constantly keep working on my timing. I knew that I would lose my timing even if I took a few days off. I would feel it.*

My secret weapon was Glen Doyle. Glen was my Kung Fu coach and he helped me translate Kung Fu into the sport of skating. He helped me figure out which muscles to work on in order to get that extra power and strength to complete the jump. I met Glen when I was 16 – and all the training on and off ice made the difference.

I also did a lot of video work. I watched the best in the world to get it into my head. I used to watch an average of 2 to 4 hours of video a day – up to 21 hours a week. Most of the time it was videos of my own skating that I watched from practice that day or other days. From time to time, I would compare my technique with the top skaters in the world. Once I saw a difference or things I needed to work on, Glen and I worked on off ice exercises to help certain muscle groups that were needed to perfect or make the jump more consistent.

B.M.   *How hard was it to learn how to do the quad triple-toe loop combination?*

E.S.   *The quad triple was tough. I almost completed it in 1994 and just stepped out of it at the end. I landed it in competition 1997. The quad-triple is difficult because the quad has to be technically perfect – you have to have the speed, balance and power to pull it off.*

It is easy to see the benefits of coaching in the sports world. The interview with Elvis illustrates how he used two coaches and had the self-discipline to watch hours of video tape to become one of the world's preeminent athletes. Coaching and the use of feedback can bring about equally effective results in leadership development.

Exercise 7-3: Have you ever had an experience where a coach helped you develop a skill or strategy in a sport or learning any type of physical activity? If so, please describe briefly how coaching helped you develop.

Coaching isn't just for athletes. An area where I still need help is in learning how to sell my services and products. A colleague offers a three-day intensive sales course that provides exceptionally good feedback. The participants are video taped making a mock sales call at the beginning of the course and they are then again video taped making the same sales call at the end of the class. I learned that even though I am a trained counselor, I talked too much and listened too little. I also learned how to ask powerful questions and have equally powerful answers. To make sure that I didn't slip back into bad habits, we had monthly coaching session for a year. I learned to see sales as a form of problem solving and negotiation and very gradually I became more comfortable with the sales process.

Exercise 7-4: State as specifically as possible the skills, strategies or combination of skills and strategies that you need to develop. Can the skills, strategies or combination of skills and strategies be translated into tipping goals?

How can coaching help you develop these skills and/or strategies?

How can you find the best coach or coaches to help you?

Mastermind Groups

One relatively easy strategy that will help you move from competence to mastery is to work within a buddy system with someone who wants to do the same thing. The buddy process is based on the psychological process of making a *commitment* to another person. For example, Jerri is more likely to engage in a new behaviour if she has previously (and publicly) promised Merrilee that she will do so. In return, according to social norm of reciprocity, Merrilee will feel an obligation not only to support Jerri in her efforts to apply what she has learned but also to make her own commitment to change. Both buddies can work on developing the same leadership skills and/or different skills. Mastermind groups and the buddy system can be especially helpful when you are trying to achieve a tipping point goal, because by their very nature tipping point goals can be hard to achieve.

> *We have plenty of men and women who can teach what they know; we have very few who can teach their own capacity to learn.*
> **Joseph Hart**

I vividly remember the second car I bought. It was a 1967 green Volkswagen Beetle. One of the reasons I remember that car so well is that I had it for 10 years and drove it on some of my most memorable trips. However, one of the things that surprised me about the car, was that once I bought it, I couldn't believe how many other VW Beetles I saw on the road. It was as if, overnight, the sales of new and used VW bugs increased 10 fold. As you probably have guessed, the sales of Volkswagens *didn't* increase 10-fold overnight – it just seemed like it because as a new VW owner, I became both more aware and more sensitive to the number of Volkswagens that were already on the road. Now what does this have to do with setting tipping point goals and compound learning?

The answer – everything, because once you have determined your tipping point goal, you will become more aware and sensitive to opportunities to learn the very things you need to learn to bring that tipping point goal to fruition. Your chances of achieving your tipping point goals increase when you write them down; alert your friends, colleagues and/or other people in your support network about what you want to accomplish and ask for their support. The difference between a buddy system and a Mastermind group, is that a Mastermind group usually has six to ten members.

Exercise 7-5: If you were going to use the buddy system or a mastermind group to help you achieve your tipping point goal(s), who would you contact, how frequently would you meet?

You also will want to create a developmental plan on how to achieve it, the resources you need to help you achieve it, the obstacles in your way, and a detailed plan to help you achieve it. The next section of this chapter will help you develop the resources, knowledge, and support you will need in order to achieve your tipping point goal(s).

Interviews

The interviews with the Master Leaders for this book not only changed the book, they changed me. I learned to see myself, leadership and the world differently. One of the biggest changes came from my interview with Annette Verschuren. Two of Annette's mantras are: "There is always another path up the mountain," and "The glass is always more than half full." I find that I repeat Annette's mantras to myself at least several times a week. The net result is that I am less stressed, more focused, more resilient and more productive. I am not sure I could have learned this important lesson nearly as well and absolutely not nearly as quickly by any other method.

> *A single conversation across the table with a wise man is worth a month's study of books.*
> **Chinese Proverb**

There are two ways you can use interviews to help accelerate your own learning to be a more effective leader. The first is to pick an area where you would like to further develop your skills and strategies, for example: becoming a more strategic decision maker; creating a stronger culture of customer service; increasing employee loyalty; or learning how to market your vision and values more effectively both inside and outside of your organization. Once you have a clearer sense of the skills and strategies you want to develop, make a list of three to five people you could interview who already have well developed expertise in the area in which you would like to grow and further develop your own skills and strategies.

Exercise 7-6: Think of someone you interviewed in the past, either formally or informally, who you found helpful in learning how to be a more effective leader. Briefly describe what you learned, how you benefited, and how you put what you learned into practice. If you haven't interviewed anybody in the past, you can go on to the next question.

List up to three topics that you would like to develop that will help you be a more masterful leader. After each topic, list the people you could interview or three people who could help you find the best person to interview.

Topic	Topic	Topic
1.	1.	1.
2.	2.	2.
3.	3.	3.

The other way to approach this exercise is to pick three leaders you admire and then list up to three topics on which you would like to interview each of these leaders.

Leader	Leader	Leader
1.	1.	1.
2.	2.	2.
3.	3.	3.

Conferences and Courses

We can learn a great deal from conferences and courses – especially if the content is appropriate for what we need to learn. However, most of us would be better off if we did a better job of implementing what we learned from the conference and/or courses we do attend. Most of us have reams and reams of notes that contain good ideas, and every year we add more notes to the pile, yet never use the information or implement the new ideas. The other mistake we can make is that we attend the same conference over and over again – it's comfortable and we know a lot of people, however, after a while the learning will drop off – just like staying in the same job and doing the same thing year after year. We also know that the learning curve picks up again when we move to a new job – even if that job is at the same level of responsibility.

An excellent way to improve your retention and application is to use the buddy system for conferences and courses.[11] You and a colleague either attend the same or difference sessions/courses and each person then selects one to three things that he or she is going to implement. Then set up weekly meetings, either in person, on the phone or by email to hold each other accountable for implementing those ideas that each person has committed themselves to. Each person in the buddy system will be responsible for making contact on the alternative dates in order to make sure that these crucial follow-ups take place.

An extension of the buddy concept is the formation of the entire group of people who want to enhance their learning into a learning community. This is commonly known as a Mastermind Group.

Exercise 7-7: List one to three ideas from conferences or course that you want to try out. What is your plan for implementing these ideas?

My ideas and plan for implementing them are:

1.

2.

3.

How could you use the buddy system or a mastermind group to improve how you implement the above ideas and other new ideas in the future?

Print Media, Audio/Video Resources, and the Internet

> Not every reader is a leader, but every leader must be a reader.
>
> **– Harry Truman**

> The man who doesn't read good books has no advantage over the man who can't read them.
>
> **– Mark Twain**

> You are the same today you will be in five years, except for two things, the people you meet and the books you read.
>
> **– Charlie Tremendous Jones**

There is a lot of wisdom in these quotations. Reading immediately opens new worlds to us and when we read about the right idea and/or experience at the right time – we benefit greatly from others' thoughts and experiences. But with the onslaught of new information venues and the explosion of information on the Internet, no matter how much we learn there is always *more* to learn. We have had to become increasingly more selective, effective and efficient to maximize our learning opportunities. I have no patience for 250 page books that could have said everything they covered in 50 pages.

Personally, I have become much more selective and focused in what I need to learn. For example, one of the best pieces of marketing advice I learned, I heard on an MP3 file. In this instance, the material I was listening to concerned how to make marketing materials scanable. At the time, I thought "scanable" meant that the material could be easily scanned into an optical scanner – however – scanable meant how to make one's materials short, concise and to the point with lots of white space so the reader can get the gist of what was being said easily and quickly.

There are also benefits in using blended learning. Blended learning means using two or more learning modalities in such a way that they complement each other. An example of blended learning occurred for me when I was consulting with a client and I was helping the client apply some of the concepts in *Good to*

Great. I had read Jim Collins' book *Good to Great* several times, and found his work so interesting I decided to visit Jim Collins' website where I discovered The Good to Great Diagnostic Tool. Before I used the tool with my client, I decided to use the tool to rate how well my business was following the principles from *Good to Great.* My employees also rated our organization, including my leadership style, using The Good to Great Diagnostic Tool. To be truthful, I never had to think about my business or my leadership of my business so intently or so thoroughly in its 25 year history.

On a colleague's recommendation, I also bought the audio CD version of the book. On the four and a half hour drive from Halifax to visit my client, I found that I began to understand some of the material at a deeper level by listening to the audio book *even though* I had already read the book several times. This is because we process information differently when we hear something than when we read it and/or the author emphasizes things differently when he or she reads the material and/or additional information is added in the various formats. In the end, both my own and my client's organization benefited markedly by becoming more systematic about not only what we are doing, but how we are doing it. This is an excellent example of blended learning, that is, written material (books), audio and Internet learning working together to enhance one's knowledge.

To help you save time, I have included valuable resources in Resources from the Masters: An Annotated Bibliography. Each resource contains an annotation so you can more easily determine which resource is the right resource for you at any given time.

You can also find updated references at *www.BradMcRae.com.* If you have any books, movies, podcasts or Internet sites or other references that you think should be added to the list, please send them along to *Brad@BradMcRae.com.*

Exercise 7-8: What are several of the most important things that you have learned about leadership from books, magazines, journals, audio/video resources and/or the Internet?

Do you want to increase what you learn about leadership from book, audio/video or the Internet? If yes, how will you go about it?

360-Degree Feedback

Feedback has a number of potentially beneficial spin-offs for an organization. First . . . it can call attention to important performance dimensions heretofore neglected by an organization, in the process of conveying organizational values. It may also be a useful intervention to enhance two-way communications, increase formal as well as informal communications, build more effective work relationships, increase opportunities for employee involvement, uncover and resolve conflict, and demonstrate respect for employee opinions on the part of top management. Because 360-degree feedback requires an element of reciprocity between managers and raters as sources of feedback, reinforcement, and improved satisfaction of customers, it can provide greater job and employability security because employees who create greater value for customers ultimately create greater value for themselves as employees[12].

– Schneier, Baird and Beatty

Three hundred and sixty degree feedback provides feedback on selected abilities from an employee's supervisor, peers, direct reports and sometimes the clients and/or customers of the person who is being assessed. The employee who is being rated also rates himself or herself on the same characteristics. Research has shown that this type of rating is more accurate and more valuable than single rater feedback or the average ratings from any one source such as a person's peers. Enhanced 360-degree feedback combines the feedback from the multiple raters listed above with feedback from psychological tests, performance reviews, and/or specific tasks or work samples that have been analyzed.

The 360-degree feedback tool developed by the Atlantic Leadership Development Institute is the Leadership/Managerial Evaluation Form (LMEF) found in Appendix A. The LMEF is comprised of 23 items rated on a seven-point scale, plus two additional items to which the respondent answers "yes" or "no"; these 25 items measure critical aspects of leadership/management behaviours. These items make it possible to do a differential diagnosis. For example, one leader/manager may give feedback that is frequent but not specific enough while another leader/manager may give feedback that is specific enough but not frequently enough. Another example would be the leader/manager who would notice if his or her direct reports were putting in 15% less effort but would not notice if his or her direct reports were putting in 15% more effort. In medicine, half of any medical cure is an accurate diagnosis; the LMEF is designed to provide information that is specific enough that a correct diagnosis can be made as to an individual's strengths and on an individual's targets for improvement.

The LMEF finishes with open-ended questions. The last three questions are: how is the leader or manager in question growing the organization's people, the business and the culture. The answers to these three questions give much-needed additional meaning to the ratings on the scaled questions and additional insight into the leader's strengths and areas that need improvement. The open-ended questions also help specify, in behavioural terms, those behaviours that need to change; and they aid in designing a developmental plan for bringing about those changes.

Information from the 360-degree feedback is often more useful and easier to interpret when there is data both from other organizations and/or from other leaders/managers at the same level in the host organization. One strategy is to have all leaders/managers in the organization undergo the same type of developmental appraisal. When this occurs, all of the employees see that everyone is treated equally and that no one has been singled out. We recommend that this procedure be implemented at the senior management level and work its way down in the organization as it will increase employee buy in.

When the LMEF is used on an organization-wide basis, and/or it is given to a particular level of management within an organization, the combined data for all employees undergoing 360-degree feedback can be used as a needs assessment, such as the training, coaching, or mentoring needs or developmental assignments for the individuals who were assessed and/or of a particular department, or level of management, or the organization as a whole.

Each year in Canada, hundreds of millions of dollars in both direct and indirect costs are spent on staff training and development. Much of this money is wasted on courses that staff do not need, and/or on courses that are needed, but that are given at the wrong time. Using an organization's data from 360-degree feedback will insure that the training courses are relevant and that the participants are eager to learn. Knowing that the individual employee's progress in improving those skills will be reassessed in six to twelve months' time also adds incentive to master the skills that are taught.

Although enhanced 360-degree feedback can do a lot to increase a leader's awareness of his or her strengths, weaknesses, or blind spots, awareness by itself does not lead to sustained change. A well-thought-out and thorough developmental plan must be developed conjointly with each person who is undergoing this type of feedback process.

A specific, detailed, results oriented developmental plan is created for each participant that contains SMART [Specific, Measurable, Attainable, Realistic, and Time-Limited] goals. SMART goals are behaviourally defined, that is, goals that have specific measurable targets for change and benchmarks so progress can be measured. Because personal change is almost always difficult, it is highly recommended that anyone undertaking this type of self-change project be supported in his or her efforts by traditional methods such as coaching or through blended learning. Blended learning uses two or more methods such as coaching, mentoring, courses, etc., to support the person who has received the feedback in achieving his or her goals. These multiple sources of feedback and support allow the candidate to compare and contrast the various viewpoints, which increases the candidate's success in changing his or her behaviour.

At the Atlantic Leadership Development Institute, when necessary or desirable, a coaching process known as ICE is implemented. ICE stands for Intensive Coaching Experience. The ICE process was designed for leaders/managers who are at risk. During the ICE process, the leader or manager is assigned three coaches, one external to the organization and two internal. Goals will be set, and the three coaches will work intensely with the participant to help give the leader or manager in question every chance to improve his or her performance. For example, one coach could be the individual's boss or supervisor. The second coach could be selected by the individual from his or her peers. The third coach could be someone from outside the organization who is known for his or her specialized abilities in the area(s) where the person in question needs to develop. Having three people act in this coaching/mentoring capacity gives a broad enough perspective to look at the problem behaviour(s) and the possible solution(s).

The best way to test for changes/improvements in the individual being assessed is to re-administer the 360-degree feedback instrument in six to twelve months' time. The time period chosen should be enough time for the individual to effectively carry out their developmental plan, but not so long that the candidate feels they will never receive closure regarding their progress, or so long that the organization has to unnecessarily delay important decisions regarding the candidate's position.

Developmental Assignments

> The simplest ... way to provide continuous stimulation and challenge is to keep moving through different assignments that demand different skills. [Hall] calls this the Mae West rule. Mae West was a sex symbol in the early film era who said, "When choosing between two evils, I prefer the one I haven't tried yet."[13]
>
> — Brad Harrington and Douglas Hall

A developmental assignment is an assignment whereby the person working on a task or project has to develop his or her skills to a higher level and/or develop new skills in order to successfully complete the assignment. Examples of developmental assignments are implementing a program or procedure, opening/ staffing a new office, working through a merger or acquisition, heading up a charity campaign, running a volunteer organization and/or working in a foreign country.

Not all learning assignments are created equal. When we look back over our career, there are always one or two assignments, often very difficult assignments, that were pregnant with teachable moments — where the learning was in fact palpable. One such assignment for me was facilitating a public meeting for the clean up of the Sydney Tar Ponds.[14] There had not been a public meeting in three years and the last meeting got so out of hand that it had to be shut down by the RCMP. When I was asked to facilitate a meeting three years later, I knew there would be a great deal of pent up anger and all of the stakeholder groups would have taken strongly opposing positions. One of the most important lessons I learned from mediating this type of deeply rooted value-laden disputes, is that I prefer to work with a colleague as co-facilitator as it often takes a team to treat a team, and this is a lesson that I do not think I could have learned in any other way.

Working in a foreign country provides a different type of developmental assignment. I have the great privilege of being able to teach negotiation and influencing skills for Michelin North America. I started working with Michelin

Canada, then Michelin US and most recently Michelin in Mexico. I thought I understood the Michelin culture very well. In fact, because I know so many of the acronyms and special programs at Michelin, many of the course participants thought I worked for Michelin full time. However, the first time I taught negotiation courses in Mexico I learned how an important cultural difference impacted the negotiation process.

In Canada and the US, the norm is that the opening statement in a negotiation is short and to the point. In Mexico there is a very long preface, where both parties inquire about the well being of each other's families. This tendency was much more pronounced than anything I had ever seen in Canada or the US. However, inquiring about the other person's family in Mexico is a cultural norm; in fact, *not* inquiring about the other person's family would hinder the negotiation.

Exercise 7-9: Are there important lessons that you have learned from developmental assignments that were instrumental in developing your leadership skills? If yes, what were the three most important lessons you learned?

1.

2.

3.

If you have not had any developmental assignments, you can create your own, either by yourself or in working with others, through creating a 100-day project.

Can you identify a developmental assignment that you could take on to help you develop your leadership skills?

Is there someone in your organization or social network you could speak to who might know of a developmental assignment?

Often, our developmental assignments occur by sheer happenstance. However, wise organizations don't wait for chance to present developmental assignments to help that organization grow its leaders. Developmental assignments can also be planned and presented at the most opportune time. An excellent way to do this type of developmental assignment is through 100-Day Projects.

The 100-Day Projects

The hundred-day project is a project that will test your leadership skills, strategies and abilities, and at the same time be of tangible benefit to your organization. As such, you must demonstrate a tangible return on investment (ROI) for yourself and your organization.

> *Unless a vision is sustained by action, it quickly turns to ashes.*
> **Warren Bennis**

At this point you may have the perfect idea of what you would like to accomplish in your project. You can also look over the exercises that you completed in this book and see if they suggest the perfect 100-day project. For example were there any projects that you identified in The Four-Factor Theory of Leadership or The Eight Competencies of Effective Senior Leaders in Strategy 3 that you want to develop further. Another option is to ask your friends, boss, supervisor, manager and/or colleagues for their advice. And yet another option is to develop your leadership at work or in your community in one of the seven areas listed below.

Exercise 7-10: Developing My Leadership at Work or In My Community

Pick one area of leadership that you would like to develop from one of the seven leadership areas listed below. In the space provided state your leadership goal, as specifically as possible, in terms of the results that you will achieve.

1. Product Knowledge Leadership

This competence includes superb product knowledge, which contributes to organizational excellence and the teaching or sharing of that knowledge with others in the company so they develop their product knowledge to the highest degree possible.

2. Organizational/Administrative Leadership

Being a leader/innovator in developing procedures and influencing/motivating others in promoting organizational/administrative excellence to the highest level possible.

3. Customer Service Leadership

Being a leader in developing, applying, and motivating/influencing others in providing both innovative and exceptional customer service at the highest levels possible.

4. Technological Leadership

Being a leader in using and promoting the best use of technology to help others maximize their value to your organization. This competency also includes providing excellent technological support to others in your organization.

5. Team Leadership

This competence includes the achievement of superior results through goal setting, providing the team members with the necessary resources to get the job done, and superior recognition for both individual and team accomplishments.

6. Leadership in Staff Development

This competence includes being the best team leader possible in terms of supervising, motivating, mentoring, and developing the careers of the team members.

7. Moral Leadership

This competence includes making moral decisions in difficult situations and humanitarian efforts to make the world a better place.

Below, is an example of one of my 100-day projects. Each section has a brief explanation for each part of the 100-day project followed by a summary of the work completed which is set out in italics.

Goal(s) for Myself and for My Organization

The goal you select must be a SMART goal. By that we mean that the goal must be Specific, Measurable, Achievable, Realistic and Time Limited.

The "S" and the "M" stand for specific and measurable; for a goal to be both specific and measurable, it must pass the Yes-No test. The Yes-No test states that the goal must be so specific and measurable that we can count whether or not the specific behaviour that the goal intends took place. For example, if a participant said, "I am going to use active listening with my subordinates for the next month," it is not specific or measurable. On the other hand, if she said, "I will use intermediate summaries three times with my associate Claire over the next three weeks," it is both specific and measurable.

"A" stands for attainable and "R" stands for realistic. Take long-distance running for example. If you were not currently training, it would be foolish to try to run a marathon. Therefore, you have to be careful that you do not set goals that cannot be met. Lastly, the "T" stands for setting a time deadline. This is based on the principle that a commitment is not a commitment unless there is a deadline attached to it.

> *Complete the proposal for the book "The Seven Strategies of Master Leaders" (SSML), the organization for the book, a tentative list of the Who's Who and write three sample chapters by December 10, 2008. Complete the remaining chapters and interviews by June 30, 2009. Get permission to use the interviews and record them in digital quality for future use in* The Seven Strategies of Master Leaders *CD.*

The ROI from Achieving My Goal(s)

In this section you must state both the direct and the indirect ROI that will accrue to you personally and to your organization from achieving their goal(s) in your 100-Day Project.

I anticipate that the net direct income from publishing the SSML will be from $10,000 to $25,000. However, the indirect income will be much more substantial. The indirect income will come from keynotes on The Seven Strategies of Master Leaders. *The sale of this book and the keynotes will also help to cross promote* The Seven Strategies of Master Negotiators *and* The Seven Strategies of Master Presenters. *Lastly, the book will help me formulate and give credibility to* The Atlantic Leadership Development Institute. *However, the real ROI for me is that the book would help me build* The Atlantic Leadership Development Institute *and that will hopefully help to make Canada in general and Atlantic Canada in particular a better place by helping to grow leaders in the public, private, not-for-profit and volunteer sectors.*

My Obstacles

There are always a number of obstacles that can potentially interfere with our ability to reach our goal(s). By defining and articulating these obstacles, they are much less likely to get in our way and we are much more likely to deal with them proactively than reactively.

Lack of time due to teaching load and the time necessary to secure, conduct and edit the interviews and my daughter thinks that I am a human taxicab. I may have to change goals if the How to Negotiate with One's Ex-Spouse *book is accepted for publication.*

My Resources

Just as we all have obstacles that can make the reaching of our goal(s) more difficult; we also have resources that can help immensely in the reaching of our goal(s). By taking the time to list our resources and by taking specific and con-crete steps to make sure we have the resources in place when we need them, we are much more likely to and can more easily reach the goal(s) we have set. Resources can include people, coaches, mentors, support networks, technology and anything else that you can access to help you achieve your goal(s).

> *I have some of the best editing and research help possible in the
> form of Katherine Coy, Marilyn Christie, donalee Moulton and
> Lawrence McEachern. I can also get expert advice from Joan
> Homewood in helping me select and work with a publisher. I will
> also ask for help conceptualizing the book from Ed Leach John
> Rocca, Shaun Newsome, Maggie Chicoine and Mia Doucet.
> I will also pilot the book with Leadership Thunder Bay and at
> Confederation College. I will integrate the information gathered
> from the interviews and integrate it with the best research on
> leadership I can find.*

Another alternative for resources is to find a mentor or hire a coach who
can help you on this specific project and/or in achieving your long-term career
goals.

My Schedule

Develop a detailed, yet flexible schedule along with specific completion dates
for the specific milestones that will be completed along the way that will bring
this project to fruition. Also make sure you include contingency plans as there
will almost always be unexpected events that you will have to contend with.

Reporting the Project Results

Present your results orally and in writing to your supervisor/director and where
appropriate to people at higher levels in your organization. State the goal(s),
the results, lessons learned, and recommendations for the future. The written
report should follow the same format and usually should not be more than ten
pages long.

Lessons Learned

State specifically what you have learned about yourself and your organization as
a result of working on your 100-Day Project.

Writing a book is a time and intensive front end loaded process. Coming up with the theoretical basis and organization of the book is a long, slow process. The interviews make the theory come alive and increase my motivation to write the book. I also used editorial help earlier in the process and that helped immeasurably in conceptualizing and organizing the book.

Recommendations for the Future

Based on your 100-day project, what are at least three recommendations you have on how to lead and achieve better results more effectively in the future.

I will note reference materials in computer files while I am reading the books and references. Be sure to include page numbers. I can then go back and fill in the details more easily afterwards. Getting permission to use some of the quoted materials from a few of the publishers will take longer than anticipated, so start as early as possible. Lastly, get the endorsements as early as possible as they are critical in "selling" the book to the publisher.

This is my eighth book and another important lesson I learned was to get feedback earlier rather than later and to get feedback that is more diverse from a wider range of people. By getting feedback earlier and from more diverse sources, I was able to "see" the book from more diverse perspectives and the book benefited greatly. I will definitely get feedback earlier and from more diverse sources, and not just for my writing projects, in the future. In summary, I learned that President Woodrow Wilson had it right when he said, "I not only use all the brains that I have, but all that I can borrow."

Commit to Life-Long Organizational Growth

Recently, I saw Carl Sagan's documentary series *Cosmos* and was fascinated with how stars are born and how they develop. In writing this book I have become equally fascinated by how Master Leaders and the organizations they lead develop. From my studies of leadership, I found a quotation by John Kotter that took on more and more meaning for me as a result of my conversations with Master Leaders profiled in the book.

> [Two] factors seemed to give people an edge by creating an unusually strong competitive capacity. Competitive drive helped create lifelong learning, which kept increasing skill and knowledge levels, especially leadership skills, which in turn produced a prodigious ability to deal with an increasingly difficult and fast moving global economy.[15]

For example, I asked Master Leader Fred MacGillivray, President and CEO of Trade Centres Limited, about his competitive drive and how it manifested itself early in his life.

F.M.   *Early in my career, at a very young age, I committed myself, that is, I made a very strong personal commitment to become the CEO of an organization before age 40, and I am happy to say that I achieved that goal.*

B.M.   *How old were you at the time that you made this commitment?*

F.M.   *It was 1965 and I must have been twenty or twenty-one. I had been working in the grocery business since I was 14 years old and I saw the opportunities that were available. By the time I was married and had responsibilities, I felt that I had the ability to achieve those goals. All I had to do was to figure out a strategy to test my abilities and to provide my family with a life they deserved.*

B.M.   *You must have been a hard worker and a high achiever at an early age.*

F.M.   *I was always a multi-tasking type of person. I paid for my tuition to a private high school and paid my way through university. I got a car at 16 years of age and paid for it myself.*

B.M.   *Why did you go to a private high school?*

F.M.   *My older brothers went there. When I told my Dad that I wanted to go to the private high school, Dad told me that he thought it was a great idea — all I had to do was figure out a way to pay for it. It was Saint Mary's Jesuit High School and the tuition was $150 per year — and in those days there was no such thing as student loans. So I convinced the Royal Bank of Canada to loan me $150 as a 14-year-old. My mother, bless her heart, had to co-sign the loan and I have now been a customer of the Royal Bank for 46 years. I worked after school and weekends at the grocery store and had a couple of jobs during the summer. I worked thirty hours a week during the school term and 6 days a week during the summers.*

In the end, this helped to motivate me. It helped me to recognize the responsibility level because I invested my own money. I learned many life lessons during this time and have applied them throughout my life.

I also read Kotter's quotation to Annette Verschuren and asked her if she thought it rang true for her. Annette answered the question by saying:

A.V.   *It is me. I am very competitive but I don't put down people. I love the game — the puzzle — of business. There is fear in me, but I love to compete and I love competing with myself. I am a very curious person and I love learning. The moment I stop learning is the moment I stop living.*

One of the things I see in people and in myself are that we are all 25% better than we think we are. My challenge is how can we get that extra 25% out and turn it into lasting results. Lowes is coming to Canada and they will be a tough competitor. I respect and have learned a lot from them. Lowes builds good looking stores — but the question is how flexible can they be in a different environment. This is their first time in a different environment and we won't make it easy.

Then Annette took a breath and added, "I would hate to compete against Home Depot in Canada."

In addition to their competitive drive and thirst to be life-long learners, there is a third factor that distinguishes the Master Leaders that I have profiled in this book. That factor is developing a teachable point of view and then weaving that point of view into their organization's culture. The idea of a teachable point of view was developed by Noel Tichy.[16] There are three main reasons why a teachable point of view is so powerful:

First, the very act of creating and testing a teachable point of view makes people better leaders. As they step back from the day-to-day ferment of business and reflect on what they know, leaders come to understand why they lead as they do - why they make certain decisions about competitive threats, for instance, or why they act in certain ways in crisis situations. In the process, leaders penetrate their underlying assumptions about themselves, their organizations, and business in general. Implicit knowledge becomes explicit and can then be questioned, refined, and honed to both the leader's and the organization's benefit.

Second, the power of the teachable point of view is in its multiplier effect and its speed. Once a leader has... [articulated his or her teachable point of view, it must be taught and embraced by the other leaders and employees in his or her organization before it becomes part of that organizations culture – that organization's DNA.]

Third and finally, the teachable point of view also expedites one of a leader's most difficult and mission-critical tasks: developing people. Typically, leaders develop other leaders by example. That can take a long time and leaves many insights unarticulated. The power of the teachable point of view is that it gives leaders an explicit body of knowledge to impart. It helps them construct a framework for their own ideas, which helps others build knowledge as well.

So in the end, Master Leaders are master learners. They move from competence to mastery by virtue of their competitive drive, strive for life-long learning, and then incorporate all that they have learned into a teachable point of view. Master Leaders use their teachable point of view to develop true learning organizations where continuous learning then becomes a part of that organization's DNA. Being part of the organization's DNA, the compound learning and teachable point of view become part of an organization's culture and by being part of the organization's culture; it becomes that leader's legacy.

CONCLUSION

After World War II, the world was a relatively simple place, after all, phones only came in one colour – black – and the most complicated direction was that sometimes you would have to dial "9" to get an outside line. There was no competition for North American Industry – most of Europe, Russia, and Asia's infrastructure were badly damaged by the war. Therefore, most organizations had one or two leaders at the top. That's all they needed based on the complexity of the problems they faced at the time.

Today's and tomorrow's problems are too complex to be solved by one or two leaders at the top. Our organizations need, as never before, teams of effective leaders who are able to work together synergistically throughout the organization. In addition, today's and tomorrow's leaders will, to an ever increasing extent, have to be able to work on virtual and/or temporary teams that will be reformulated and repopulated so we will constantly have the right group of leaders and followers working on the right problem, at the right time. They will also have to be prepared to work in different roles and with different people on different projects as the need arises.

However, developing our own leadership skills and strategies is not enough. Having all of our leaders within each of our organizations working together collaboratively and synergistically is a step in the right direction, but that isn't enough either. All of our leaders in the private, public, volunteer and not-for-profit sectors must work together far more effectively than they have done in the past. Equally critical, Canada must step up to the plate and develop its leadership potential and this must extend to our cities, municipalities and towns working more effectively with each other and with their respective provinces, and our provinces must learn to work together with each other and the provincial governments must learn how to work together with the federal government. In other words we must develop leaders at every level and in every sector who can and will work together to solve today's and tomorrow's complex problem.

I sincerely hope that you have benefited from reading about the Master Leaders you met in this book and that you will continue to develop and enhance your own leadership skills and strategies as well as the leadership skills and strategies of those with whom you come into contact.

Brad McRae

Notes

Introduction

[1] McCall, M., Lombardo, M., and Morrison, A.; *The Lessons of Experience: How Successful Executives Develop on the Job*. NY: Lexington Books, 1988.

[2] Bennis, W & Nanus, B.; *Leaders: The Strategies of Taking Charge*. NY: Harper Collins, 1997, p. 20.

[3] Robinson, Francis; *Effective Study* (4th ed.). New York: Harper & Row Publishers, 1970, p. 22.

[4] Marcia Kaye, "One Man's Mission", 50 Plus, April 2005. pp. 12-14.

[5] The website for the Stephen Lewis Foundation is *www.stephenlewisfoundation.org*.

[6] Grassroots, the Stephen Lewis Foundation Newsletter, Winter 2008.

[7] Stephen Lewis was selected as MacLean's Magazine first annual Canadian of the Year in 2003.

Strategy 1: Inspire by Vision/Fuel with Passion

[1] www.mec.ca

[2] Today Sarah Golling is a retired lawyer in Roseland, BC, and is still an active kayaker.

[3] Maclean's, April 29, 2002.

[4] MEC actually has a Charter, the last part of which contains its vision.

[5] The information in quotes in this section is from MEC's website at *www.mec.ca*.

[6] The consultant who worked with Rania Cassar-Awe on evolving the new corporate learning strategy is Sheryl Herle, at BBIS.

[7] More information of the transformation of CN and Paul Tellier role in that transformation is documented in McRae, B.; *The Seven Strategies of Master Negotiators*, Toronto, ON, Northbridge Publishing, 2005.

[8] As of November 1, 2007; U.S. dollars as stated in *Change, Leadership, Mud and Why*, Volume II by E. Hunter Harrison, Canadian National Railroad Company, 2008, p. 3

[9] Ibid.

[10] A nonprofit public policy center founded by Jimmy and Rosalynn Carter to fight disease, hunger, poverty, conflict, and oppression around the world.

[11] I wish to acknowledge that this technique was developed by Yvonne Dolan and its use here is with her kind permission.

[12] Collins, J.; *Good to Great: Why Some Companies Make the Leap and Other Don't*, NY: Harper Business, 2001.

[13] Ibid, page 95.

[14] Martin Seligman spoke at the HRANS Human Resource Association Bi-annual conference on May 30, 2003.

[15] Seligman, M.; *Authentic Happiness: Using the New Positive Psychology to Realize Your Potential for Lasting Fulfillment*, NY: The Free Press, 2002, p. 263.

[16] Ibid, p. xiii.

[17] Buckingham, M. and Clifton, D.; *Now, Discover Your Strengths*, NY: The Free Press, 2001, p. 128.

[18] Ibid. p. 133.

[19] Collins, J.; *Good to Great: Why Some Companies Make the Leap and Other Don't*, NY: Harper Business, 2001, p. 165.

Strategy 2: Step Up to the Plate

[1] Knowledge as Advantage: Building Advantage through Canada's universities. A submission to the TD Forum on Canada's Standard of Living, by David Johnston, President, University of Waterloo, pp 4-5.

[2] The Innovation Quotient: Building Advantage through Canada's Universities. Submitted to the TD Forum on Canada's Standard of Living by David Johnston, President, University of Waterloo, October 2002

[3] Ibid.

[4] Former Vice-President and environmental activists Al Gore has made similar comments about Wal-Mart in the US.

[5] Kouzes, J. M. and Posner, B. Z.; *A Leader's Legacy*. NY: John Wiley & Sons, 2006.

[6] The "Top 40 under 40" is complied each year by the Globe and Mail newspaper.

[7] If you would like to find out more, there is a National Film Board documentary of Hetty's efforts in Serbia entitled "Teaching Peace in a Time of War" and you can visit the PSI website www. peacefulschoolsinternational.org.

[8] The Capital Health District also includes Dartmouth General Hospital, Eastern Shore Memorial Hospital, Hants Community Hospital, Twin Oaks Hospital, Musquodoboit Valley Memorial Hospital, Nova Scotia Hospital, East Coast Forensic Psychiatric Hospital and Cobequid Community Health Centre.

[9] Hansen, R. and Taylor, J.; Rick Hansen: Man in Motion, Vancouver, BC: Douglas & McIntyre,1987, page 86.

[10] Ibid, page 87.

[11] Ibid, page 149.

[12] www.rickhansen.com.

Strategy 3: Assess Your Leadership Style

[1] Reprinted by permission of Harvard Business Review. From "In Praise of the Incomplete Leader." by Deborah Ancona, Thomas W. Malone, Wanda J. Orlikowski, and Peter M. Senge, February 2007,p. 92. Copyright ©2007 by the Harvard Business School Publishing Corporation: all rights reserved.

[2] Davies, et al.; Successful Manager's Handbook, Minneapolis, MN: Personnel Decisions, Inc., 1992, p. v.

[3] Spencer, L.M and Spencer, S.M.; *Competencies at work: Models for Superior Performance*. NY: John Wiley & Sons, 1993.

[4] Goleman, D.; *Working with Emotional Intelligence*, NY: Bantam Book, 1998.

[5] Bowers, D. C. and Seashore S. E.; "Predicting Organizational Effectiveness with a Four Factor Theory of Leadership." Administrative Science Quarterly, Vol. II, No. 2, 1966, pp 238-63.

[6] You can find information about Kidsfest at www.kidsfest.com.

[7] Material from Klemp and McClelland's article, "What Characterizes Intelligent Functioning Among Senior Managers" is from Sternberg, R. J. and Wagner, R. K.; *Practical Intelligence: Nature and Origins of Competence in the Everyday World*, Cambridge University Press, 1986.

[8] Ibid, p. 38-39.

[9] Grescoa, P.; *Flight Path: How Westjet is Flying High in Canada's Most Turbulent Industry*, Toronto, ON: John Wiley & Sons, 2004, p. 257.

[10] Ibid, p. 170.

[11] Off, C.; *The Lion, the Fox & the Eagle: A Story of Generals and Justice in Yugoslavia and Rwanda*. Toronto, ON: Random House Canada Limited, 2000.

[12] The Big City Mayor's Caucus.

[13] Sternberg, R. J. and Wagner, R. K.; *Practical Intelligence: Nature and Origins of Competence in the Everyday World*, Cambridge University Press, 1986, p. 41.

[14] F. John Reh's article on the Internet entitled "You Can't Manage What You Don't Measure". http://management.about.com/b/2006/07/14/you-cant-manage-what-you-dont-measure.htm

[15] Sternberg, R. J. and Wagner, R. K.; *Practical Intelligence: Nature and Origins of Competence in the Everyday World*, Cambridge University Press, 1986, P. 41.

[16] Deal, T. and Kennedy, A.; (1982). *Corporate Cultures: The Rites and Rituals of Corporate Life*. Reading, MA: Addison-Wesley Publishing Co., 1982, p.

[17] Sternberg, R. J. and Wagner, R. K.; *Practical Intelligence: Nature and Origins of Competence in the Everyday World*, Cambridge University Press, 1986, P. 40.

[18] Ibid, pp. 40-41.

[19] Quoted from the Canadian Environment Awards 2008, Citation of Lifetime Achievement.

[20] However, you will get a better sense of her passion in influencing others to join her in mitigating the harmful effects of climate change by going to the following link and hearing Shelia speak in her own words at www.cbc.ca/thisibelieve/audio/ap_TIB_Cloutier.mp3, which originally aired on the CBC on May 23, 2007.

[21] Sternberg, R. J. and Wagner, R. K.; *Practical Intelligence: Nature and Origins of Competence in the Everyday World*, Cambridge University Press, 1986, p. 41.

[22] McRae, B.; The Seven Strategies of Master Negotiators: Featuring Real-Life Insights from Canada's Top Negotiators, Toronto, ON: Northbridge Publishing, 2005. Available at www.bradmcrae.com.

[23] Sternberg, R. J. and Wagner, R. K.; *Practical Intelligence: Nature and Origins of Competence in the Everyday World*, Cambridge University Press, 1986, p. 42.

[24] Reprinted by permission of Harvard Business Review. From "Reshaping an industry: Lockheed Martin's survival story." by Norman R. Augustine, February 1997, p. 83-94. Copyright ©1997 by the Harvard Business School Publishing Corporation: all rights reserved.

[25] Profit Magazine, Nov. 2007

[26] Sternberg, R. J. and Wagner, R. K.; *Practical Intelligence: Nature and Origins of Competence in the Everyday World*, Cambridge University Press, 1986 p. 42.

[27] Moss Kanter, R.; *Confidence: How Winning Streaks and Losing Streaks Begin and End*, NY: Three Rivers Press, 2004.

[28] Collins, J. *Good to Great: Why Some Companies Make the Leap… and Others Don't*, NY: Harper Business, 2001.

Strategy 4: Become a Purposeful Learner

[1] McCall, M., Lombardo, M., and Morrison, A.; *The Lessons of Experience: How Successful Executives Develop on the Job*, NY: Lexington Books, 1988.

[2] Newsroom, Canada Post Corporation 2008.

[3] ATV is an affiliate of CTV in Atlantic Canada.

[4] The purpose of Transparency International Canada Inc. (TI-Canada) is to inform businesses, government, and the general public of the effects of corruption in national and international marketplaces, and to provide support and resources for public and private sector initiatives to prevent corrupt business practices. You can learn more about Transparency International Canada by going to their website at www.transparency.ca.

[5] Anna Fels; Do Women Lack Ambition? Harvard Business Review, Cambridge, MA.: Harvard Business School Publishing Corporation, April, 2004.

[6] McCall, M., Lombardo, M., and Morrison, A.; *The Lessons of Experience: How Successful Executives Develop on the Job*, NY: Lexington Books, 1988, pg. 71.

[7] Adapted from M.W. McCall, Jr., & M.M. Lombardo. Off the track: Why and how successful executives get derailed. Technical Report No. 21 (Greensboro, NC: Center for Creative Leadership, January 1983.

[8] Richard Norris. "Fail to Succeed Action." Published in the Steps International Business Coaching Newsletter, August, 2004. www.action-international.com.

[9] I had read his book, *Shake Hands with the Devil*, so when I decided to see the movie with the same title; I did not expect to learn much more. I could not have been more wrong. The movie portrays Dallaire's leadership and heroism during the genocide in Rwanda. What I was not prepared for, was how much of the movie dealt with Dallaire's suffering and PTSD (Post Traumatic Stress Disorder). The film documents how Dallaire, with the help of a therapist, was able to purposefully learn to transform his pain and suffering into empowerment and hope.

[10] Dallaire, R.; *Shake Hands with the Devil: The Failure of Humanity in Rwanda*, Toronto, ON: Random House Canada, 2003, p. 520.

[11] Ibid, p. 6.

[12] Richard E. Farson. "Praise Reappraised." Harvard Business Review, September 1, 1963, pp. 103-108. Copyright ©1963 by the Harvard Business School Publishing Corporation: all rights reserved.

[13] A participant in one of my workshops on Maintaining Peak Performance was surprised to see he increased his motivational potential score from 24 to 252 when he left his old job and went into business for himself.

Strategy 5: Become a Master Decision Maker

[1] Tichy, N. M. and Bennis, W. G.; *Judgment: How Winning Leaders Make Great Calls*, NY: Penguin, 2007, p. 4.

[2] DEVCO stands for The Cape Breton Development Cooperation which was a federal crown cooperation. It ceased operations in 2001.

[3] Eisenhardt, K., Kahwajy, J., and Bourgeois, L.J., "How management teams can have a good fight", Harvard Business Review, Cambridge, MA.: Harvard Business School Publishing Corporation, July-August, 1997.

[4] Useem, M.; *The Go Point: When It's Time To Decide Knowing What To Do and When To Do It*, NY: Crown Business, 2006, p. 95.

[5] Reasons why mergers and acquisitions can fail, Jacksonville Business Journal, August 25, 2000.

[6] Morgan, P., Frantic Free: 147 Way to Calm Down & Lighten Up, Calgary, AB, Light Hearted Concepts, 2005.

[7] This form was adapted with permission from Tom Stoyan, Coaching and Sales Institute Inc.

Strategy 6: Build a Culture of Excellence

[1] Gershon, R.; *Telecommunications Management: Industry Structures and Planning Strategies*, Oxford, UK, Taylor & Francis, 2001, p310.

[2] Kaplan, R. W. and Norton, D. P.; Measuring the Strategic Readiness of Intangible Assets, Harvard Business Review, Cambridge, MA. Harvard Business School Publishing Corporation, February, 2004.

[3] Deal, T. & Kennedy, A.; *Corporate Cultures: The Rites and Rituals of Corporate Life*, Reading, MA: Addison-Wesley Publishing Company, Inc., 1982, p. 4.

[4] Surowiecki, J.; *The Wisdom of Crowds*, NY: Anchor Books, 2005.

[5] WestJet website, www.westjet.com

[6] http://www.autoblog.com/2008/01/15/detroit-2008-michelin-challenge-design-winners/

[7] As cited in Richard Morais, "The Old Lady is Burning Rubber." Forbes.com Nov. 26, 2007. Michelin spends "3.6% of sales on research and development, compared with 3% at Bridgestone and 1.8% at Goodyear, and has, over the decades, invented everything from steel-belted radials to "regenerating" tires (as the tread wears, new water-planing grooves emerge, extending tire life by 25%).

[8] Ibid.

[9] Foot, D., and Stoffman, D.; *Boom, Bust, & Echo: How to Profit From the Coming Demographic Shift*, Toronto, ON: Macfarlane Walter & Ross, 1997.

[10] Roger Taylor, If Halifax were a stock, would you buy it?, The Chronicle Herald, October 2007.

[11] Tracey Staedter, Smart Bandage: How a smart bandage works, May 2003, Technology Review, Published by Massachusetts Institute of Technology; and Robbie Ward, Engineer creates 'smart' bandages to test cholesterol, blood without needles, Bagley College of Engineering News, Mississippi State University, February 2008.

[12] If you would like to see some of the features of Apple TV, go to www.apple.com

[13] Pine, J. and Gilmore, J. H.; *The Experience Economy: Work is Theater & Every Business a Stage*, Cambridge MA: Harvard Business School Press, 1999.

[14] Ray Ivany was the Principle of Nova Scotia's Community College system (NSCC) from 1998 to 2005.

[15] Michelin annual report 2006.

[16] Ibid.

[17] MacDonald, L.; *The Bombardier Story: Planes, Trains, and Snowmobiles*, Toronto, ON: John Wiley & Sons, 2001.

[18] Ibid, p. 235.

[19] Exhibition Park is part of the World Trade Centre which also runs the World Trade and Convention Centre in Halifax, Nova Scotia.

[20] The Flat Rate Box can only be used with a Canada Post Flat Rate Box shipping label created, purchased and printed through eBay's Online Shipping tool. http://pages.ebay.ca/flatratebox/index.html

[21] Goleman, D. Boyatzis, R. McKee, A.; *Primal Leadership: Realizing the Power of Emotional Intelligence*, Boston, MA: Harvard Business School Press, 2002.

[22] Susan Hughes. "On leading well: Rudolph Giuliani, Louis Gerstner, and Derrick Bell set the example." Quill & Quire, January 2003.

[23] Moss Kanter, R.; *Confidence: How Winning Streaks & Losing Streaks Begin and End*, NY: Three Rivers Press, 2004, p. 306.

[24] www.fedcan.ca/english/policyandadvocacy/win/publicatioins.cfm

[25] http://www.cbc.ca/canada/story/2008/06/29/gay-pride.html

[26] One organization that is doing a great job at increasing inclusiveness is the Aboriginal Human Resources Council. You can find out more about the council's work by going to www.aborignalhr.ca.

[27] Gallop Management Journal Q&A with Roy Spence, president of advertising agency GSD&M interviewed by Jennifer Robinson: December 8, 2005, from an article entitled, "What's Your Company's Purpose?" in Geoffrey Brewer & Barb Sanford (Eds.), *The Best of Gallup Management Journal: 2001-2007*, NY: Gallup Press, 2007.

[28] The Enterprise of the Future, IBM Global CEO Study, 2008, p. 61

[29] Tim Sanders November 10, 2008 Globe & Mail

[30] From Meeting Professionals International report, Corporate Social Responsibility: Where We Stand www.mpiweb.org/cms/mpiweb/Uploads/DocLibrary/208982_4302008_75109_PM_.pdf.

[31] Moss Kanter, R.; *Confidence: How Winning Streaks & Losing Streaks Begin and End*, NY: Three Rivers Press, 2004, p. 162.

Strategy 7: Transform Competence to Mastery

[1] Frager, Rovert. "The psychology of samurai." Psychology Today, January, 1969.

[2] Gladwell, M.; *The Tipping Point: How Little Things Can Make a Big Difference*, NY: Little Brown and Co., 2000.

[3] CAM-X is an industry trade Association representing Call Centres and Telephone Answering Service companies

[4] John Kotter, J.; *Leading Change*, Cambridge, MA: Harvard Business School Press, 1966, p. 181.

[5] Battley, S.; *Coached to Lead: How to Achieve Extraordinary Results With an Executive Coach*. NY: Jossey-Bass, 2006.

[6] Does Internal Coaching Work, a research study by Results Coaching Systems, August 2005, www.resultscoaches.com.

[7] If you are considering coaching, it is worthwhile taking The Coaching Readiness Quiz online at www.coachedtolead.com.

[8] Source, www.wikipedia.org.

[9] I interviewed Doug Leigh by telephone on June 4, 2008. Doug is clearly recognized as Canada's premier skating coach interviewed, and is internationally acclaimed as a leader in the field. Doug has coached Brian Orser, Jennifer Robinson, Steven Cousins, and Jeffrey Buttle. Among Doug's awards are: 9 CAC Awards (Coaching Association of Canada), the 1996 Canadian Coach of the Year, and he was inducted into The Sports Hall of Fame – Figure Skating, in 1998.

[10] I interviewed Elvis Stojko on August 14, 2008. Elvis currently lives in Mexico and in addition to skating is a recognized motivational speaker.

[11] Broad, M. and Newstrom, J.; *Transfer of Training: Action-Packed Strategies to Ensure High Payoff from Training Investments*, Reading MA: Addison-Wesley Publishing Company, 1992, pp 93-94.

[12] Schneier, C.E., Baird, L.S., and Beatty, R.W.; *The Performance Measurement, Management and Appraisal Sourcebook*, Amherst, MA, 1995, p. 214.

[13] Harrington, B. & Hall, D.; *Career Management & Work–Life Integration: Using Self-Assessment to Navigate Contemporary Careers*, Los Angles, CA: Sage Publications, Inc., 2007, p. 1

[14] The Sydney Tar Ponds are the largest toxic industrial waste site in Canada.

[15] John Kotter. J.; *Leading Change*. Boston, MA: Harvard Business School Press, 1996, p. 178.

[16] Noel Tichy is a professor of organizational behavior and human resource management at the University of Michigan Business School in Ann Arbor. He is the coauthor, with Eli Cohen, of *The Leadership Engine* (HarperBusiness, 1997). The quotes used in this section were originally published in March-April 1999 Harvard Business Review.

The Who's Who of Master Leaders

Louise Arbour, United Nations High Commissioner for Human Rights[1]
Louise Arbour received the Eleanor and Franklin Roosevelt "Freedom from Fear" Award for her work as prosecutor for the International Criminal Tribunal for the Former Yugoslavia and for Rwanda. She then became a judge on the Supreme Court of Canada before being selected as the High Commissioner for Refugees at the United Nations. Louise Arbour is not only a champion of human rights in Canada and in the world; she is one of the most strategic thinkers and leaders in the world. She is also the first person in the world to indict a sitting president of a country for crimes against humanity. By doing so she set a precedent that will help make the world safer, more just and more humane. Louise Arbour is currently the president and CEO of the International Crisis Group.

Jamie Baillie, President and CEO, Credit Union Atlantic
Jamie Baillie is the President & CEO of Credit Union Atlantic (CUA). Credit Union Atlantic is a customer-owned financial institution providing banking services and financial solutions to individuals and businesses and is the largest credit union in Nova Scotia. Since Jamie became the CEO of Credit Union Atlantic, it has become an industry leader by completing a successful equity offering and introducing a number of innovative new products. Before joining CUA, Jamie worked in various leadership roles in Nova Scotia business and government, including three years as Chief of Staff for Premier John Hamm and as a partner in an executive search firm. Jamie's leadership in both the public and private sectors was recognized when he was named one of Atlantic Canada's Top 50 CEOs.

---

[1]   Each person's job title is the title that he or she had at the time of his or her interview or, in the few cases where an interview was not possible, the person was profiled in the book.

Jim Balsillie, Founder, Co-CEO and Chairman, Research In Motion (RIM)

Jim Balsillie became the co-CEO and chairman of Waterloo-based Research In Motion in 1992, less than a decade before the small pager company created the device that has led it to be called one of the four technological horsemen with the other three being Microsoft, Apple and Google. Today RIM is one of the world's most successful high tech companies. At the same time competition and convergence are increasing on a daily basis. Jim, a noted philanthropist, has donated $10 million to help found the Perimeter Institute for Theoretical Physics, $30 million to establish the Centre for International Governance Innovation, and $50 million to the University of Waterloo, Wilfrid Laurier University and the Centre for International Governance Innovation as part of a $100 million initiative to create the Balsillie School of International Affairs which is a collaboration between his centre and the University of Waterloo and Wilfred Laurier University. As an avid hockey fan, Jim is working to bring a National Hockey League club to Hamilton and the Southern Ontario region.

Clive Beddoe, Founder and former President and CEO, WestJet

Clive Beddoe started a new airline during one of the worst times in the history of aviation. Although most new airlines fail, WestJet succeeded beyond anyone's expectations. One of the main reasons for its success is the leadership style of Clive Beddoe. There are many types of leadership models. One of the most powerful is leadership that establishes an empowered workforce and a culture of excellence in customer service and in these endeavours, Clive Beddoe and WestJet have succeeded admirably.

Pierre Beaudoin, President and CEO, Bombardier Inc.

Pierre Beaudoin studied industrial relations at McGill University and has worked at Bombardier since 1985. He became President and CEO on June 4, 2008. Bombardier is one of Canada's largest manufacturers specializing in trains and planes. Pierre Beaudoin has worked in every division of the company. Planes and trains are an interesting mix.   Both industries can be very cyclical.

Pierre's biggest accomplishments and his biggest challenges await as he takes on the leadership of one of Canada's most renowned companies in times of major economic uncertainty.

Rania Cassar-Awe, Director of Learning and Development, Pfizer Canada

Rania Cassar-Awe has energetically championed change at Pfizer Canada for 17 years. Her 21-year career in the pharmaceutical industry spans diverse management roles in sales, operations, government affairs and human resources. Rania believes that the articulation of ambitious goals motivates individuals to apply their strengths in new ways to solve new and challenging problems. In her current role as subject matter expert, Rania has pioneered an innovative learning culture that allows individuals and teams to adapt quickly to a changing business environment, by combining latest technology and time-tested learning practices.

David Cheesewright, President and CEO, Wal-Mart Canada

David Cheesewright became the President and CEO of Wal-Mart Canada in 2005. Previously he was the COO for Wal-Mart Canada from 2004 to 2005. Prior to that he had 20 years of retail and manufacturing experience in the UK. As of May, 2009, Wal-Mart Canada had a total of 312 retail units, 255 Wal-Mart Discount Stores, 57 Wal-Mart Supercentres and nearly 80 thousand employees, spectacular growth for a company that started in Canada in 1994 when it took over 122 Woolco stores. Wall-Mart Canada has made a significant commitment to environmental sustainability, which has caused many of its suppliers to do the same.

Lieutenant-General Roméo Dallaire

Lieutenant-General Roméo Dallaire was the head of UNIMAR, the United Nations Peacekeeping operation in Rwanda and is the author of *Shake Hands with the Devil: The Failure of Humanity in Rwanda*. However, instead of keeping the peace, he witnessed a genocide where 800,000 men, women and children lost their lives. Tragically, even after countless efforts, he could not get the United Nations or the first world powers to intervene. Although he could not do anything to prevent the genocide that took place in Rwanda, he has done everything in his power to make sure that there will never be another Rwanda by holding the United Nations and the first world powers accountable for the fact that they passively sat back and let the genocide take place. He continues to give riveting speeches giving witness to the genocide that took place in Rwanda and challenges all of us not to let genocide happen ever again.

Warren Evans, Chief Fund Raiser, Laura's Hope

In October, 2001, Warren Evan's daughter, Laura died of Huntington's Disease, a genetic degenerative brain disorder. Laura's last hope was that her older sister, Andrea would not become stricken with Huntington's. Up until Laura's death there had been no treatment for Huntington's and it always proved fatal. By the end of 2001, Warren decided to start Laura's Hope as a charity to raise money to fund clinical trials to find a cure for Huntington's. Doing most of the work himself and with volunteers he has recruited along the way, close to a million dollars had been raised. It is also noteworthy that none of the money raised goes towards administrative costs to manage Laura's Hope; all of the administration is done by Warren and other volunteers.

Phil Fontaine, National Chief of the Assembly of First Nations

As a leader and healer, Phil Fontaine has dedicated his life to the advancement of First Nations people and is currently finishing his third term as the National Chief of the Assembly of First Nations. One of his greatest honours occurred when he received the National Aboriginal Achievement Award for his public service. Phil Fontaine courageously helped to bring to light the terrible sexual abuse by revealing that he had been sexually abused by the priests who ran the residential schools. Although Phil Fontaine has many accomplishments, his focus is squarely on building a better future for his people. As he so eloquently states, "Canada deserves nothing less."

Ruth Goldbloom, Order of Canada Recipient, Pier 21

Ruth Goldbloom is the driving force in the development of Pier 21. She led the fundraising efforts that raised over $9 million so Pier 21 could be re-opened. The Pier 21 National Historic Site is a tribute to the immigrants who have passed through its doors and helped develop Canada into a diverse and strong nation. Between 1928 and 1971 over one million immigrants, 58,000 war brides and close to half a million military personnel who served overseas during the Second World War, passed through its doors. One out of five Canadians can trace their roots through Pier 21. Ruth continues her fundraising with the

Pier 21 Foundation. In 2007, Pier 21 was selected as one of the seven wonders of Canada. In June 2009, Pier 21 was designated a National Museum of Immigration, only the second museum outside of Ottawa to be given this designation.

Moya Greene, President and CEO, Canada Post Corporation

Moya Greene is the President and Chief Executive Officer of Canada Post, a $7.5 billion company that delivers over 40 million pieces of mail every business day. She has worked for 17 years in the federal public service and was a senior officer in three of Canada's largest multinational companies: TD Securities, CIBC and Bombardier. She was named one of Canada's top 40 female corporate executives by the Richard Ivey School of Business for her "strong track record in strategic planning, complex negotiations and relationship building."

Kevin Hamm, President and COO, DownEast Communications

Kevin Hamm is the President and COO of DownEast Communications. DownEast Communications offers a wide variety of communications solutions including cellular phones, two-way radios, pagers, satellite communications, and corded and cordless phones. DownEast Communications has 46 retail locations in Nova Scotia, Newfoundland and New Brunswick. Kevin has more than 20 years of leadership experience in the retail and marketing sectors. He is a proven business developer and team player with a solid track record of building brands, opening new business markets and delivering results.

Rick Hansen, President and CEO, The Rick Hansen Foundation

Rick Hansen is a fundraiser, role model and humanitarian. For over two years Rick Hansen stroked his wheelchair 48,000 times a day through a 34-country, 40,075-kilometre journey around the world. His twin goals were fundraising for spinal cord research (he raised over $20 million), and consciousness raising among both disabled and non-disabled. Rick says, "My disability is that I cannot use my legs. My handicap is your negative perception of that disability, and thus of me." Rick's story is a testament to perseverance in the face of obstacles, which included everything from flat tires, injuries, and wheeling in desert to blizzard conditions. Rick continues to raise funds for spinal cord injury research and to help people who have been injured adapt and lead a full and productive life. The Rick Hanson Foundation has raised over $200 million for spinal cord injury related programs and initiatives.

General Rick Hillier, Former Chief of Defence Staff

Rick Hiller was the Chief of Defence Staff – the highest-ranking position in the Canadian Forces – from February 4, 2005 to July 1, 2008. Much of the current military success is being attributed to General Rick Hillier. In 2008, for the first time in 30 years, there were no problems in recruiting into Canada's armed forces. In fact, the armed forces were achieving 100 to 110% of their recruiting objectives. During Rick's time as Chief of Defence Staff, he also saw modernization of equipment. All these results came at a time when much was being asked of the men and women who served. General Hiller is currently the Chancellor of Memorial University of Newfoundland which is also his alma mater.

Ray Ivany, Past President, NSCC

Ray Ivany brought new life and a sense of entrepreneurism to the Nova Scotia Community College system during his tenure as President and CEO of NSCC from 1998 to 2005. A native Nova Scotian, Mr. Ivany joined the NSCC from the University College of Cape Breton where he had served as Executive Vice President. He has been active in shaping post-secondary education and economic development policy within the region. *Atlantic Business* magazine has twice named him one of Atlantic Canada's top 50 CEOs. Currently Ray Ivany is the president of Acadia University.

David Johnston, President, University of Waterloo

David Johnston completed his university studies in three countries: the US (Harvard), England (Cambridge), and Canada (Queens). This may help to explain why David Johnston is such an innovative and eclectic thinker. Dr. Johnson is also one of the strongest advocates for higher education, research and innovation in Canada – at the University of Waterloo in particular and in Canada in general. He is also a strong advocate of "The Waterloo Way" which works for the advancement of higher education through the largest cooperative education program in the world and in developing strategic partnerships with industry and government, an example of which is the six-way public-private partnership, the Research & Technology Park, located on the University of Waterloo campus.

Craig and Marc Kielburger, CEO, Free the Children

Craig Kielburger became a leader and child rights activist railing against child labour in the third world when he was only 12 years old. He then established Free The Children (FTC) to take action. He was determined to help free children from poverty, exploitation, and powerlessness. The organization began as a small group of classmates but quickly grew with chapters being established all over the world. Craig was later joined by his brother Marc and today FTC is the largest network of children helping children through education in the world. FTC has built more than 500 primary schools to provide education to over 40,000 children. Free The Children also works in the areas of education, alternative income, health care, water and sanitation provision, and peacebuilding. FTC has formed strategic partnerships with organizations such as the United Nations and Oprah's Angel Network.

Michael Lazaridis, Founder and Co-President/CEO of Research In Motion

Mike Lazaridis is the University of Waterloo's most famous dropout. He left his studies in his fourth year to start Research In Motion which is the maker of the Blackberry and is now one of the world's most successful high-tech companies in the world. Michael is also a noted philanthropist. He personally donated over $200 million to found the Perimeter Institute for the study of theoretical physics and the Institute for Quantum Computing at the University of Waterloo. In an interesting turn of events, he served two terms as Chancellor of the University of Waterloo and still is one of that universities staunchest supporters.

Stephen Lewis, Former UN Special Envoy for AIDS/HIV in Africa

Stephen Lewis has held the offices of the Canadian Ambassador to the United Nations, Special Adviser to the UN Secretary General on Africa, Assistant Secretary General with UNICEF and adviser to the Executive Director of the

Joint United Nations Programme on HIV/AIDS (UNAIDS). Mr. Lewis is a world-renowned orator who uses words of eloquence to make the world, and especially Africa, a better place. When the world's governments refused to offer enough economic aid to fight the HIV/AIDS pandemic, he started his own fundraising organization – The Stephen Lewis Foundation. When drug companies refused to lower the cost of drugs that could be used to contain AIDS, he shamed, cajoled, begged, and negotiated agreements where these drugs would be made available to help prevent the transmission of HIV/AIDS from infected mothers to their unborn children. He campaigned tirelessly on behalf of the countless number of people whose lives have been devastated by the pandemic in Africa.

Fred MacGillivray, President and CEO, Trade Centre Limited

Fred MacGillivray is one of the most strategic and visionary leaders in Canada. He became President and CEO of The World Trade Centre in Halifax in 1994. At the time, the World Trade and Convention Centre had an annual debt of $2 million. Within three years, Fred wiped out the deficit and now the World Trade and Convention Centre generates an annual profit of $2 million. Fred has a vision of making Halifax a world event destination centre and is well on his way to bringing that vision to fruition. Not only does Fred believe strongly in Halifax reaching its full potential, as a true leader he has convinced countless others that anything is possible – from building a house for charity in one day to winning the hat trick of having Halifax host the 2003 World Junior Hockey Championship, the 2004 World Women's Hockey Championship, and co-host the 2008 World Men's Hockey Companionship.

Hazel McCallion, Mayor of Mississauga

On November 11, 2003, Hazel McCallion started her 10th term as Mayor of Mississauga, Ontario, Canada's sixth largest city. She was first elected Mayor of Mississauga in November, 1978, and is the longest serving mayor in the city's history. Hazel was acclaimed in 1980, re-elected in 1982 and 1985, acclaimed again in 1988 and re-elected in 1991, 1994, 1997, 2000, 2003 and 2006. She was runner-up for World Mayor in 2005. When Mayor McCallion first became mayor, Mississauga was a bedroom community for Toronto. Today, 80,000 to

100,000 people commute into Mississauga for work. In her role as chief sales-person for Mississauga, Mayor McCallion has helped to recruit 90 Fortune 500 companies to locate their head offices in Canada in Mississauga. At the time of the interview, Mayor McCallion was 87 years young and showed no signs of slowing down.

David Rathbun, Executive Vice President, Bell Aliant and President, xwave

As president of xwave, a full range information technology company David is responsible for the organization's overall business direction and growth strat-egy. Prior to coming to xwave, David was Senior Vice President Corporate Resources & Chief Talent Officer of Aliant, as such David was instrumental in the merging of the 4 Atlantic Canadian telephone companies which eventu-ally became Bell Aliant. He is also well known for his contribution to numer-ous business and community organizations, a member of the Acadia School of Business Administration Advisory Board, a Board Member of the Information Technology Association of Canada and a Board Member of the Prior Learning Assessment Centre.

Jim Reid, Founder & CEO, Green Solutions North America Inc.

Jim Reid created GSNAI to be a successful business that also does something good for the world. Building on his experience as a prominent business leader in the United Kingdom and Canada, Jim founded GSNAI in 2006. GSNAI is now expanding across Canada and the US. GSNAI repurposes furniture, computers and other valuable assets that would have gone into landfill and move those assets to where they are most needed both domestically and over-seas. Two of his most innovative programs are "School in a Box" and "Doc in a Box." whereby assets that would have needlessly be disposed in a landfill are transported in shipping containers where they can permanently alter the lives people in the communities they are sent too. At the same time, many organiza-tions would like to balance their environmental and social strategies within a corporate social responsibility (CSR) framework; however they do not have a process in place to easily carry this out. Jim founded GSNAI to do just that – help companies do the right thing by providing an environmentally sensitive and socially responsible solution to dispose of corporate assets, thereby "turning policy into process."

Heather Riesman, President and CEO, Chapters/Indigo

You can't help but get a sense of pride when you walk into any Indigo store and climb the circular staircase to the second floor, because on the wall is a listing of famous Canadians and their contributions to Canada and the world. The title of the display is, "The World Needs More Canadians," and in this sentiment Heather could not be more right. At the same time, the Canadian book industry is facing a myriad of challenges including the fact that there are fewer and fewer publishing houses that can give voice to Canadian writers and the migration to non-print information formats. Among her most important projects is her efforts to add 17 billion to the Canadian economy by decreasing the illiteracy rate in Canada.

Peter Robinson, Former President and CEO, Mountain Equipment Co-op

Peter Robinson was President and CEO of Mountain Equipment Co-op from 1999 to 2007. During his tenure, MEC became the biggest cooperative in Canada with over three million members. MEC has combined sustainability and profitability and is known as a company that lives its values, often locating in downtown areas and thereby helping to revitalize Canada's downtowns. Peter Robinson left MEC at the end of 2007 to become the President and CEO of the David Suzuki Foundation.

Roy Romanow, P.C., O.C., Q.C., Chair and Chief Spokesperson for the Canadian Wellness Index

Roy Romanow is one of Canada's most respected public servants. He is a former Premier of Saskatchewan and was appointed to head the Commission on the Future of Health Care in Canada. In 2002, Roy recommended sweeping changes to ensure the long-term sustainability of Canada's health care system. Roy is currently the chair and principal spokesperson for the Canadian Index of Wellbeing, which is a groundbreaking initiative designed to give Canada one of the most advanced systems which will be able to measure and thereby help improve Canada's physical, economic, social and community health.

Cora Tsouflidou, Founder, Cora's Restaurants
Cora was born into a modest family in a little village in the Gaspé Peninsula. From an early age Cora had a passion for fine art, but her father wanted her to study stenography so she could become a "good secretary." Little did he know that Cora would become one of the most successful leaders and entrepreneurs in Canada. When her husband deserted Cora and her family of three teenagers, Cora bought a small snack bar in Montreal. After a few months, Cora transformed the snack bar into a whole new breakfast concept that blended the best of traditional breakfasts with new health food trends. At last count Cora's had 92 restaurants from St. John's, Newfoundland, to Victoria, British Columbia.

Hetty Van Grup, Peace Activist, Founder Peaceful Schools International
Peaceful Schools International (PSI), was established in 2001 by Hetty van Gurp, an internationally recognized educator and author. Hetty was inspired to found PSI as a result of the tragic death of her son Ben. Ben died as a result of an incident of aggression by a boy who had been bullying him. Peaceful Schools International is based in Nova Scotia and includes about 300 schools in 14 countries as members and the purpose is to create a culture of peace in schools. Hetty was named as a Canadian hero by TIME magazine in June, 2006.

Annette Verschuren, President, The Home Depot Canada and Asia
The Home Depot Canada is a subsidiary of Home Depot Inc. in the U.S. and operates 179 stores in Canada with estimated sales of $2.3 billion. When Annette Verschuren joined The Home Depot Canada in 1996, they had 19 stores. Annette has built The Home Depot Canada into one of this country's most successful "big box" retailers. Her latest challenge is bringing The Home Depot to the hyper-competitive Chinese market.

Pamela Walsh, President of the College of the North Atlantic
Pamela Walsh was the President of the College of the North Atlantic from 1999 to 2005. It was under her initiative that the College of the North Atlantic won a 10-year $500 million contract to develop the community college system in Qatar. Currently Pamela Walsh is the Director of Operations at Athabasca University. In addition to her duties Pamela is completing her doctorate on the Internationalization of Higher Education at the University of Calgary.

Brian Warren, President and CEO, Kidsfest

Brian Warren is a CBC – Canadian by Choice. He is a former Canadian Hall of Fame football player who came to Canada to play football in the Canadian Football League and stayed. Today, Brian is the President and CEO of Kidsfest. Kidsfest is a charity that helps inner city and disadvantaged children become more physically active and better readers. One day a week, these children stay after school to run, exercise and read and they have "coaches" for all of these critically important activities. The children are also supplied with all of the materials they need to succeed in the program such as brand-name running shoes and books.

Shelia Watt-Cloutier, Environmental Activist

Shelia Watt-Cloutier grew up in Northern Quebec. At the age of 10 she was sent to school in Nova Scotia. She subsequently became increasingly concerned about the effect climate change was having on Arctic communities and the threat it was having on the Inuit's way of life and cultural survival. Shelia travels extensively speaking about climate change as an early warning system of worse things yet to come. In 2005 she was acknowledged with the Champion of the Earth Award from the United Nations and in 2006, she received a citation of lifetime achievement from the Canadian Environment Awards. She was nominated in 2007 for the Nobel Peace Prize along with Al Gore. Shelia Watt-Cloutier resides in Iqaluit, Nunavut and is the past Chair of the Inuit Circumpolar Council (ICC), which represents 155,000 Inuit.

Resources from the Masters:
An Annotated Bibliography

The man who doesn't read good books has no advantage over the man who can't read them.

— Mark Twain

Ancona, D., Malone, T., Orlikowski, W., and Senge P. 2007. "In Praise of the Incomplete Leader." Harvard Business Review, pp 92-100.

The premise of this seminal article is that, "No leader is perfect. The best ones don't try to be—they concentrate on honing their strengths and find others who can make up for their limitations." The authors describe four different types of leader: Sensemaking, Relating, Visionary, and Inventing. Sensemaking leaders are valuable because they are able to make sense out of chaos – they see the world as it really is. Relating leaders have the ability to build trusting relationships and use that synergy to achieve higher-order results. Visionary leaders see the world as it could or should be and then inspire others to achieve more than they thought possible. Inventing leaders create. They move, "... from the abstract world of ideas to the concrete world of implementation." In summary, organizations often need all four types of leadership. However, they are unlikely to get all four types of leadership in one person. As well, different times and different circumstances often necessitate more emphasis on one type of leadership to help that organization grow and/or survive. The real-life examples used to illustrate each of the four types of leadership bring the theory to life.

Badaracco, J. 1977. *Defining moments: When managers must choose between right and right.* Boston, MA: Harvard Business School Press.

Perhaps the most neglected aspect of manager and leadership development is the development of character. As character is one of the most difficult concepts to write about, the fact that so few authors have written about it is not surprising. What is surprising, however, is not only has Badaracco written about character, but that he has done it so well. *Defining Moments* is theoretically solid and the examples the author uses to illustrate dilemmas where a person has to chose between what's right and what's right that are as intriguing to read as the most well written mystery novel.

Badaracco, J. 2002. *Leading quietly: An unorthodox guide to doing the right thing*. Boston, MA: Harvard Business School Press.

"This book is the result of a four-year study of quiet leadership. It presents a series of stories describing quiet leaders at work and draws practical lessons from their efforts. Underlying these stories is an unorthodox view of leadership. It builds on the heroic approach, but offers a much broader perspective on what counts as responsible, effective leadership in organizations." This book includes a number of insightful examples from Albert Schweitzer to case studies that most of us have never heard of. However, they all led quietly and in doing so achieved significant results.

BusinessWeek. 2007. *Marketing power plays: How the world's most ingenious marketers reach the top of their game*. NY: McGraw-Hill.

BusinessWeek's *Marketing Power Plays* is one of the best books you can read on marketing. The book is divided into 15 articles about some of the most innovative marketing trends and strategies from how to market hip-hop to how IKEA became a global cult brand. Many of these ideas can be tweaked and applied to your business or organization. Any business or organization that wants to insure that it gets its message out, gets attention and has sticking power would do well to read this book. As an added bonus, each of the 15 case studies are 6 to 14 pages long and are self-contained which means they can be read in short bursts.

Collins, J. 2001. *Good to great: Why some companies make the leap . . . and others don't.* NY: Harper Business.

Every once in a while a business book comes along that revolutionizes our thinking and becomes a classic. *Good to Great* is just such a book. The book starts with the provocative statement "Good is the enemy of great." Collins then develops objective criteria that differentiate the good from the great companies and notes that there is a point at which great companies start behaving remarkably differently from their good counterparts. Among the factors that differentiated the great companies were level 5 leadership, hiring the right people and letting go of the wrong, confronting all of the facts — especially the brutal ones — developing an incredible focus and a culture of discipline, using technology accelerators, and developing momentum that reaches a critical mass. This book will challenge your view of the world — as it did mine — and we will all be better off for having read it.

Collins, J. 2005. *Good to great and the social sectors: Why business thinking is not the answer.* Boulder, CO: Self-Published.

Greatness is not a function of circumstance. Greatness, it turns out, is largely a matter of conscious choice, and discipline.

— Jim Collins

Good to Great and the Social Sectors is a monograph that was designed to accompany the book *Good to Great*. After writing *Good to Great*, Collins was inundated with questions as to whether the principles that he wrote about so elegantly in his book applied to the social sectors. Collins skillfully points out where there are similarities and differences among long-term business success and long-term social success. For example, great organizations, business or social, "deliver superior performance and make a distinctive impact over a long period of time." While "[i]n the social sector, the critical question is not 'How much money do we make per dollar of invested capital?' but 'How effectively do we deliver on our mission and make a distinctive impact, relative to our resources?'" This monograph is an excellent resource on how the principles from *Good to Great* can be applied in the social sector.

Collins, J. 2009. *How the mighty fall: And why some companies never give in.* NY: HarperCollins.

At first this seems like a strange book to come from Jim Collins as the book is actually the inverse of *Good to Great*. One of the strongest metaphors Collins uses in the book is that of running up a mountain in the Rockies outside of Boulder Colorado. It is one of those magical days and he is being left behind by his wife, Joanne, who is a very accomplished runner. Collins sees her far up ahead, the absolute picture of health. A mere two months later, Joanne has a double mastectomy to remove the cancer that had been silently growing within her. Collins' research documents that companies can seem equally robust, yet silently slipping toward disaster. To counteract this trend, Collins' demonstrates that there are five stages of decline: Stage 1, Hubris Born of Success; Stage 2, the Undisciplined Pursuit of More; Stage 3, Denial of Risk and Peril; Stage 4, Grasping for Salvation, and Stage 5, Capitulation to Irrelevance or Death. By identifying these stages, organizations can be on the lookout for signs of decline and with the right leadership rise again to prominence.

Eisenhardt, K., Kahwajy, J., and Bourgeois, L.J. 1997. "How management teams can have a good fight." <u>Harvard Business Review</u>, July-August, pp. 77-85.

The authors studied conflict and decision making in high technology companies all of which "competed in fast changing, competitive global markets . . . [and] had to make high-stakes decisions in the face of considerable uncertainty and under pressure to move quickly." The study concluded that there are six tactics for managing interpersonal conflict. The most successful companies: "1) worked with more, rather than less, information and debated on the basis of facts; 2) they developed multiple alternatives to enrich the level of debate; 3) shared commonly agreed-upon goals; 4) injected humour into the decision process; 5) maintained a balanced power structure; and 6) resolved issues via qualified consensus." For keen insights into modern-day decision-making, this article is a must read.

Fink, S. 1986. *Crisis management: Planning for the inevitable.* NY: AMACOM.

Crisis Management examines the anatomy of crises and suggests more effective ways of dealing with them. Fink examines the four stages every crisis goes through and gives sage advice on how to deal effectively with each stage. The discussion of the critical importance of effective leadership, communication and negotiating skills during each stage make it a fascinating read. Detailed examples such as the Three Mile Island crisis, the Johnson & Johnson's Tylenol poisoning, and Union Carbide's catastrophe in Bhopal, illustrate both how to use these skills and the perils that await any CEO and management team who do not use them.

Freedman, D.H. 2000. *Corps business: The 30 management principles of the U.S. Marines.* NY: HarperBusiness.

Why do the US Marines exist? After all, the US Army, Navy and Air Force carry out the same functions. The answer is that the US Marines have traditionally taken on the most harrowing and difficult assignments from invasion to disaster relief because no other organization does it better or faster. In this insightful book, the author looks at the 30 best management/leadership principles and practices of the Marines and richly illustrates how they can also be applied to businesses and organizations. The need for speed, flexibility, competence and leadership development is the hallmark of the Marines. Because many of the examples occur in a military setting, the author helps the reader see where these principles and practices could be imminently helpful in civilian organizations of all types. For example, one of the principles on decision making that is explained in the book is the 70% Rule. Learning and implementing this rule has helped me, my family and my business make significantly better decisions — and it will do the same for you.

Goleman, D. 1998. "What Makes a Leader." <u>Harvard Business Review</u>, November-December, pp. 93-102.

In this seminal article, Daniel Goleman reviews the literature on leadership and emotional intelligence and demonstrates that effective leaders are alike in one crucial way: they all have a high degree of emotional intelligence. At higher levels of leadership, emotional intelligence accounts for 90% of their effectiveness. Emotional intelligence is also linked to performance. "In a 1996 study . . . [it] was found that when senior managers had a critical mass of emotional intelligence capabilities, their divisions outperformed yearly earnings goals by 20%. Meanwhile, division leaders without that critical mass underperformed by almost the same amount." If you want to raise both your EQ and your ability to lead, this article is a must read.

Goleman, D., Boyatzis, R., and McKee, A. 2002. *Primal leadership: Realizing the power of emotional intelligence*. Boston, MA: Harvard Business School Press.

The authors state that, "Even if they get everything else just right, if leaders fail in this primal task of driving emotions in the right direction, nothing they do will work as well as it could or should." They then go on to document how leaders create resonance or dissonance within the people and organizations in which they lead. Although there is nothing new in this statement, what the authors do better than anyone else, is to document their findings with solid research that is relevant to and can be applied in the real-world. If you would like to further explore the relationship between emotional intelligence and leadership, this book is most highly recommended.

Heward, L. and Bacon, J.U. 2006. *Cirque du Soleil: The spark*. NY: Currency Books.

If you have been fortunate enough to see any of the Cirque du Soleil shows, there are times during the performance when your brain literally can't believe what your eyes are seeing. In the book the authors take us behind the scenes where we can see how Cirque du Soleil maintains and enhances its creative and innovate spark. There are proven lessons in creativity and innovation for individuals and for the organizations in which they work. Although the story is written as a parable, it is a parable of the first order. The book is incredibly well crafted just like Cirque du Soleil's shows. You will find that this book is as innovative as it is fun to read.

Kellerman, B. 2004. *Bad leadership: What it is, how it happens, why it matters*. Boston, MA: Harvard Business School Press.

Most of the leadership books available are on what makes a good leader. This book is on what makes a bad leader. The premise is that we must recognize both good leaders, so we can emulate them, and bad leaders, so we can better prevent bad leadership from occurring and/or stopping it. This book contains well written and insightful stories of incompetent, rigid, intemperate, callous, corrupt, insular and evil leaders. Following each type is an insightful analysis of the role that the leader, the followers and other important people such as board members played in allowing the bad leadership to develop and even flourish. I found the first part of the book to be a bit boring, but once you get into the case studies of the different types of bad leadership it is a very interesting and insightful read.

Kelley, T. with Littman, J. 2005. *The ten faces of innovation: IDEO's strategies for beating the devil's advocate & driving creativity throughout your organization*. NY: Doubleday.

We all know how helpful it is to change perspectives when we are trying to innovate and/or solve problems. The authors suggest that we go one step further and change personas or roles to help us think more creatively about innovation. The book looks at innovation through the persons of the anthropologist, experimenter, cross-pollinator, hurdler, collaborator, director, experience architect, set designer, caregiver, and storyteller. Illuminating examples from each persona bring the book to life. This book belongs on your reading list if you want to become more innovative yourself, help your organization become more innovative, develop a more innovative culture and achieve more innovative results.

Kotter, J. 1996. *Leading change*. Boston, MA: Harvard Business School Press.

Effective leaders need to have a very good understanding of the process of change. I knew intuitively that there was a phenomenally big difference between leading change and managing change. However, I was incredibly fortunate to be able to attend Harvard Business School's Leadership Best Practices Program, where I learned the real difference between leading change and managing change, as we spent an entire day with Professor Kotter. John Kotter is the world's leading authority on leading change. He eloquently describes his theory of and develops an eight-step action plan for leading change in his book *Leading Change*. The eight steps are:

1. Establishing a Sense of Urgency
2. Creating the Guiding Coalition
3. Developing a Vision and Strategy
4. Communicating the Change Vision
5. Empowering Broad-Based Action
6. Generating Short-Term Wins
7. Consolidating Gains and Producing More Change
8. Anchoring New Approaches in the Culture

Kotter, J. and Cohen, D. 2002. *The heart of change: Real-life stories of how people change their organizations*. Boston, MA: Harvard Business School Press.

In *The Heart of Change*, Kotter and Cohen further demonstrates how the eight-step leading change model works. The in-depth case studies bring the model to life and make it readily apparent that if all of the eight steps are not followed, the change is not likely to stick and the organization will revert to business as usual. They also point out that most organizations start with a vision and this is not the right place to start. Without a strong sense of urgency and a guiding coalition, the change effort will not be powerful enough to overcome homeostasis, which is the strong tendency to revert back to the old ways.

Kotter, J. and Rathgeber, H. 2005. *My iceberg is melting: Changing and succeeding under any conditions.* NY: St. Martin's Press.

My Iceberg is Melting is a parable that illustrates Kotter's eight-step model. And although I found it light when compared to his first two books, I soon came to realize that this book is an excellent way to communicate the eight-step process to individuals who would never read the first two books. So it is in fact a wonderful way to help build the critical mass that is necessary to get enough people onboard in order to develop the momentum to bring a successful change to fruition.

Kotter, J. 2008. *A sense of urgency.* Boston, MA: Harvard Business School Press.

John Kotter's most recent book in the leading change series is *A Sense of Urgency.* In far too many cases the enemy of a successful change effort is complacency and/or a sense of false urgency that leads to panic and fruitless, frenetic activity. The current world economic crisis has certainly brought a renewed sense of urgency to the world. How much of the ensuing change will make a positive and sustained difference is yet to be seen. However, we now have a real living laboratory in which we can see how well John Kotter's eight-step model of leading change is applied or not. In other words, there has never been a better time to study, learn from and apply the body of work that is outlined in these four books.

Kouzes, J. and Posner, B. 1995. *The leadership challenge: How to keep getting extraordinary things done in organizations.* San Francisco, CA: Jossey-Bass Publishers.

This book can save you an infinite amount of time because the authors have done one of the most thorough reviews of all of the leadership literature and integrated their findings in this insightful book that illustrates the 13 best practices of effective leaders. In this book you will learn how leaders have learned to make a difference by developing their vision, skills, credibility and character. As an added bonus, each of these areas is illustrated with real-life examples. For all aspiring leaders, this book is a must read.

Kouzes, J.M. and Posner, B.Z. 2006. *A leader's legacy.* San Francisco, CA: Jossey-Bass.

Kouzes and Posner are two of the most respected researchers and authors on leadership. In this book they synthesize 20 years of work in the field by examining the underlying results of leadership that is a leader's legacy. They offer a unique and powerful perspective by looking at the process of leaving a legacy as opposed to the end result of that legacy. The major premise of the book is, "The legacy you leave is the life you lead." The authors further state that, "changing the way [we] do things requires hard work and some heartache." This book is above all else a challenge for all of us to be the best leaders and followers we can be. To be the best leader or follower requires courage: courage to be open to feedback, to continuously challenge assumptions, and to foster authentic leadership throughout organizations and communities. *A Leader's Legacy* is not so much a book to be read as it is a book to be savoured and used as a reference book; a north star to help guide us as we continually develop and refine our abilities to lead, follow, and continuously develop others' abilities and capacities to lead.

Larson, C.E. and LaFasto, F.M. 1989. *Teamwork: What must go right/What can go wrong.* Thousand Oaks, CA: Sage Publications.

Effective teamwork is one of the essential ingredients that is necessary to achieve high performance organizations. The book *Teamwork* adds incisive knowledge of the factors that are necessary to develop high performing teams. To accomplish this task, the authors conducted in-depth research on various types of teams. Among those included in the study were a cardiac surgery team, a team of epidemiologists and the team that developed the IBM personal computer. From the findings of their research, the authors were able to discern nine essential characteristics that high performance teams have in common: 1) a clear, elevating goal; 2) a results-driven structure; 3) effective communication; 4) competent team members; 5) a unified commitment; 6) a collaborative climate; 7) standards of excellence; 8) external support and recognition, and 9) principled leadership. Detailed examples are used to illustrate each of these characteristics.

Larson, C.E. and LaFasto, F.M. 2001. *When teams work best: 6,000 team members and leaders tell what it takes to succeed.* Thousand Oaks, CA: Sage Publications.

In this book, Larson and LaFasto probe more deeply into the factors that contribute to effective leaders working together with effective teams. Many of the insights come from the 6,000 team members and team leaders they studied. This book covers: what makes a good team member, team relationships, team problem solving, what makes for a good team leader, and the role of the organizational environment in fostering good leaders and good team members. For any leader who wants to work more effectively and more synergistically with his or her team, this book is highly recommended.

Mayo, A.J. and Nohria, N. 2005. *In their time: The greatest business leaders of the Twentieth Century.* Boston, MA: Harvard Business School Press.

Just as men and women have a marked impact on history, history and the historical context into which we are born and in which we work has a marked impact on us all. *In Their Time* helps the reader see the effects of the time, or context, in which these leaders lived by profiling one hundred leaders, managers and entrepreneurs over a 100 year period. Although it is harder to see how context affects us during the times within which we are living, this book advises us to try because we will become more effective leaders by studying how context affected leaders in the past and by learning how to pay closer attention to context in the present.

McCall, M., Lombardo, M., and Morrison, A. 1988. *The lessons of experience: How successful executives develop on the job.* NY: Lexington Books.

The Lessons of Experience is an outstanding book based on research at the Center of Creative Leadership. The authors conducted groundbreaking research, which investigated how managers, executives and leaders learn. What makes this book doubly fascinating is that the authors were able to quantify the sources of learning. They demonstrate that 50% of what executives learn is learned from experience. The authors call this "trial by fire", which means that "job challenge and specifically difficult assignments are indeed the best teachers..." and "The essence of development is that diversity and adversity beat repetition every time."

The authors state that 20% of what leaders and executives learn is learned from good, bad, and flawed bosses. From the good bosses one can learn what to do, from the bad bosses one can learn what not to do, and from the flawed bosses one can learn that everyone has weaknesses or flaws, and if we do not keep our weaknesses and flaws under control, they will lead to our downfall. An additional 20% is learned from failure and hardship. The reason that hardship and failure are listed as a separate type of experience is that it is such a powerful, and at the same time, one of the most difficult ways to learn. The last 10% of what is learned stems from formal education. Although this only accounts for 10%, it can be an incredibly important 10% if the education relates to the overall learning goals and objectives of the individual in question.

The last point to consider is that compound learning works just like compound interest. Almost everyone wishes to maximize either his or her short-term learning and to compound his or her long-term learning. Most of us do this. However, much of one's learning takes place in a hit-or-miss fashion. Reading *The Lessons of Experience* and applying the lessons therein can help anyone to better understand how accelerated learning works and how to apply these principles to our own development.

Moss Kanter, R. 2004. *Confidence: How winning streaks and losing streaks begin and end.* NY: Three Rivers Press.

When people have confidence in one another, they are willing to lead and be led by the team.

— Rosabeth Moss Kanter

In this seminal book, renowned Harvard Professor Kanter examines the role that leaders play in building or destroying confidence in their organizations and how that confidence relates to the beginning and ending of winning and losing streaks in businesses, schools and professional sports teams. She also examines the critically important roles of accountability, collaboration and initiative in starting a winning streak and in turning around a losing streak. If you want to read a well researched, well written and well thought-out book on one of the most important aspects of leadership, this book is for you.

Neff, T.J. and Citrin, J.M. 1999. *Lessons from the top: The search for America's best business leaders.* NY: Doubleday.

In the research for *Lessons from the Top*, the authors interviewed 50 of America's best business leaders from a cross-section of industries such as: Dell Computers, Caterpillar, Johnson & Johnson, Walt Disney and Campbell's Soup, who share their expert advice. For example, Gillette has developed an innovative approach to people development. Only 10% of promotions can be vertical, that is, where an employee moves into his or her boss's job. The other 90% are diagonal which fosters building talent and breadth, and at the same time breaks down artificial walls between departments — all of which greatly strengthens organizations. For anyone interested in leadership, strategy and the negotiations necessary to put them into place, this book is a great read.

Newhouse, J. 2007. *Boeing versus Airbus: The inside story of the greatest international competition in business.* NY: Alfred A. Knopf.

This book demonstrates that leaders and their organizations have to know when to and how to innovate because often the very existence of an organization depends on it. The book also gives us valuable insight into the dynamics, opportunities, pitfalls and politics of global collaboration and global supply-chain management through an in-depth examination of one of the greatest international competition of our times.

Perkins, D., *et. al.* 2000. *Leading at the edge: Leadership lessons from the extraordinary saga of Shackleton's Antarctic expedition.* NY: AMACOM.

Leading at the Edge examines how a select number of individuals learned how to lead, negotiate and persuade in extreme conditions where their survival and that of fellow members of the expedition were at stake. The lessons the author draws from this riveting story can be extrapolated to help each of us and the organizations we work for perform at peak performance. Among the ten lessons that are exquisitely illustrated from real life tales of survival are: "1) Never lose sight of the ultimate goal, and focus energy on short-term objectives, 2) Set a personal example with visible, memorable symbols and behaviors, 3) Instill optimism and self-confidence, but stay grounded in reality, 4) Maintain your stamina and let go of guilt, 5) Reinforce the team message constantly: 'We are one – we live or die together,' 6) Minimize status differences and insist on courtesy and mutual respect, 7) Master conflict–deal with anger in small doses, engage dissidents, and avoid needless power struggles, 8) Lighten up! Find something to celebrate and something to laugh about, 9) Be willing to take the Big Risk, and 10) Never give up – there's always another move." If you would like to learn about leadership, peak individual and team performance and the negotiating and influencing skills that are necessary to bring them to fruition in a well-written book with ample servings of drama and adventure, then this book is for you.

Phillips, D. 1992. *Lincoln on leadership: Executive strategies for tough times.* NY: Warner Books.

Lincoln on Leadership is a remarkable book about the leadership, mediation, and negotiating style of one of America's greatest presidents. Although well known for his ability as a statesman and communicator, in this book Lincoln's style of leading, negotiating, and problem solving is analyzed with modern management and leadership theories. Because these theories are applied to the behaviour of an historic figure and in the historic context in which he lived, the theories stand out much more graphically than when they are applied in a modern day setting to today's leaders. Particularly interesting is Lincoln's ability to confront others without the need for those people to lose face. *Lincoln on Leadership* is a very informative and readable book about the use of principled leadership and negotiation in extremely difficult times during the United States Civil War. Lincoln knew that the way in which this dispute was settled would be the foundation on which a "new and free nation would stand."

Roberto, M.A. 2005. *Why great leaders don't take yes for an answer: Managing for conflict and consensus.* Upper Saddle River, NJ: Pearson Education, Inc.

In *Why Great Leaders Don't Take Yes For an Answer*, Roberto states that leaders, "must cultivate conflict so as to enhance the level of critical and divergent thinking, while *simultaneously* building consensus so as to facilitate the timely and efficient implementation of the choices that they make." I would stipulate that most leaders are inherently better at one of these two critical processes than the other, but that Master Leaders can do both. Roberto then artfully makes his case in theory and in practice with real-life case studies. The book is divided into four parts: "Leading the Decision Process", "Managing Conflict", "Building Consensus" and "A New Breed of Take-Charge Leader." This book is a must-read for anyone who aspires to lead in today's turbulent environment.

Russo, E. and Schoemaker, P. 1989. *Decision traps: The ten barriers to brilliant decision-making and how to overcome them.* NY: Doubleday.

Leaders have to make countless decisions and the better the quality of the decision-making, the better the outcome. This book analyzes ten principles that aid in effective decision-making and each principle is illustrated with memorable examples. In helping you become a better decision-maker, this book will help you become a better leader.

Russo, E. and Schoemaker, P. 2002. *Winning decisions: Getting it right the first time.* NY: Doubleday.

This book takes up where the authors' previous book, *Decision Traps: Ten Barriers to Brilliant Decision Making*, leaves off. The book adds more depth and an excellent decision making model and examples that will help the reader examine his or her own decision making and learn how to make better decisions. Since we are the sum total of all of the decisions we make, this is a most important and often overlooked subject. Although it is not the most readable book in the world, reading it is well worth the effort.

Senge, Peter. 1990. *The fifth discipline.* NY: Doubleday.

In the 1990's, Peter Senge became a major figure in organizational development when he wrote *The Fifth Discipline. The Fifth Discipline* is one of those rare seminal books that continues to have far-reaching influence many years after it was written. This book essentially launched the movement toward the learning organization. According to Senge, to be a learning organization, learning has to take place on an individual level, on a team and/or department level, *and* on an organizational or systems level. Negotiating to arrive at this level of commitment takes visionary leadership plus strategic thinking. For example, one of the questions he asks his readers is "Who is the leader on a ship?" Most people say the captain, or the navigator, however, Senge makes a strong case for the naval architect, the person who designed the ship, since that person designed the systems on which the ship runs. How leaders and negotiators understand and develop systems have a lasting impact on an organization's culture. This book is a must read for anyone wanting to see how systems work as a whole. One of the most valued attributes of a leader is farsightedness. *The Fifth Discipline* and the other books that are based on it will help the reader look at the larger picture and to better appreciate its importance.

Surowiecki, J. 2005. *The wisdom of crowds*. NY: Random House.

This book is like reading a great detective story, only the subject is not *who* did it, but *how* they did it. In this book the author examines when decision-making works effectively and when it does not through rich and finely detailed examples. Moreover, the author concludes that most leaders do not pay enough attention to developing a culture, and this includes a culture of accurate, viable and timely decision making, that will help their organization grow and succeed long after that particular leader has retired or moved on. If you want to sharpen your understanding of human behaviour, group dynamics as it relates to one of the most important aspects of our lives, namely accurate and viable decision making, *The Wisdom of Crowds* is a fascinating, multi-faceted and well written book that you can not afford to miss.

Useem, M. 1998. *The leadership moment: Nine true stories of triumph and disaster and their lessons for us all*. NY: Random House.

There are times when leaders must negotiate and times when negotiators must lead. *The Leadership Moment* is about those times. Of particular interest are those moments in which a leader is defined by his or her decisions and the impact those decisions have on others. One of the best examples is the decision Merck Pharmaceuticals had to make regarding a medication that would eradicate river blindness in Western Africa. The only problem was that those who needed the medication could not afford to pay for it. The humanitarian reasons to donate the drug were countered by the fact that the amount of money necessary to donate the drug was equal to the amount of money necessary to bring a potentially profitable and necessary new drug to market and that shareholders and retirees had invested their retirement savings in Merck stock. You can come to your own conclusions as to whether or not you would donate the medication if you were the president and CEO of Merck. You can then compare your decision with that of the company's CEO. This book contains fascinating stories of real leaders making both wise and disastrous decisions at crucial leadership moments.

Useem, M. 2006. *The go point: When it's time to decide – knowing what to do and when to do.* NY: Crown Business.

In this in-depth book, Michael Useem examines the crucial role that decision making and seasoned judgment play in our lives. Useem is a master story teller, and he illustrates his points with diverse examples from fire-fighting, to business, to the American Civil War to show that, "Poor preparation predictably leads to poor choices." Useem then goes on to develop a robust model of decision making and from time to time asks the reader to consider how he or she would behave at a critical point in time and then lets the reader compare his or her answer with the actual outcome. This book is well researched, well written and well thought out. Since we are the sum total of all of our decisions, it is a good idea to make as many good, and eliminate as many bad decisions as possible. This book was designed to help you do exactly that.

Williams, D. 2005. *Real leadership: Helping people and organizations face their toughest challenges.* San Francisco, CA: Berrett-Koehler Publishers, Inc.

This is one of the best books on leadership you will ever find. The major premise of the book is that there are real leaders and counterfeit leaders. Real leaders solve real problems and use valuable resources wisely, while counterfeit leaders solve false problems and waste valuable resources. Williams richly illustrates his ideas with examples of real leaders such as: Eleanor Roosevelt, Andre Sakharov and Nelson Mandela. On the other hand, an excellent example of counterfeit leadership was in 1692 when the town leaders of Salem Massachusetts burned "witches" at the stake.

The book then goes on to identify six challenges of real leadership and analyzes what makes successful activist leaders, developmental leaders, transitional leaders, maintenance leaders, creative leaders and leaders facing crises. Riveting examples of each type of leader brings Williams' theories to life.

Movies with Leadership Themes

Bloody Sunday (2002)

Bloody Sunday is the story the Irish can't forget and the British don't want to remember. The purpose of the film was to develop a common story and a common account that can be recognized across the islands of Britain and Ireland, because it is only by developing a common account that the wounds will begin to heal.

— Jim Sheridan, Executive Producer

This movie shows a re-enactment of the events of January 30, 1972 when, during a civil rights demonstration, 13 civilians were killed by British police in the streets of Northern Ireland. The film makes a brave attempt to be as realistic as possible. As the movie progresses, it constantly switches back and forth between the thoughts and actions of the opposing sides. In watching the film, it becomes heartbreakingly clear how the conflict escalated and in this terrible escalation, there are valuable lessons for all. I strongly advise looking at the special features on the DVD. They contain fascinating segments on how the movie was made. A highlight is an interview with Ivan Cooper, the Protestant civil rights leader at the centre of the movie, who based his movement on the work of Martin Luther King Jr. and Gandhi.

Catch a Fire (2006)

"It takes one spark for an ordinary man to become a hero." Based on a true story, "Catch a Fire" is the story of one man's political consciousness raising based on what happened to him and his family when he becomes wrongfully accused of committing a terrorist act against the apartheid government in South Africa. "Catch a Fire" is also the story of two tribes at war, the white tribe and the black tribe, which is similar to the conflict in Northern Ireland between the Catholics and Protestants, and the civil war in Iraq between the Shias and Sunnis. At the time of this incident, 3 million whites held all of the power over 27 million blacks and they intended to keep it that way using any means that they saw fit — moral or immoral, ethical or unethical, honourable or dishonourable. Paradoxically, the use of immoral, unethical, and dishonourable behaviour hastened the end of the apartheid regime that the Afrikaners were trying to protect. The lessons contained in this movie are universal.

Freedom Writers (2007)

Based on true events, "Freedom Writers" is the story of Erin Gruwell, a first-year high school teacher assigned to teach students considered to be at risk, unreachable and unteachable. After a great deal of difficulty, against almost impossible odds and many false starts, Erin learns how to relate to her students by trying to understand their world before she asks them to try to understand hers. She then bridges the gap between these two worlds by showing them how intolerance, prejudice and violence in a larger context of the holocaust was a larger and more sinister version of what was happening to them. The students respond by keeping their own diaries about violence and other negative influences in their lives and in so doing transform their lives and the world around them.

Good Night, and Good Luck (2005)

In the early 1950's, the threat of Communism created an air of paranoia in the United States; exploiting those fears was Senator Joseph McCarthy of Wisconsin. However, CBS reporter Edward R. Murrow and his producer Fred Friendly decided to take a stand and challenge McCarthy, exposing him for the fear monger he was. Of particular interest in this film is that Senator McCarthy plays himself through the clever use of historical film clips. Edward R. Murrow demonstrates leadership and the courage to negotiate for what he believes in. Murrow also has the oratorical skills to get his message across and he uses parts of Senator McCarthy's own speeches to expose McCarthy for the tyrant he was.

Munich (2005)

"Munich" is Steven Spielberg's semi-fictional movie about the Israeli retaliation after the massacre of 11 Israeli athletes at the 1972 Olympics. In the film, Israel's Prime Minister, Golda Meir, authorizes a small group of agents to find and kill 11 of the people who masterminded the Israeli massacre. The group is led by an agent named Avner. Avner must find a source — a paid informant — whom he can trust to reveal the names and locations of the 11 terrorists.

However, Avner and his group also become the hunted. Can the Israelis trust their informants? If they don't trust and use the informants, their mission is over because they will not have the identities and location of the terrorists. If they do trust their informants, they could be putting their own lives in jeopardy. This predicament, to trust or not trust, becomes even more pressing after one of their own members is found murdered.

The question to trust, not to trust or to partially trust is at the heart of most difficult situations. It takes seasoned judgment to know the correct approach. This film's power comes from the tension between its central themes of trust and ambiguity in the negotiation process on the one hand, and the seeming necessity versus the long-term futility of revenge killings on the other.

The Reader (2008)

The Reader is the story of a 15-year-old-boy, Michael Berg, who has an affair with a 36- year-old woman named Hanna Schmitz. They both have secrets, he from his family, and her from her past. Years later, Michael finds himself in a situation where he can help Hanna when she is put on trial for war crimes during the Holocaust. In the end, the audience must decided for himself or herself, how much of her crime is a result of personal responsibility or of a country that allows its citizens to grow up illiterate. And, how much responsibility did Michael share for choosing to remain silent. I find that these questions still haunt me — long after I have seen the movie.

Shake Hands with the Devil (2007)

I have seen Roméo Dallaire speak twice and there is no doubt that he is a master presenter. I had also read his book, *Shake Hands with the Devil,* so when I decided to see the movie, which has the same title, I did not expect to learn much more. I could not have been more wrong. The movie accurately portrays Dallaire's leadership and heroism during the genocide in Rwanda. What I was not prepared for, was how much of the movie dealt with Dallaire's suffering and PTSD (Post Traumatic Stress Disorder).

The film documents how Dallaire, with the help of a therapist, was able to transform his pain and suffering into empowerment and hope. Although there was nothing he could have done to prevent the genocide in Rwanda, because of the complete lack of support he received from the UN and the world powers. However, Dallaire found a new purpose in life — and that purpose is to prevent future genocides, stop countries from using child soldiers and be a strong advocate for mental health and make the issue of PSTD — not as something that should be swept under the carpet — but a mental health issue that no one should be ashamed about and that for which proper treatment should be put into place. If you want to see leadership, heroism in action and also the story about a man who was able to overcome his own demons and find a new purpose in life, I don't think you will be able to find a better example or a better movie.

The White Masai (2005)

This is a true story about Corinne Hofmann, a Swiss-German tourist who falls in love with a Masai warrior from the Samburu tribe. When they decide to marry and live together in Africa, a myriad of difficulties arise from the ensuing culture clash. Watching this couple try to navigate their cultural differences provides great insight into a social anthropologist's observation that ninety percent of what we think is culturally and linguistically determined. For anyone who wants to gain a deeper perspective on the role that culture plays in our lives, and in all of our communications and negotiations, this movie is a rare treat.

Additional Movies with Leadership Themes

Apollo 13 (1995)

Breaker Morant (1979)

The Bridge on the River Kwai (1957)

Das Boot [The Boat] (1982)

Gallipoli (1981)

Gandhi (1982)

Hoosiers (1986)

In Search of Excellence (1985)

The Insider (1999)

Norma Rae (1979)

The Parable of the Sadhu (1983)

A Passion for Excellence (1985)

Patton (1970)

Pride (2007)

Schindler's List (1994)

Stand and Deliver (1988)

Twelve Angry Men (1957)

Twelve O'Clock High (1949)

Young Winston (1972)

The West Wing (TV Series September 1999 to May 14, 2006)

Appendix A:
Leadership/Managerial Evaluation Form™

Manager's Name:_____

Please rate_____on the following scales. If you do not have enough
information at the present time to rate your manager fairly on any of the scales,
please circle N/A to the right of the scale.

I find that the goals_____wants me to work for are:

    Unclear   Clear
    _____ N/A
    1   2   3   4   5   6   7

As a person to work for, I find_____to be:

    Disorganized   Organized
    _____ N/A
    1   2   3   4   5   6   7

As a person to work with,_____ is:

    Unmotivated   Very Motivated
    _____ N/A
    1   2   3   4   5   6   7

In terms of decision-making,_____:

    Needs improvement   Is Excellent
    _____ N/A
    1   2   3   4   5   6   7

I receive feedback from_____:

Infrequently   Frequently
_____ N/A
1   2   3   4   5   6   7

I receive feedback from _____that is:

Vague   Specific
_____ N/A
1   2   3   4   5   6   7

My manager's technical understanding of the work I do:

Needs improvement   Is excellent
_____ N/A
1   2   3   4   5   6   7

My manager's understanding of my needs as an employee:

Needs improvement   Is excellent
_____ N/A
1   2   3   4   5   6   7

In dealing with staff, I find_____ to be:

Discourteous   Courteous
_____ N/A
1   2   3   4   5   6   7

_____ delegates the workload:

Unfairly   Fairly
_____ N/A
1   2   3   4   5   6   7

_____ behaves in a way that enhances my feelings of personal worth and importance:

Not at all Descriptive   Very Descriptive
_____ N/A
1   2   3   4   5   6   7

_____ behaves in a way that encourages all members of the group to develop close, mutually satisfying relationships.

Not at all Descriptive   Very Descriptive
_____ N/A
1   2   3   4   5   6   7

_____ behaves in a way that stimulates enthusiasm for meeting the group's goal of excellent performance.

Not at all Descriptive   Very Descriptive
_____ N/A
1   2   3   4   5   6   7

_____ behaves in a way that helps achieve goal attainment by such activities as scheduling, coordinating, providing resources, materials and technical knowledge.

Not at all Descriptive   Very Descriptive
_____ N/A
1   2   3   4   5   6   7

In terms of his/her ability to listen carefully to what I have to say, I find that _____:

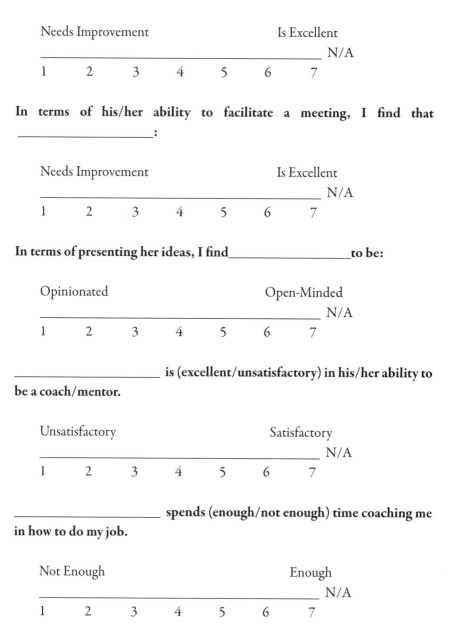

Needs Improvement   Is Excellent
_____ N/A
1   2   3   4   5   6   7

In terms of his/her ability to facilitate a meeting, I find that _____:

Needs Improvement   Is Excellent
_____ N/A
1   2   3   4   5   6   7

In terms of presenting her ideas, I find_____to be:

Opinionated   Open-Minded
_____ N/A
1   2   3   4   5   6   7

_____ is (excellent/unsatisfactory) in his/her ability to be a coach/mentor.

Unsatisfactory   Satisfactory
_____ N/A
1   2   3   4   5   6   7

_____ spends (enough/not enough) time coaching me in how to do my job.

Not Enough   Enough
_____ N/A
1   2   3   4   5   6   7

In   terms   of   teamwork   and   team   building,   I   find   that
_____:

Needs Improvement   Is excellent
_____ N/A

1   2   3   4   5   6   7

I find _____ to be (supportive/unsupportive) of the efforts of
other departments within this organization.

Unsupportive   Supportive
_____ N/A

1   2   3   4   5   6   7

_____ spends (enough/not enough) time coaching me
on how to advance in my career.

Not enough   Enough
_____ N/A

1   2   3   4   5   6   7

In terms of performance management, I am evaluated:

Unfairly   Fairly
_____ N/A

1   2   3   4   5   6   7

Would your manager notice if you put 15 percent more effort into your
job?

Yes _____   No _____   N/A _____

Would your manager notice if you put 15 percent less effort into your job?

Yes _____   No _____   N/A _____

Please list three specific things you enjoy about working with _____:

Please list three specific things you have learned from working with _____:

Please list three specific things that _____ could do to improve his/her managerial performance in your department:

Please make any suggestions you have for improving this working relationship:

Please list any other suggestions that you have that would help
_____ 1) Grow the Business, 2) Grow the People, and
3) Grow the Culture.

THANK YOU

Appendix B:
Eight Competencies Feedback Forms

In 360-degree feedback, you rate yourself, and you are also rated by your boss, manager or supervisor, peers, direct reports and/or by your customers/clients. The rating form for these eight competencies are below. You may want to consider asking someone in human resources or some other independent third party to collect this information for you as the information will tend to be less biased and more honest if it is collected by a neutral third party. Use this form and reproduce it for each of the persons you have requested feedback from and then tabulate the results on the fourth page of this appendix.

1. Planning/Causal Thinking: "Planning/causal thinking is essentially hypothesis generation. It involves seeing either the potential implication of events or the likely consequences of a situation based on what has usually happened in the past."

I do not enjoy nor am I good at developing hypotheses and seeing the consequences for a situation based on what has happened in the past.

I enjoy and I am good at developing hypotheses and seeing the consequences for a situation based on past events.

1	2	3	4	5	6	7	8	9	10

2. Diagnostic Information-Seeking: "Diagnostic information-seeking is pushing for concrete data in all sorts of ways, using a variety of sources to get as much information as possible to help with solving a particular problem. People who are good at diagnostic information-seeking are naturally curious and they ask questions to help them get the most data/information possible."

I do not typically ask very many questions nor am I seen by others to engage in a great deal of diagnostic information seeking.

I typically ask a great many questions. Others see me engaging in a great deal of diagnostic information seeking.

1	2	3	4	5	6	7	8	9	10

3. Conceptualization/Synthetic Thinking: "Conceptualization/synthetic thinking is theory-building in order to account for consistent patterns in recurring events or for connections between seemingly unrelated pieces of information. It is enhanced by diagnostic information-seeking."

I am not good at nor do I enjoy building theories from seemingly unrelated events or data.					I am good at and I enjoy building theories from seemingly unrelated events or data.				
1	2	3	4	5	6	7	8	9	10

4. The Need or Desire to Influence Others: "The need for influence is an alertness to the potentialities for influencing others. Concern for influence appears in such statements as, 'When I walked into that meeting, I was trying to figure out how to persuade them to agree to my proposal.'"

I do not have a strong need or desire to influence others.					I have a strong need or desire to influence others.				
1	2	3	4	5	6	7	8	9	10

5. Directive Influence: Directive influence measures the ability to "confront people directly when problems occur, [to] tell people to do things the way [you want] them done."

I am not comfortable using my personal authority or expert power to make sure that something gets done.					I am comfortable using my personal authority or expert power to make sure something gets done.				
1	2	3	4	5	6	7	8	9	10

6. Collaborative Influence: Collaborative influence measures the ability to "operate effectively with groups to influence outcomes and get cooperation, to build 'ownership' ... among key subordinates by involving them in decision-making."

I need improvement in building relationships for the good of both parties.					I am good at building relationships for the good of both parties.				
1	2	3	4	5	6	7	8	9	10

7. Symbolic Influence: Symbolic influence "is indicated by a use of symbols to influence how people act in the organization. A senior manager with this competency can, by personal example or a statement of mission, create a sense of purpose for the whole organization, which engenders individuals' loyalty and commitment to it." Symbolic is also related to "walking the talk".

I have difficulty leading others by enrolling them with a sense of mission.					I can easily lead others by enrolling them with a sense of mission.				
1	2	3	4	5	6	7	8	9	10

8. Self-Confidence: Leaders with strength in this competency, although recognizing difficulties, never expressed any doubt that they would ultimately succeed. In behavioural interviews, they display strong self-presentation skills and come across as very much in charge. They act to make others feel comfortable, and they respond quickly and confidently to requests in key situations. By contrast, the average senior managers are more tentative. Moreover, the outstanding managers expressed self-confidence by being stimulated by crises and other problems, rather than distressed or overwhelmed by them.

I have a low degree of self confidence.					I have a high degree of self confidence.				
1	2	3	4	5	6	7	8	9	10

Comparison of My Ratings on the Eight Competencies

	Self	Direct Reports	Peers	Boss/ Manager	Clients/ Customers
1. Planning/ Causal Thinking:					
2. Diagnostic Information- Seeking:					
3. Conceptualization /Synthetic Thinking:					
4. The Need or Desire to Influence Others:					
5. Directive Influence:					
6. Collaborative Influence:					
7. Symbolic Influence:					
8. Self- Confidence:					

Appendix C: Delegation Record for _____

Date Assigned	Goal and/or Project	Priority	Due Date	Progress	Date Completed	Follow-up: What worked	Follow-up: Targets for improvement

Appendix D:
Meeting Improvement Form

1. Please rate your individual effectiveness in making the meeting a success the following on a scale from 1 to 5, where 1 indicates very ineffective and 5 indicates very effective.

1	2	3	4	5

2. Please rate the effectiveness of the meeting as a whole, where 1 indicates I would never want to meet with this group again to 5, which means that I would be blessed if I could work with this group for the rest of my career.

1	2	3	4	5

3. Please list 1 specific thing that has helped make this meeting successful.

4. Please make 1 specific suggestion that would improve our meetings.

Index

Dr. Brad McRae, CSP, Director, Atlantic Leadership Development Institute

Brad is the Director of the Atlantic Leadership Development Institute in Halifax, Nova Scotia and Kingston Jamaica. Brad has a doctoral degree in Counseling Psychology from the University of British Columbia and a baccalaureate and master's degree from California State University, Chico. He is a registered psychologist, consultant, and best-selling author. He was trained in negotiating skills at the Harvard Project on Negotiation and is a graduate of Harvard Business School's Leadership Best Practices Program. He also has extensive training in career development.

Brad has earned his CSP (Certified Speaking Professional) designation and was a Platinum Level Presenter with Meeting Professionals International for six consecutive years. He has taught at: the British Columbia Institute of Technology, Carleton University, Saint Mary's University, and the University College of the Caribbean. Brad has also worked as a subject matter expert in negotiating and influencing skills at the Pearson International Peacekeeping Centre.

Brad gives over 100 presentations a year and has lectured across Canada and the United States, and in Australia, Mexico, Africa, England, and the Caribbean. Brad is a member of the Canadian Society for Training and Development, the Canadian Association of Professional Speakers and the International Federation for Professional Speakers.

He is also the author of eight books: *How to Write A Thesis and Keep Your Sanity*; *How To Study For Comprehensive Exams And Keep Your Sanity*; *Practical Time Management: How to Get More Done in Less Time*; *Negotiating and Influencing Skills: The Art of Creating and Claiming Value*; *The Seven Strategies of Master Negotiators*; *The Seven Strategies of Master Presenters*; *From our Grandmother's Lap: Lessons for a Lifetime*, and *The Seven Strategies of Master Leaders: Featuring Key Insights from 32 of Canada's Top Leader* and the editor of The Atlantic Leadership Development Institute Newsletter. On a personal note, Brad is, an avid cyclist, reader, adventure traveler and a noted philanthropist in Canada and Jamaica.

ALDI   *Great Leaders*
Great Organizations
Lasting Results

Programs provided by the Atlantic Leadership Development Institute:

➢ Become a Master Leader

➢ Become a Master Presenter

➢ Become a Master Negotiator

➢ Living Your Legacy

These programs are available as:
- 1 hour keynotes
- half or full day workshops
- 2 and 2 ½ day seminars.

These programs are customizable to your organization or meeting group.

Contact Brad at Brad@BradMcRae.com to discuss your specific needs

For more information visit us at *www.BradMcRae.com.*

Dr. Brad McRae gave a Platinum Level Presentation to our MPI Chapter and hit a home run with ratings of 6.5 out of 7 on content and 6.7 out of 7 on style.

Anne Urban, North Florida Chapter President
Meeting Professionals International

Also by Dr. Brad McRae

Complete the series by ordering:

The Seven Strategies of Master Negotiators

Whether negotiating a multi-million dollar contract, terms with a new supplier, a raise with the boss, or your child's allowance, everyone finds themselves striking partnerships and "making deals" on a daily basis. In *The Seven Strategies of Master Negotiators* Brad McRae interviewed 21 top negotiators to gain insight into their negotiating secrets. Combined with his own experience teaching thousands of people to negotiate, he presents the seven key strategies and 21 skills that will help you become a Master Negotiator.

The Seven Strategies of Master Presenters

In this book, Platinum Level Presenter Brad McRae and co-author David Brooks, 1990 World Champion of Public Speaking with Toastmasters International, interviewed 28 of the best presenters across North America. By reading this book, you will learn the seven key strategies that made them masters. The book also contains specifically designed exercises will help you create presentations that are twice as good, in half the time, with half the stress.

To order copies of
- *The Seven Strategies of Master Leaders*
- *The Seven Strategies of Master Negotiators*
- *The Seven Strategies of Master Presenters*

This Master Series is Also Available as E-Books along with:
- *Are You Managing Your Career or Is Your Career Managing You?*

Visit our online store at *www.BradMcRae.com* for more information.

For bulk orders contact Brad at Brad@BradMcRae.com.

More Advanced Praise for
The Seven Strategies of Master Leaders

The Seven Strategies of Master Leaders **speaks to the very core of what leaders do** and reminds us that we are constantly challenged to grow and move on to greater achievements. Dr. McRae has chosen to single out a diverse group of Canadians, fellow citizens, whose contributions continue to inspire us.

– Joan Kean-Howie, PhD
Director General   IMB/INH
National Research Council of Canada

Developing community leadership is an investment in the well-being of our cities and our citizens. When we needed to select a Canadian book for Leadership Thunder Bay's participants to study, we made our selection very carefully. Our key criteria? Diverse examples of contemporary corporate, public and charitable leadership in action. **We found the perfect book in *The Seven Strategies of Master Leaders: Featuring Key Insights from 32 of Canada's Top Leaders.***

– *Maggie Chicoine*
Lead Facilitator
Leadership Thunder Bay

There are very few books that address leadership from a Canadian perspective, and fewer still that are as inclusive as *The Seven Strategies Master Leaders.*

– *Crystal Kosa*
National Director
Corporate Training and Inclusion Strategies

In tough economic times, effective leadership is more important than ever. Increasingly, people are turning to our community colleges, not only to provide training for our youth, but retraining for large numbers of older workers who have been downsized. In class our students are taught job-related skills but more importantly we also train the student in management and leadership. **At Confederation College, we are proud to be using a Canadian text that profiles Canadian examples of first rate leadership – Dr. McRae's Book, *The Seven Strategies of Master Leaders.***

– Allen Richert
Professor & Coordinator, Business-Marketing Programs
Confederation College

There are many books written about leadership but very few written about Canadian leaders. Kudos to Dr. Brad McRae for filling this void. As our world becomes increasingly competitive and more complicated, we will need more people to step forward and show true leadership. *The Seven Strategies of Master Leaders* shows all of us how we can become more masterful leaders.

– Dr. Carole Olsen
Superintendent
Halifax Regional School Board

The wide variety of contemporary Canadian leaders profiled in *The Seven Strategies of Master Leaders* make **this book an invaluable tool for *everyone* striving to be a better leader.**

– *Warren Evans CSP Hall of Fame,*
President and CEO of The Service Excellence Group